From Peasant Struggles to Indian Resistance

From Peasant Struggles to Indian Resistance

The Ecuadorian Andes in the Late Twentieth Century

Amalia Pallares

University of Oklahoma Press : Norman

Library of Congress Cataloging-in-Publication Data

Pallares, Amalia, 1965–
    From peasant struggles to Indian resistance : the Ecuadorian Andes in the late twentieth century / Amalia Pallares.
    p. cm.
    Includes bibliographical references and index.
  ISBN 978-0-8061-3459-8 (hardcover) ISBN 978-0-8061-9492-9 (paper)
    1. Indians of South America—Ecuador—Politics and government.
2. Indians of South America—Ecuador—Sierra—Ethnic identity.
3. Indians of South America—Ecuador—Sierra—Government relations.
4. Indian activists—Ecuador—Sierra.   5. Self-determination, National—Ecuador—Sierra.   6. Sierra (Ecuador)—Politics and government.
7. Sierra (Ecuador)—Race relations.   I. Title.

F3721.1.S54 P35 2002
322.1'19808661—dc21

                                                2002019423

The paper in this book meets the guidelines for permanence and durability of the Committee on Production Guidelines for Book Longevity of the Council on Library Resources. ∞

Copyright © 2002 by the University of Oklahoma Press, Norman, Publishing Division of the University. All rights reserved. Manufactured in the U.S.A.   Paperback published 2024.

To my parents, Victor and Carlota

Contents

Preface	IX
List of Acronyms and Abbreviations	XIII
1. Something Old, Something New: Indigenous Resistance and the New Indio Identity	3
2. Theorizing Indigenous Resistance: Explaining the Shift	25
3. Uncertain Development: Post–agrarian Reform Politics and the New Racial Order	36
4. Representing the Rural Poor: Citizenship and Political Identity in Cotacachi	72
5. Our Own Teniente Político: Gaining Indigenous Autonomy in Cacha	110
6. Seeking Respeto: Racial Consciousness and National Indian Politics	144
7. From Pluriculturalism to Plurinationalism: The Politics of Disruption	184
8. Indians in the Public Sphere: Comparative Reflections on the Negotiation of Difference	218
Appendix. Sixteen Demands Proposed by the CONAIE in the 1990 Uprising	228
Notes	229
Glossary of Spanish and Quichua Terms	249
References	253
Index	267

Preface

At the outset of my fieldwork in Ecuador, I spent four months in Quito learning Quichua. I was the guest of a family whose friendship with my mother's family dated back fifty years. One afternoon as I was leaving the house, I ran into my host's nephew who had just arrived from my native city of Guayaquil. He was a wealthy architecture student who spent weekends in Quito visiting his girlfriend. He asked where I was going. When I said that I was going to my Quichua class, his eyes opened in bewilderment and he burst out in laughter, immediately replying in a display of quick coastal humor: "How do you say computer in Quichua?" I did not respond, in part because I was not able to answer (my Quichua was and remains quite basic) and in part because I was surprised by his familiar response. My silence completed the joke and prompted more laughter from him.

I have since thought often about this encounter. It exemplifies an endemic problem in Ecuadorian society: the shared belief that Indians and modernity are incompatible. The young man regarded his comment as a joke precisely because of the contradiction involved in placing the computer—a symbol of modernity—and Quichua—a symbol of primitiveness and antimodernity—in the same sentence. The omitted punch line of the joke was, "Of course, there is no word in Quichua for computer, nor can there be."

This incident alludes to an underlying paradox: whereas Ecuadorian Indians are considered primitive and premodern, the contemporary Indian movement and the creation of the *nuevo indio* (new Indian) as a distinct political identity are fundamentally modern processes. The politicization of Indian identity and the creation of one of the strongest panethnic indigenous movements in the region stem from a process of consciousness formation that was facilitated by post–land reform economic and political changes. Hence, at no time has the gap between the stereotype and reality been larger. As the young Ecuadorian, among many others, continued to freeze Indians in time, Indian organizations were becoming political actors, creating autonomous organizations, and entering the political process in local, national, and transnational arenas.

The political emergence of Indians as Indians is the central concern of this book. The 1990 national uprising marked the entrance of Ecuadorian Indians into the national political scene. The scale and level of indigenous mobilization was unprecedented in the country and in Latin America. Within a decade indigenous movements in Mexico, Guatemala, and Bolivia would follow suit, staging numerous mobilizations in their quest for empowerment.

As one of the strongest and most enduring contemporary movements, the Ecuadorian case provides important lessons on the formation of an "Indian" political identity. For the first time in the twentieth century Indians are not merely the objects of policies, political debate, and discussion but are becoming political subjects and engaging in direct negotiations with the state. Their public voice is autonomous: indigenous political actors speak and act for Indians, reproducing distinct "Indianities" in the process.

Indian movements in Latin America are both old and new. They are old insofar as indigenous populations across the continent have participated extensively in uprisings, labor conflicts, land invasions, and other forms of protest during the colonial and postindependence periods. They are new because they are articulating new ideologies and practices of resistance that draw on a panethnic national and transnational identification as the source of political solidarity. As old and new movements, they provide rich case studies of identity shift and transformation. Unlike the environmental or animal rights movements, long-standing indigenous participation in peasant struggles provides both a basis for historical comparison and a confirmation that groups (even those most essentialized) can rely on different axes of identity to construct a political imaginary. Hence, Indian movements today are so distinct from nineteenth- and early-twentieth-century forms of resistance that they must be theorized as more than the continuation of an ongoing, millenarian struggle. Instead, the transition from a *campesinista*, or peasant-based, identity to an *indianista*, or Indian-based, one and from more localized struggles to panethnic resistance in the region needs to be explained as a thoroughly modern phenomenon.

This study focuses primarily on indigenous activism in the Ecuadorian highlands region. This region was selected for two principal reasons. First, it is the stage of a long-standing if often tense relationship between Indians and the Left; second, it is the site of transition from specific forms of campesino organization to *indianismo* (Indianism). I conducted fourteen months of field research in 1992, 1993, and 1998 at the national and local levels. My national analysis covers the development of the Indian movement in relation to the state and to a changing political economy. I also analyze two local movements spearheaded by the Unión de Organizaciones Campesinos e Indígenas de Cotacachi (UNORCIC) and the Federación de Cabildos Indígenas de la Parroquia de Cacha (FECAIPAC) in the provinces of Imbabura and Chimborazo respectively. I conducted approximately one hundred forty hours of structured interviews with more than fifty activists and informants in six highland provinces: Pichincha, Imbabura, Cañar, Azuay, Loja, and Chimborazo. I defined as activists people who spend at least ten hours a week in political work in an indigenous communal, intercommunal, provincial, or national organization. Using a snowball technique, I developed a representative list of national and provincial activists, asking each activist to recommend five other activists who had been extensively involved in indigenous politics. This technique was necessary as there is not always a direct correspondence between organizational titles and length or depth of political involvement because of the rapid turnover in high-level leadership in many organizations. Finally, I interviewed several mestizo informants who were active in religious institutions or government or development organizations. I also engaged in participant observation in national assemblies, encounters, meetings, and consciousness-raising courses and workshops, festivals, and commemorations. While I often cite national and local activists and informants when they are expressing views for which they are well known, for reasons of political sensitivity, I have maintained the confidentiality of many sources whose critical insights were invaluable.

This book draws extensively from my Ph.D. dissertation. I would like to thank all those at the University of Texas who helped to make this first effort possible, including my co-adviser Henry Dietz, Gretchen Ritter, Aline Helg, Milton Jamail, Fran Buntman, Manuel Orozco, Shannan Mattiace, Clare Sheridan, Terri Davis, Roger Frahm, Jay McCollough, Azza Salama Layton and Camille Bussette. I would like to especially thank my co-adviser, mentor, and friend, Michael Hanchard, for all his assistance throughout this project and for his unconditional support.

During my fieldwork in Ecuador, the activists Luis Macas, Auqui Tituaña, Pedro de la Cruz, Mercedes Gualacata, Cornelio Orbe, Miguel Robalino, Segundo Andrango, Alberto Andrango, and Enrique Morán gave generously of their time and hospitality. The hospitality and support of the Saltos-Falquez family, Sister Ruth, Cecilia Falquez, Maria del Carmen Montesdeoca, Esteban and Alfonso Quirola, Xiomara de Triana, and Juan Carlos Muñoz were invaluable. I also benefited greatly from the advice of fellow scholars, among them, Hernán Ibarra, Hernán Carrasco, Andrés Guerrero, Adrian Bonilla, Tania Korokvin, Jorge Leon, and Pablo Hospina. Throughout my stay, I was extremely fortunate to have the companionship of Marta Roldós and Emma Cervone, with whom I shared crucial conversations and exchanges about field experience and theoretical inquiry.

The final manuscript was developed at the University of Illinois at Chicago, where I received the assistance of colleagues Andy McFarland, Rasma Karlkins, Stephen Engelmann, Norma Moruzzi, and Nilda Flores-Gonzalez and editorial assistant Jennifer Rexroat. I am especially indebted to Audie Klotz and Marc Becker, who read the manuscript at a time when it was most necessary.

Finally, I thank my family for always being there: my siblings, Carla, Jerry, and Victor, and my son, Antonio. My parents, Victor and Carlota, instilled in me a passion for Ecuadorian history and culture and encouraged my academic endeavors. I also want to acknowledge my *compañero*, Omar González, without whom the completion of this journey would not have been possible.

Acronyms and Abbreviations

ACAE	Asociación de Campesinos Agricultores del Ecuador (Association of Agricultural Peasants of Ecuador)
ACAL	Asociación de Campesinos Agricultores del Litoral (Association of Agricultural Peasants of the Coast)
CEDOC	Confederación Ecuatoriana de Organizaciones Clasistas (Ecuadorian Confederation of Classist Organizations)
CEOSL	Conferencia Ecuatoriana de Organizaciones Sindicales Libres (Ecuadorian Conference of Free Syndicalist Organizations)
CIA	Central Intelligence Agency
CIEI	Centro de Investigación para la Educación Indígena (Indigenous Education Research Center)
COICE	Coordinadora de Indígenas de la Costa Ecuatoriana (Coordinator of Coastal Indians of Ecuador)
CONACNIE	Coordinadora Nacional de Nacionalidades Indígenas del Ecuador (National Coordinator of Indigenous Nationalities of Ecuador)
CONAIE	Confederación de Nacionalidades Indígenas del Ecuador (Confederation of Indigenous Nationalities of Ecuador)
CONFENIAE	Confederación de Nacionalidades Indígenas de la Amazonia Ecuatoriana (Confederation of Indigenous Nationalities of the Ecuadorian Amazon)
CTE	Central de Trabajadores Ecuatorianos (Ecuadorian Workers Union)
DINEIB	Dirección Nacional de Educación Intercultural Bilingue (National Directorate of Bilingual Intercultural Education)

ACRONYMS AND ABBREVIATIONS

DNPI	Dirección Nacional de Pueblos Indígenas (National Directorate of Indian Peoples)
DP	Partido Demócrata Popular (Popular Democratic Party)
ECUARUNARI	Ecuarunapac Riccharimui (Ecuadorian Indian Awakens)
FADI	Frente Amplio de Izquierda (Broad Leftist Front)
FECAIPAC	Federación de Cabildos Indígenas de la Parroquia de Cacha (Federation of Indigenous Councils of Cacha Parish)
FEI	Federación Ecuatoriana de Indios (Ecuadorian Federation of Indians)
FENOC (FENOC-I)	Federación Nacional de Organizaciones Campesinas e Indígenas (National Federation of Peasant and Indian Organizations)
FEPOCAN	Federación de Poblaciones Indígenas de Napo (Federation of Indigenous Populations of Napo)
FEPP	Fondo Ecuatoriano Populorum Progresio (Ecuadorian Fund for Popular Progress)
FICI	Federación Indígena y Campesina de Imbabura (Federation of Indians and Peasants of Imbabura)
FODERUMA	Fondo para el Desarrollo Rural Marginal (Fund for Rural Marginal Development)
FOIN	Federación de Organizaciones Indígenas del Napo (Federation of Napo Indigenous Organizations)
FTAL	Federación de Trabajadores Agrícolas del Litoral (Federation of Agricultural Workers of the Coast)
FULC	Frente Unido de Lucha Campesina (United Front for Peasant Struggle)
FURA	Frente Unitario por la Reforma Agraria (United Front for Agrarian Reform)
FUT	Frente Unitario de los Trabajadores (United Workers' Front)
ID	Izquierda Democrática (Democratic Left)
IERAC	Instituto Ecuatoriano de Reforma Agraria y Colonización (Ecuadorian Institute for Agrarian Reform and Colonization)
ILV	Instituto Lingüístico de Verano (Summer Institute of Linguistics [SIL])
INCAYAC	Instituto de Culturas Aborígines y Acción Comunitaria (Institute of Aboriginal Cultures and Community Action)
INCRAE	Instituto Ecuatoriano de Colonización y Reforma Agraria (Ecuadorian Institute for Colonization and Agrarian Reform)

ACRONYMS AND ABBREVIATIONS

ISAL	Iglesia y Sociedad en America Latina (Church and Society in Latin America)
MICH	Movimiento Indígena de Chimborazo (Chimborazo Indigenous Movement)
MIT	Movimiento Indígena de Tungurahua (Tungurahua Indigenous Movement)
MNCL	Movimiento Nacional de Cristianos por la Liberación (National Movement of Christians for Liberation)
MPD	Movimiento Popular Democrático (Popular Democratic Movement)
MRIC	Movimiento Revolucionario de Izquierda Cristiana (Christian Left Revolutionary Movement)
NGO	Nongovernmental organization
OAI	Oficina de Asuntos Indígenas (Office of Indigenous Affairs)
ONAI	Oficina Nacional de Asuntos Indígenas (National Office of Indigenous Affairs)
OPIP	Organización de Pueblos Indígenas de Pastaza (Organization of Indigenous Peoples of Pastaza)
PCE	Partido Comunista Ecuatoriano (Ecuadorian Communist Party)
PRE	Partido Roldosista Ecuatoriano (Ecuadorian Roldós Party)
PSC	Partido Social Cristiano (Social Christian Party)
PSE	Partido Socialista Ecuatoriano (Ecuadorian Socialist Party)
SEDRI	Servicio de Desarrollo Rural Integral (Integral Rural Development Service)
UDP	Unión Democrática Popular (Popular Democratic Union)
UNASAY	Unión Campesina del Azuay (Azuay Peasant Union)
UNE	Unión Nacional de Educadores (National Union of Educators)
UNORCIC (UNORCAC)	Unión de Organizaciones Campesinas e Indígenas de Cotacachi (Union of Peasant and Indigenous Organizations of Cotacachi)

From Peasant Struggles to Indian Resistance

CHAPTER ONE

SOMETHING OLD, SOMETHING NEW

Indigenous Resistance and the New Indio Identity

In June 1990 the indigenous movement of Ecuador announced its presence in an unprecedented fashion. Thousands of Ecuadorian Indians participated in a national mobilization that paralyzed most of the country. In several cities throughout the highlands, local activists participated in massive marches, took over town squares, held public trials, made demands of local authorities, and blocked areas of the Pan American Highway. In Quito, indigenous activists of national stature occupied the Santo Domingo church for days, refusing to leave until the government agreed to negotiate with them. Among the demands presented by the Confederación de Nacionalidades Indígenas del Ecuador (CONAIE) were the resolution of land conflicts, bilingual and bicultural education, cultural rights, and economic rights. Not all the demands were immediately met, but the platform laid out a course of action as well as a basis for future discussions between government officials and national indigenous leaders.

This uprising was soon followed by other major events. In April 1992 lowland Amazonian Indians marched for thirteen days from Puyo to Quito, gathering substantial indigenous and popular support en route. They remained in the Ejido Park in downtown Quito for days until the government guaranteed significant land concessions to indigenous organizations in Pastaza province (Whitten 1997, 1–3). In the 1994 national uprising, Ecuadorian Indians once again paralyzed the country to avert the privatization of water rights called for in the government's new rural modernization law. In 1996 CONAIE joined a coalition of social movements to create a new political party called Pachakutik–Nuevo País. The party secured

10 percent of national or provincial congressional positions and a total of seventy-six other positions, including gains in local offices (Mijeski and Beck 1998, 4).

In the late 1990s the national indigenous movement continued to stage several massive protests and mobilizations to protest economic measures and the rising cost of living. Increasingly, Indian activists protested major policies that affected all low-income Ecuadorians. After years of staging independent mobilizations, the movement formed coalitions with workers, teachers, cab drivers, and students to obstruct structural adjustment policies. Finally, in January 2000, after Ecuador experienced the severest economic crisis in a decade, national indigenous activists in CONAIE joined forces with junior military personnel to oust President Jamil Mahuad. Although the temporary government they helped to create lasted only three hours, their current role as the strongest social movement in the country—and perhaps the only one able to alter the course of national politics—is undeniable.

The initial 1990 uprising marked the transition from *campesinismo*, or peasant politics, to indianismo. The development of a panethnic contemporary Indian movement based on a common identification as Indians is a marked departure from previous forms of activism in which indigenous peasants' insertion as peasants into the socioeconomic structure was the central axis of political identification. This new politicized Indian identity does not involve a mere change in name. It simultaneously represents a new institutional basis, new organizational forms, new modes of leadership, and new political strategies.

In this book I ask why and how indigenous activists formed a collective identity as Indians.[1] In contrast to popular depictions in the Ecuadorian press, indigenous activism is not novel; the historical record shows that numerous indigenous revolts, labor disputes, and land invasions have taken place since colonization. The contemporary movement, however, relies on a newly politicized indio (Indian) macro identity, departing not only from the peasant political identity formerly prevalent in the highlands but also from local identities that often constituted the sole basis for political mobilization in earlier periods. The regional and cross-regional identification and the creation of an imagined community among different groups is a distinctly modern phenomenon that is deeply linked to economic and political modernization. Like other ethnic and racial movements, this one is characterized by a politics of mobilization in which, as Ernest Laclau and Chantal Mouffe (1994) contend, labor and capital are not the main opposition, as former "class" concerns become rearticulated in new discourses and practices.

By focusing on this shift from campesinismo to indianismo, I seek to both acknowledge the history of resistance and explain what is distinct and significant about the current politicization of Indian identity in Ecuador. I also seek to analyze the meaning and implications of this shift for the politics of national and transnational indigenous activism in Ecuador and Latin America. As a case study Ecuador is optimal because its contemporary movement that is older than other movements in the region. It also provides a rich history of joint activism with the left in the form of peasant unions, workers' organizations and national fronts. Indigenous movements are particularly helpful in elucidating the relationship between identity and resistance. Unlike women's or grassroots groups, which are relatively new, the long-standing existence of indigenous activism provides an excellent window into the historical connections among ethnic and racial formation, consciousness, and political agency.

This book studies the discourse and political practice of indianismo in the post–land reform period, beginning with the creation of the first highland regional organization, Ecuarunapac Riccharimui (ECUARUNARI), in 1973 and ending with the national elections of 1996, in which indigenous candidates participated on a broad scale for the first time, consolidating their new role as formal political actors. The primary focus of my empirical research is the post-1964 period, which witnessed rural modernization, the restructuring of the rural land and labor market, and the development of new types of indigenous organizations.

During this period, the distance between indigenous activism and the traditional Left widened as indigenous activists began to rely on new political practices and to develop new ideologies in which antiracism, the attainment of social and political autonomy, and cultural recovery received attention not previously granted by the Left, which had emphasized land and labor rights exclusively. The distancing need not be understood, however, primarily or simply as a separation between leftists and Indians but as a changing of consciousness of indigenous activists in ways that facilitated new ideologies of resistance and carved the path for novel types of organization, unprecedented forms of mobilization, and a new generation of indigenous leadership. The birth of this nuevo indio can be linked directly to the economic, political, and social transformations that took place in the Ecuadorian highlands between the 1960s and the 1990s. The basis for this new form of political solidarity is to be found in a common political history and struggle, a common experience of modernization, and a common racialization.

THE INDIGENOUS POPULATION IN ECUADOR

Calculations of the percentage of Ecuadorians who claim indigenous descent vary greatly depending on the source, from 40 percent in CONAIE documents to 12 percent in census reports based on self-reporting of native language. Estimates based on projections by the geographer Gregory Knapp (1991) are closer to 22 percent.[2] There are nine ethnic indigenous nationalities throughout the three main regions of the country. The lowland or Amazonian region, consisting of five provinces, has the greatest variety of groups, including the lowland Quichua (90,000), the Huaoranis (2,000), the Sionas and Secoyas (600), the Cofanes (600), the Achuar (500), and the Shuar (40,000). Together they make up approximately 38 percent of the lowland population. The coast (five provinces) has much smaller ethnic groups such as the Awa (3,500), the Chachis (7,000), and the Tsachilas (1,400), which constitute less than 1 percent of the national population (Benítez, Lilyan, and Garcés 1993).

The mountainous highland region (ten provinces) has the highest proportion of Quichua-speaking indigenous people, located in the provinces of Chimborazo, Imbabura, Cotopaxi, Carchi, Bolivar, Loja, Azuay, Cañar, Pichincha, and Tungurahua. Knapp (1991) places the Quichua population at 836 to 1.3 million in 1987, whereas Zamosc (1995, 27) places it at 747,400 in 1990. The most accurate figure would still undercount the Quichua population, as estimates usually exclude urban Indians as well as Indians living in predominantly mestizo rural parishes and cantons.

By adding the populations of designated Quichua majority zones (in which 33 percent or more of the population speaks Quichua), Zamosc (1995:23) concludes that Indians were 37.85 percent of the highland rural population in 1990, up from 35.44 percent in 1962. The provinces with the largest Indian population are Chimborazo (66.35 percent), Cañar (55.31 percent), Cotopaxi (53.06 percent) and Imbabura (49.38 percent). The provinces

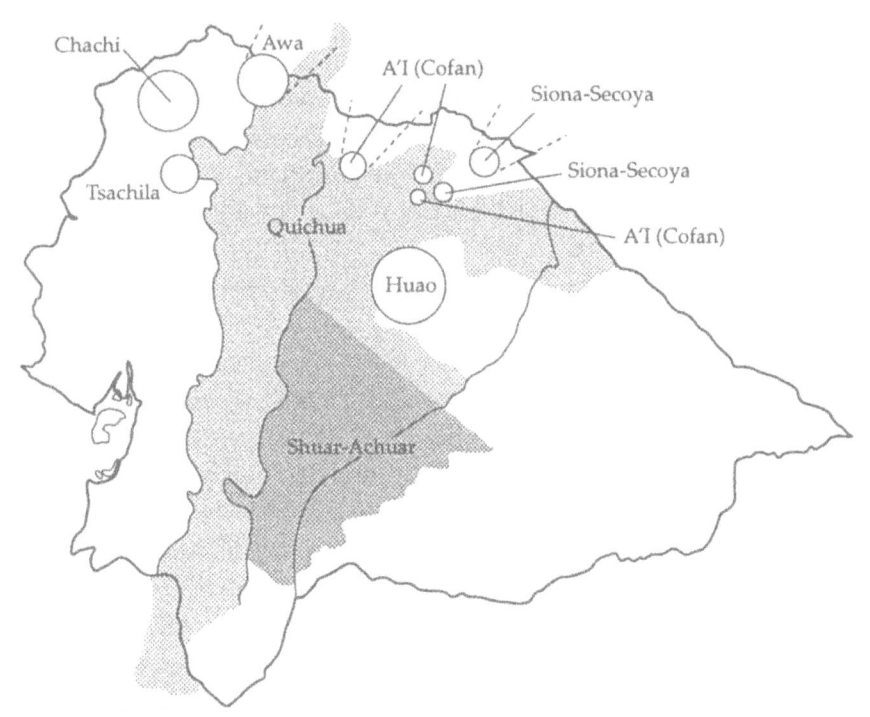

Indigenous Nationalities in Ecuador. Source: *Las nacionalidades indígenas en el Ecuador: Nuestro proceso organizativo*. Quito: Ediciones Tincui-Abya-Yala, 1989.

of Carchi, Loja, Azuay, and Bolivar are predominantly mestizo (Zamosc 1995, 223).

There are obvious cultural differences between the indigenous highland and lowland groups, as well as within regions. Unlike lowland groups, all highland Indians belong to one broad ethnic category: the Quichua. However, this is a broad category that subsumes groups of very different origin and distinct traditions who speak Quichua.[3] Before the arrival of the Spaniards, the Inca conquest of most of the highlands had produced important and abrupt demographic changes. Furthermore, the formation of encomiendas and haciendas during the postcolonial period divided many of the extant ethnic groups as labor opportunities and economic reorganization led to massive migration. Through this process, many preexisting ethnic formations were dissolved, and in many zones any sense of common origin has been lost (Ramón Valarezo 1993). Cultural identity became attached primarily to the community rather than to a common origin. Moreover, Quichua identity is rendered even more complex because of the subethnic identities of certain groups (e.g., Otavaleños, Saraguros, Salasacas, and Cañaris) who, for various reasons, share a sense of common origin and consider themselves distinct from other highland Quichua-speaking Indians. This factor, along with the life conditions that characterize different ethnic formations in the highland region, has led to the primacy of more specific or local identities as equally if not more important than the Quichua identity.

The role of race in shaping life chances and class difference in the Ecuadorian highlands is evident in contemporary statistical indicators. Although modernization has brought improvements in some basic socioeconomic respects to the Indian population, stark differences between mestizo and indigenous peasants remain significant. In an effort to assess the socioeconomic status of highland Indians, Zamosc (1995, 42–43) correlates cantons and parishes with large indigenous populations with basic socioeconomic indicators (see table 1). He finds a high level of spatial concentration (or segregation) of predominantly Indian parishes in specific cantons. He also finds that Indians are less integrated into the market than are mestizos and that mestizo agricultural products are more highly valued (Zamosc 1995, 42).

To produce a rough indicator of class and determine whether there are distinctions among Indians by class, Zamosc divides land plots into two sizes: less than 1.5 hectares and more than 1.5 hectares. Indian areas are overrepresented in the *minifundista* (small-plot owner) category, with 62.59 percent, whereas mestizo areas have 52.76 percent minifundistas. Zamosc (1995, 36) concludes that land reform has led to a breakdown of predominantly Indian zones into excessively small units.

In all the socioeconomic indicators shown in table 1, Indians fare considerably worse than non-Indians or mestizos.[4] Moreover, although a comparison of the campesinos and minifundistas in the mestizo population reveals a clear difference between the two in terms of basic socioeconomic indicators, a comparison of Indian campesinos and minifundistas does not. There is a much smaller difference between the two categories among Indians. In fact, Indians with more than 1.5 hectares have higher poverty, malnutrition, mortality, and illiteracy rates than do small landowners. This suggests that class difference, as measured by plot size, has little or no effect on social welfare and life chances among rural Indians, but it does affect mestizo indicators. This means that whereas land reform benefits indigenous peasants in securing their right to land, this land is not enough to

TABLE 1.
Average Values of Indicators of Social Conditions in the Sierra Cantons, Grouped According to Ethnic Sectors in the Rural Setting (N=73)

	Poverty[a]	Malnutrition[b]	Mortality[c]	Illiteracy[d] Males	Illiteracy[d] Females	Public Expenditures in Municipality[e] (sucres)
Average	55.4	44.14	46.10	13.85	23.18	20,635
Mestizo majority	49.1	41.77	40.99	11.50	18.73	22,384
Indian majority	74.3	47.47	62.95	21.55	37.84	12,872
Majority Mestizo Population						
<1.5 hectares	61.6	43.95	49.74	11.60	21.35	24,971
>1.5 hectares	39.6	40.39	35.33	11.45	17.04	20,711
Majority Indian Population						
<1.5 hectares	70.9	44.44	62.04	19.19	33.93	15,397
>1.5 hectares	78.2	50.88	63.99	24.21	42.25	14,282

Notes: [a] Rank of cantons according to eight indicators of poverty used by the Central Bank of Ecuador, 1979 (FIDA 1988: 2:59–61).
[b] Percent malnutrition among children less than two years old, 1986 (FIDA 1988: 2:63–65)
[c] Index of child mortality per 100,000, 1990 (Landin and Varela 1992)
[d] Percent illiteracy among men or women ten years old and older, 1990 (INEC 1990).
[e] Municipal budget in relation to rural population (Landin and Varela 1992).

Source: Zamosc (1995).

equalize their life chances relative to mestizos who own equal amounts of land. This disparity can be explained by other factors, primarily the differential access of mestizos and Indians to the labor market, public lands, and other goods. Further, a key difference is the disparity in access to municipal expenditures. Table 1 also shows that public expenditures are noticeably lower in Indian cantons than in predominantly mestizo cantons. In sum, these figures confirm the existence of a racial hierarchy in highland Ecuador, and underscore the role of race and ethnicity in structuring economic and social relations and hierarchies.

HISTORICAL ANTECEDENTS

Most highland Indian groups were conquered by the Incas in the fifteenth and sixteenth centuries. Before the Inca conquest, the highlands consisted of a number of regions each under the control of a different leader and with a distinct ethnic and political identity. During Spanish colonial rule, the Real Audiencia de Quito, present-day Ecuador, was divided into a republic of Indians and a republic of citizens. Indians, considered minors in need of the Crown's protection, were expected to pay a tribute to the crown in exchange for protection of their communal lands. Due to the lack of a mining economy, the hacienda economy was consolidated much earlier in Ecuador than in Peru or Bolivia, dominating the highland landscape in the seventeenth century and employing more than two-thirds of the indigenous population (Ramón Valarezo 1993, 21). The haciendas provided goods to mining communities in Peru and Bolivia. Hacienda owners had access to the labor of personal servants as well as forced workers, or *mitayos*, which included most male Indians over the age of eighteen who lived in their communities (Moreno and Oberem 1981). However, this was not sufficient, and landowners also employed peons, first called *conciertos* and later *huasipungueros*. Unlike a wage laborer, a concierto exchanged his work for the right to use a parcel of land in the hacienda's territory. This relationship has been characterized as debt peonage, as it was usually the concierto's indebtedness to the landowner that initiated and prolonged the relationship. Many landless peasants with no other way to gain access to land became conciertos. A concierto could also be bought with a hacienda or acquired in prison. The concierto's entire family was expected to work in exchange for the use of land. If a concierto did not fulfill his obligation, he faced imprisonment.

After independence in 1822, the concierto system continued, as large landholdings expanded. The abolishment of the mita in 1812 and of slavery in 1855 led to further dependence on concierto labor. Officially, Indians lost their special status in 1857, when the tribute was abolished. In theory, this meant the extension of ordinary citizenship to Indians. According to Guerrero (2000), this marked the point when the Indian disappeared as an object of national state records and state concerns. The administration of indigenous affairs and indigenous-mestizo issues was left to local officials and landlords, which led to a privatization and decentralization of ethnic domination. This process made it possible for conflicts between Indians and mestizos to be interpreted as natural and individualized, devoid of political content (Guerrero 2000, 46). Privatization of rural affairs made resistance difficult but not impossible.

In the twentieth century, highland Indians shared a history of social and economic subordination, racialization, and political struggle. Whereas previous indigenous uprisings in Ecuador were local or regional rebellions against census taking and taxation, by the early twentieth century, the hacienda had become the focus of local conflicts and strikes.

Pre-Land Reform, 1926–1964

Mid-twentieth-century highland communities were characterized by a closed, corporate system in which haciendas ensured the social control of Indians by providing needed goods and services that increased their debts and by preventing them from seeking work in villages and cities. Parish officials, chapels, and local police authorities exercised fragmented but powerful authority over huasipungueros. Interaction between Indians and mestizos was relatively common in villages but rare in cities and large towns. Many indigenous peoples remained unexposed to broader societal institutions and rarely had contact with provincial and national governmental units. Most labor conflicts were local, and only those that were large and intense were reported in national newspapers and news magazines.

While indentured workers and their relatives were dependent on the hacienda, residents of free communities faced another set of power relations.

In these communities most Indians were small landholders dominated by local merchants and *caciques*, or chieftains, with more dispersed but nonetheless significant political and economic control. In addition, labor was more diversified, combining incipient migrant work, handicraft and agricultural production, and work as domestics and peons for elites in adjoining white-mestizo towns.

The *concertaje*, or concierto system, was legally abolished by liberal policy makers in 1918, but the *huasipungo* system persisted until the 1964 land reform. The expropriation of church land by the state in the early twentieth century created the opportunity for indigenous peasants to struggle with tenants for the ownership of state haciendas in the canton of Cayambe, Pichincha province. With the assistance of leftist activists from the urban middle class, indigenous activists organized in small unions that focused on nonpayment or underpayment of salaries and unacceptable working conditions, as well as land rights. By the 1920s and 1930s there was significant rural protest against working conditions in haciendas throughout the highland region.[5]

In February 1926 Indians at the Changalá hacienda in Cayambe occupied land they claimed for themselves as legal heirs. The struggle with government forces led to a violent conflict. This is considered the first organized land protest action in Ecuador (Becker 1997, 161). An important development that stemmed in part from the 1926 Cayambe revolt was the rise of the Partido Socialista Ecuatoriano (PSE). In the context of a growing national labor movement, the coalition of middle-class radical intellectuals, workers, and elites who founded the PSE saw the revolt as an opportunity for a socialist transformation. PSE members traveled to several communities in the highland region, helping to organize indigenous peoples into unions and promoting the use of strikes.[6] At the national level, the PSE incorporated a few indigenous leaders into its central committee, promoted ties among indigenous organizations and labor, supported a platform that proposed the return of community lands to peasants, and in some administrations legislated policy designed to improve conditions for indigenous peasants. The PSE saw the organization of Indians as instrumental in the struggle against its main enemy, *gamonalismo*, a system characterized by the economic, political, and social domination of indigenous peasants by the few landholders who owned most of the land. Gamonalismo was blamed for preventing Ecuador from modernizing and from unleashing the productive energies that would expedite the development of capitalism and thus produce the necessary conditions for revolution. Hence, gamonalismo could be destroyed only with the elimination of the coercive relations of production that exploited native communities.

The PSE believed that the protagonists of the social revolution would be both the radicalized Indian and the urban worker, and it perceived the establishment of commonalities and connections between these two movements as one of its main goals. As the socialists won elections at the congressional level in the 1930s and 1940s, they broadened the narrowly elitist party system, offsetting the liberal/conservative pendulum and pressuring the state to either accede to some social demands or risk losing legitimacy. Despite the worker-peasant alliance, most state reforms passed by the more progressive regimes (with the exception of the rural section of the labor code) were designed to benefit primarily urban workers. Landholding patterns were left alone, for fear of disrupting the interests of conservative landholders, and most indigenous claims were met with state repression.[7]

The 1940s and 1950s witnessed greater institutionalization of indigenous resistance, from local cooperatives and unions to the Federación Ecuatoriana de Indios (FEI), founded by the Communist Party with the participation of urban mestizo intellectuals and a few indigenous activists. Unions and cooperatives were able to obtain ownership of a few public haciendas in the northern highlands and fought for improvements in wages, a shorter workweek, improved working conditions, payment for women's labor, and an end to personal service in landowners' homes (Becker 1997, 240). The FEI played a crucial role in the construction of cross-regional and cross-sectoral coalitions for land reform. Its activities in the countryside were primarily targeted to selected haciendas with labor conflicts. While free communities competed with haciendas for land and water rights, they had few political resources, as the FEI and cooperatives were focused on hacienda disputes.

Throughout the 1940s and 1950s, indigenous activism in hacienda disputes continued. The influence of the Communist Party on local syndicates as well as on the FEI led to an increasing focus on the procurement of land rights for huasipungueros and on land reform. With the Central de Trabajadores Ecuatorianos (CTE) and student movements, the FEI organized a massive indigenous march on Quito on December 16, 1961. Twelve thousand Indians and peasants called for land reform and the end to the huasipungo system. Leftists supported the march wholeheartedly (Becker 2000, 284) and leftist president Carlos Julio Arosemena promised to pursue reform. Before Arosemena could act, however, he was deposed by a military coup. It was not until three years later that a military government enacted the agrarian reform law designed to end the huasipungo system and give peasants access to land.

After land reform, many indigenous mobilizations and invasions of land pressured landowners to implement the law, particularly in the central highlands, where landowners were more reluctant to comply. In addition to the continuing but declining presence of the FEI, the Federación Nacional de Organizaciones Campesinas (FENOC) formed in 1968 as a classist peasant organization that focused on land reform and related issues. FENOC, which arose from a Catholic political movement that had shifted considerably to the Left by the 1960s, supported several intercommunal organizations in their pursuit of land and infrastructure for rural development.

Campesinismo

This period between the first Cayambe revolt and the passage of land reform was one characterized by campesinismo. By "campesinismo," I refer to a broad ideological construct that informed indigenous organization and mobilization during this period in several Latin American countries. Until the 1970s, for most indigenous peoples campesinista politics was the sole conduit to a public identity and to the exercise of citizenship. The main premise of campesinismo is that indigenous peoples' location in relations of production as debt peons or, in free communities, as small landholders should be the basis of their public and political identity. While ethnic identity is not necessarily negated or rejected, it remains in the background. Campesinismo is characterized by specific organizational forms, objectives, leadership, and alliances.

Campesinista organizations stress their class consciousness as peasants and focus primarily on those material demands that have been defined as class based: wages, working conditions, and land. The first campesinista organizations were the syndicates or unions created in haciendas in the northern highlands in the 1930s and 1940s. They did not question the huasipungo system per se but challenged landowners who did not fulfill huasipungueros' expectations of reciprocity and had therefore broken the hegemonic pact between landowner and huasipunguero.[8] For example, landowners who paid too little, extracted excessive labor, denied expected access to land for pasture and water, or threatened to remove huasipungos were often targeted by these syndicates. When the FEI was founded, it also focused primarily on wages and conditions in the haciendas. It was made up of syndicates, cooperatives, and cultural institutions but not indigenous communes, which the Ministry of Social Welfare and Labor rejected as a condition for accepting FEI's statutes (Becker 1997, 238). Both the FEI and FENOC provided legal assistance to local organizations engaged in land disputes.

Campesinista organizations were also characterized by what I call a constitutional link to the Left. A leftist party or workers' organization plays a key role in the conceptualization, formation, and development of a campesinista organization. Such was the case of the PSE and the syndicates in the northern highlands, the Communist Party and FEI, and the Confederación Ecuatoriana de organizaciones Clasistas (CEDOC) and FENOC. The party continued to play an important ideological and functional role in the campesinista organization, and the latter remained an affiliate of the party. Hence, since their inception, campesinista organizations were not autonomous. With a few exceptions, the top leadership in national campesinista organizations was not indigenous. In addition, class discourse played a key role in connecting campesinista organizations with other leftist organizations.

Finally, campesinista organizations frequently engaged in coalitions with nonindigenous classist organizations in pursuit of specific political objectives. While these alliances are not exclusive to campesinista organizations, the racial politics involved in class politics usually led to white and mestizo mediation for Indians and control over political agendas and strategies. The nature of class discourse did not provide much recourse for indigenous leaders who might have protested this imbalance of power. If there was little or no acknowledgment of the specificity of Indian identity or of an indigenous platform, there was no basis to argue against mestizo leadership or for more parity in leadership decisions within coalition politics.[9]

Post–Land Reform Activism, 1964–1996

Social movement activism, popular and international pressure, and the initiatives of landowning elites led to the land reform laws of 1964 and 1973.

While the 1964 law called for expropriation of haciendas and abolishing the huasipungo and the precapitalist labor relations that accompanied it, the 1973 law allowed neighboring communities to demand expropriation of haciendas because of demographic pressure. Through land reform and related rural development projects, the state became a permanent and direct presence in the lives of Indian communities (both free and former hacienda ones), expanding its previous role as police authority and occasional regulator of disputes between landowners and indigenous peasants. The state regulated and oversaw land and water conflicts, as well as the institutionalization of economic, political, and legal resources that could be accessed by indigenous peasants to challenge landowner power.

The economic and political effects of land reform that debilitated landowner control over local resources—increased access to education, economic expansion and modernization that accompanied oil exploration in the 1970s, state involvement in the countryside and in the Amazonian region, and the development of the Christian Left and of liberation theology—all promoted indigenous activism in the 1970s. The new local and national organizations that developed in this period had a distinct agenda that focused on indigenous peoples, combining cultural, political, and economic demands. While some indigenous organizations maintained their allegiance with the organized Left, developing contemporary forms of campesinismo, other activists opted for indianismo, the adoption of a panethnic identification as Indians and the creation of a new discourse that focused on difference from the white-mestizo society as a point of departure in the quest for self-determination. Ecuador Runacunapac Richarimui, or ECUARUNARI (a highlands regional organization whose name means "the Ecuadorian Indian Awakens"), and the lowlands Shuar Federation, created in 1972 and 1964 respectively, were the first of a number of federations and confederations founded on the premise that Indian, not peasant identity, was foremost in the definition, specification, and defense of indigenous people's interests.

Finally, the democratic transition of 1979 led to further changes in the relationship between the state and indigenous organizations. First, the vote was expanded to include illiterates, extending citizenship to many indigenous peasants who previously had been excluded. Second, the Roldós (1979–81), Hurtado (1981–84), and Borja (1988–92) administrations advocated indigenous bilingual education and rural development, using a grass-roots participatory approach to organizations.[10] As the national government wrested economic and political power from local elites and encroached further into rural policy, it provided indigenous activists with unprecedented and unmediated access to state officials. State-aided mobilization and the incorporation of politicized activists increased their demands for institutional and political access and helped to generate profound critiques of the distribution of power and resources in the country.

In the 1980s regional and national indigenous organization building was consolidated. Each regional or national federation was grouped into one of three major regional federations: Confederación Nacional de Indigenas Amazonicos (CONFENAIE), Coordinadora de Indígenas de la Costa Ecuatoriana (COICE), and ECUARUNARI. By 1986 these new Indian organizations had coalesced with lowland provincial organizations to form one national organization, CONAIE, which, together with the efforts of regional organizations and local organizations, generated an unprecedented uprising in 1990 and subsequent mobilizations in 1992 and 1994. This new movement was characterized by its emphasis on self-determination, ethnic autonomy, and cultural rights and by its ability to develop cross-regional, cross-ethnic allegiances and extensive grassroots support.

INDIGENOUS ACTIVISM IN THE 1990s

Before as Indians they didn't notice us, but now they see us as Indians with rights, with proposals, as different Indians, not like what they thought we were, but how we can be and how we are.[11]

In April 1990 CONAIE called for dozens of provincial and local organizations to join in a national uprising scheduled for early June. On June 4, 5, and 6, 1990, the largest Indian uprising in twentieth-century Ecuador took place. While two hundred Indians staged a hunger strike in the Santo Domingo Church in Quito, hundreds of thousands took over the plazas and blocked main roads of all the provinces. By most accounts, even CONAIE leaders were astounded by the massive response. The *levantamiento*, or uprising, was particularly intense in Chimborazo, Cotopaxi, Bolivar, and Tungurahua provinces, less so in Pichincha and Imbabura. Chimborazo Indians occupied one hacienda and Cotopaxi Indians took over two others. Mobilizations were staged in the cities of Latacunga, Riobamba, Guaranda, and Ambato and to a lesser extent in the Amazonian region, particularly in Napo province. For four days, Indian activists and nonactivists, local and provincial leaders, and women, children, and the elderly blocked roads, refused to take their produce to the markets, and staged massive marches in dozens of plazas throughout the highlands.[12]

The country was at a virtual standstill during this week. The government responded with military action, but the military was instructed to withhold excessive force. The CONAIE presented a platform of sixteen demands, including resolution of land conflicts, an end to the exploitation of Indians, a decrease in the cost of living, health care, relief from market tensions, satisfaction of credit needs, and an end to the invasion of Indian communities by public and private institutions. A coalition of human rights organizations and the Catholic Church became the intermediaries between the government and the CONAIE. The hunger strike in the church ended on June 6, 1990, when the government agreed to meet with national Indian leaders at the negotiation table if actions were stopped immediately.

The movement's ability to get some major long-standing land conflicts addressed (if not resolved) was a significant gain. The uprising and its aftermath also addressed racial discrimination and inequities in local power relations at the provincial level. While racism and local power issues were not part of the official platform, they were the motivating factor behind the actions of many communities with and without land. These concerns were evident in several public trials held during the uprising in the towns and cities of several highland provinces. When Indians went en masse to the main plaza, they presented their own platforms, consisting of several specific demands that aimed to transform local power relations. In addition, they held public trials of provincial officials, highlighting the racial discrimination against Indians and the exclusion of Indians from positions of power. One of the most notable trials of local public officials occurred in the city of Latacunga, Cotopaxi province, where Alberto Taxco, a *yachac*, or medicine man, discussed the second-class treatment experienced by Indians, linking it specifically to the lack of respect from public authorities:

> How we sweat, how we stay up all night! And yet when we ask authorities to help us, they deny this help. When we ask for a phone, they say the phone is out of order. As soon as we approach them, they laugh at us, we are aware of this. . . . But enough is enough, we will no longer be the soles of their shoes. It is we Indians who support this country. Where are the bluebloods while we are growing the potatoes and the oats?[13]

The trial lasted several hours. At one point, Taxco turned to the police chief and said:

> If you take an Indian prisoner, you must treat him as you would treat a deputy. Would you kick the deputy as you arrested him? No! What would you do to the *runas* [Indians]? Kick them, kick them! If you caught a landowner's son, you would hold him by the hand, and make arrangements with his father. This is neither just nor equal."[14]

These concerns resonated in dozens of indigenous communities. After reading similar statements in several public trials throughout the highlands, activists pressured local officials to sign the platform and commit to meeting the demands. Most of the officials present signed and made an oral commitment to follow through. Although the actual outcome of these demands was mixed, they served to create multiple sites of contestation, pressure, and negotiation instead of only one negotiation at the national level. Moreover, the experience reinforced the belief of many CONAIE leaders that even when they were rebuffed by national-level public officials, the struggle could continue at the local levels and that local changes in power relations in dozens of towns and cities could lead to significant empowerment.[15]

The local uprisings led to new and renewed demands for Indian *tenientes políticos* (sheriffs; political lieutenants) and council members. In several cases, local activists were successful in pressuring provincial governors to select Indian tenientes or allow locals to elect one. By 1994 of the thirteen Indian tenientes políticos in highland provinces with large Indian populations, nine were selected after the uprising. In addition, after the uprising, Indian council-members were selected in Saraguro, and one was added to the city council slate in Cotacachi in Imbabura province. Despite these significant changes, local activists continued their efforts as mestizos continued to dominate local and regional politics.

In addition to seeking land, the end of racial discrimination, and shifts in local power, indigenous activists sought territory, autonomy, and the recognition of Ecuador as a pluricultural state. The vulnerable relationship between the CONAIE and the state was complicated further when the CONAIE presented a declaration written by the Organización de Pueblos Indígenas de Pastaza (OPIP) titled "Agreement concerning the Territorial Rights of the Indian Peoples of Pastaza." In addition to the concession of land rights, the document called for self-rule, political autonomy, and

Indian participation in decisions concerning oil exploration in Indian-inhabited lands. It also opposed military intervention in indigenous people's affairs, asking for the revision of military statutes. Although the government had been willing to open up a discussion about economic demands, the political ones, particularly those focused on self-determination, seemed out of the question, as President Borja accused the OPIP of wanting to create a parallel state. Other popular movements as well as sectors of the Left also warned against the threat this movement presented to national sovereignty. Many intellectuals and analysts began to claim that the Indians had gone too far. The struggle for pluriculturalism would continue through 1998, when the new Ecuadorian constitution declared Ecuador a pluricultural country.

Between 1990 and 1992 the Ecuadorian Indian movement met with both success and failure. It was successful in changing the political discourse and practice with regard to Indians and in pressuring the state to adopt a concept of pluriculturalism that included land rights and other economic demands. This process allowed for the resolution of highland land conflicts and the concession of land grants to Quichua Indians in Pastaza province after a massive march to Quito in 1992. It failed, however, in achieving its goal of political empowerment at the national level. The extent to which Ecuadorian Indians remained excluded from any national decision-making process was painfully evident in 1994, when extensive lobbying of congress to review the Indians' agrarian law proposal (alongside the one proposed by the chamber of Agriculture) led to no action whatsoever. The second largest indigenous uprising, the "mobilization for life," was held in June of that year. The massive event reminded the state and civil society that the indigenous movement remained vital. Several days of protest were not able to stop the new law, which rendered agrarian reform defunct. The sole concession activists were able to obtain was to halt the privatization of water rights.

If the early 1990s marked the eruption of the indigenous social movement on the national scene, the late 1990s were characterized by two main developments: the creation of an indigenous political movement and increased indigenous involvement in political affairs that affected *all* Ecuadorians. Both developments involved coalition building with nonindigenous popular organizations. This was a significant departure from the indigenous politics of the 1980s and early 1990s, which had stressed organizational and ideological autonomy.

In November 1995 the CONAIE formed a coalition with other social movements (environmental, women's, anticorruption, human rights, and some workers' organizations) with substantial support from the Socialist Party, the Communist Party, and the Izquierda Democrática (Democratic Left), creating Pachakutik–Nuevo País (New Country, in Quichua and Spanish, respectively). Indian activists' previous lack of participation in the formal political sphere was due to activists' fear of contaminating themselves with "politics as usual" and to their pursuit of "autonomist" politics. The creation of Pachakutik–Nuevo País meant the formalization of coalition politics with whites and mestizos, the abandonment of an exclusive focus on protest politics, and an unprecedented engagement in electoral and institutional politics. In 1996 Pachakutik–Nuevo País won eight of eighty-two congressional seats. Four were won by Indians, including Luis Macas, then president of the CONAIE, and Miguel Llucu, former president of ECUARUNARI. The movement also won seventy-one elected positions at the local and provincial levels in thirteen provinces, most of them by Indian candidates. The party's focus on gaining local positions to build an electoral machine from the bottom up was effective. Pachakutik–Nuevo País won seven of every ten races it entered.[16] According to an exit poll conducted by Natalia Wray, 80 percent of indigenous voters voted for indigenous candidates, and most of those questioned said they were participating because Indians were on the ballot.[17]

Indianismo

Indianismo, the set of ideologies of resistance that posit the racial domination of whites and mestizos over Indians as the main impediment to Indians' socioeconomic advancement, stresses Indian/white polarities over class polarities and in general pursues Indian self-determination, cultural recuperation, socioeconomic rights, and the legitimization of a multinational state. In indianista politics, indigenous activists stress a shared identity as Indians in opposition to non-Indians. This umbrella identity incorporates not only indigenous peasants but migrant workers, merchants, and urban professionals, among others. "Indian," which had become a derogatory term, was now assigned a positive value, as indigenous activists reclaimed it as a source of pride and a basis for political mobilization. Indianismo is characterized by specific organizational forms, objectives, and strategies.

In contrast to campesinista organizations, indianista organizations were not founded by the Left, nor did they rely on the Left for substantial institutional, financial, or ideological support. Many indianista organizations stemmed from church, literacy, or other forms of grassroots activism. Several intercommunal and regional organizations were promoted by the state, which preferred them over leftist organizations. Financial and institutional support for many of these organizations came from international foundations and nongovernmental organizations (NGOs). Campesinista organizations operated either at the local level as syndicates or at the national level, as did the FEI and FENOC. Indianista organizations, by contrast, can be divided into the following categories: first-degree organizations at the community level; second-degree, or intercommunal, organizations that usually represent several communities; and third-degree organizations, several intercommunal organizations at the provincal level. Whereas the FEI was characterized by selective campaigns in which its leaders worked with a community that had land or labor issues, indianista organizations are far more decentralized and engaged in multiple demands at very different levels. In addition, indianista organizations are characterized by exclusive indigenous leadership. While mestizo supporters may be active in assisting organizations in various ways, they do not share positions of leadership with indigenous activists. While some activists had some connection with the Left, most local- and national-level activists became involved through their work as literacy educators or catechists.

The objectives of indianista organizations also vary significantly from campesinista organizations. Indianista organizations address a wide range of issues that include but go beyond land claims. Moreover, traditional material issues, such as land, are cast in a different light and interpreted as cultural demands. In addition, indianista organizations have made it their purpose to enter the political sphere as well as engage with and alter the political process.

Finally, a major distinction between indianista and campesinista organizations is the former's focus on political autonomy. Between 1972, the year ECUARUNARI was created, and 1995, when Pachakutik was created, indianista organizations struggled to achieve unprecedented autonomy as political actors speaking for and representing themselves in exchanges and negotiations with state authorities. Many of the internal debates about campesino versus Indian political identity addressed questions about the value and political necessity of establishing a separate political identity that required a separate politics from traditional forms of rural organization. While the post-1996 period has been characterized by the establishment of new coalitions with nonindigenous organizations, this has occurred after indigenous organizations have obtained organizational and ideological autonomy and considerably shifted the interracial power dynamics among social movement organizations.

From Campesinismo to Indianismo

The transition from campesinismo to indianismo is a complex phenomenon that has deeply shaped indigenous politics in Ecuador and the region. There is no single or simple explanation for a development that has international and domestic dimensions and that has been shaped by changes in the political economy, racial relations, state-society relations, and social movement politics. To explain this shift, this book analyzes the factors that played a role in this transition at the national and local levels.

Chapters 2 and 3 provide the theoretical and historical foundations for the study. Chapter 2 argues for a theory of political identity that studies how the intersection of macrostructural change and specific forms of consciousness have shaped indigenous identity and resistance. Chapter 3 examines changes in the political economy and racial order that laid the basis for the contemporary movement. I analyze the unequal insertion of Indians in the post–land reform period during the 1960s and 1970s, arguing that the political and economic changes produced by rural modernization policies transformed both the relations of production in the region and the relationship between Ecuadorian Indians and the state.

Chapters 4 and 5 introduce two local movements to explicate how different local forms of indianismo are informed by the interplay among political, economic, and racial structures and consciousness. Both the UNORCIC and FECAIPAC were created to combat racism, and both seek to achieve indigenous autonomy. However, they represent two very different paths of resistance. UNORCIC pursued a strategy of class politics based on alliances with nonindigenous politicians, whereas FECAIPAC fought against racial subordination by "rediscovering" a unique ethnic identity, eroding all links with non-Indians, and creating its own Indian parish.

Chapters 6 and 7 explore the role of indigenous consciousness and related modes of resistance in shaping the national movement. In chapter 6 I trace the origins of indianista discourse on the national level in the 1970s. The creation of an "Indian" political identity was a complex process that emerged both in internal debates and in relationships with other social sectors, including the state, the Left and the church. Characterized by a discourse of autonomy, antiracism, nationalism, and anti-imperialism, indianismo initially coexisted in a tense relationship with campesinismo, leading activists to become engaged in the politics of double consciousness.

Chapter 7 analyzes how this new indianista activism and the state influenced and shaped each other in the 1980s and 1990s. As activists become disillusioned with the constraints of cultural policy, they developed a more radical discourse that moved beyond the notion of a singular pueblo indio and adopted self-definitions as nationalities, incorporating new conceptions of autonomy, territory, and multinationalism in their political repertoire.

In chapter 8 I discuss the implications of this case for the study of identity formation and social movement politics in Latin America. I address the theoretical implications of this study for the understanding of the role of Indian movements and politics in the region and the relationship between identity and resistance in contemporary social movements.

CHAPTER TWO

Theorizing Indigenous Resistance

Explaining the Shift

The contemporary Indian movement is deeply linked to shifts in structures and consciousness that led to the formation of an indianista identity. Surely political identity is not the only component of social movement activism: mobilization of resources, organizational strength, solidarity networks, and political opportunity also determine the likelihood of prolonged collective action. Nevertheless, a set of common identifications is a necessary condition for the development of shared goals and long-standing solidarities. The creation of the new politics of indianismo remains largely unexplained in Ecuadorian social science literature.

Before the 1990 uprising, indigenous activism was a neglected topic of study.[1] Traditionally, scholars portrayed Ecuadorian mobilizations as atomized and local, excessively legalistic, and often falling prey to the clientilistic interests of public officials and landowning elites.[2] This portrayal was shaped in part by Ecuadorian and Latin American leftist visions of what a national political struggle should be: uniting social sectors across regions, confronting the nation-state, and seeking a revolutionary transformation. Most scholarly assessments of Ecuadorian indigenous mobilizations produced before the 1990 uprising fall within two broad categories. I call the first and (until recently) most common approach class centered. The second, newer approach is ethnicity centered.

Rooted in orthodox Marxism, the class-centered perspective is represented by Albornoz (1971), Quijano (1979), Sylva (1986), Velasco (1979), and Donovan (1989). Class-centered studies draw their empirical support from a preagrarian reform history of highland indigenous coalitions with the Left. This approach views the indigenous struggle as prepolitical, dispersed, and lacking in mature reflection. It argues that to develop the necessary revolutionary consciousness, peasants had to be "awakened" and guided by urban socialists and communists.

Most class-centered studies share the conviction that although the inclusion of ethnic struggles under the broader umbrella of a socialist-popular movement may be extremely difficult, it is the most effective way to contest state power. Furthermore, an implicit (but sometimes explicit) assumption is that the nature and goal of this coalition should be defined and directed by urban intellectuals of the Left and not by "prepolitical" peasants. When looking at the problematic and unfulfilled aspects of the indigenous-Left coalition in the past, class-centered perspectives usually blame mistakes either on peasants' inability to attain a truly revolutionary consciousness or on the Left's failure to garner the support of indigenous leaders. Sylva (1986) claims that peasants are unable to represent themselves because they lack a cohesive strategy. Albornoz (1971) argues that the peasant-worker coalition failed because indigenous leaders' claims do not go beyond the immediate concerns of the single issues of land and agrarian reform, while Iturralde (1988) contends that peasants do not have a clear working-class consciousness that would allow them to differentiate themselves from the bourgeoisie. Other works focus on the inability of different sectors of the Left to sustain a stable coalition and adequately incorporate indigenous people's demands in their platforms during the indigenous-Left alliances between the 1920s through the 1970s.

The limitations of the class-centered approach lie in its exclusive concern with indigenous people's insertion into the economy as peasants. Despite the purported focus on class consciousness, indigenous people's consciousness as "peasants" is frequently dismissed, assumed, or naturalized, rarely interrogated or explained. This approach, which has prevailed in studies of highland indigenous people, has not only reduced them to being followers of a mestizo vanguard but has also neglected cultural and political processes and their role in supporting or deflating peasant resistance. For example, in Fernando Velasco's (1979) classic work, Indians were under such cultural domination that they were incapable of mobilizing on the basis of ethnicity. Therefore, they could produce change only when struggling as a class (p. 85).

Velasco's argument reflects a central problem with class studies: they start with the premise that class refers primarily to location in relations of production and that a change in relations of production will eliminate a specific social antagonism. However, after land reform, class analysts were faced with the continued subordination of indigenous populations despite changes in landownership. Land reform was not the panacea that many analysts predicted, and this has presented new theoretical challenges. As the postslavery organization of labor in Brazil has shown, one's location in relations of production can be shaped by racial hierarchies and processes of racial exclusion (Hasenbalg 1985). Likewise, land reform and the end of the huasipungo did indeed transform the agrarian class structure but did not end racial subordination.

The ethnicity-centered perspective, by contrast, is represented by Sánchez-Parga (1986) and Ramón Valarezo (1993). This approach stems from scholarly reaction to the reinvigoration of cultural claims and to the proliferation of new and distinctive indigenous organizations in the past two decades. Ethnicity-centered studies draw on these developments to explain the primacy of "ethnic rationality," which they define as an indigenous worldview characterized by distinct ideological perspectives, organizational forms, and political strategies. They claim that ethnic rationality and the political rationality of labor unions and parties are not only incompatible, but incommensurable. In this light, the Left's efforts to organize indigenous people are considered instrumentalist, paternalistic, and illegitimate and ultimately riddled with insurmountable contradictions because non-Indians and Indians have different political traditions, cultures, and rationalities.

While this perspective is best in its critique of the Left, it does little to analyze earlier forms of organization on their own terms without constantly positing them against presumably more "enlightened" and genuine contemporary forms. In fact, it appears as if earlier struggles are often not studied in and of themselves but are used to occupy a space in an evolutionary scale in which the contemporary movement represents the highest level of consciousness. Most important, the ethnicity-centered school cannot explain changes in indigenous organization. Indeed, if earlier forms of protest are only the product of Indians blindly emulating the political rationality of the Left, then how were the blinders removed, and when exactly did "ethnic rationality" emerge?

This limited perspective of ethnic processes cannot explain changes in the Indian movement because it places the ethnic outside of the political, portraying distinct communities' cultures and practices as self-contained and separate from the state. Not only does this represent a dangerous reification of the division between the social and the political, it also rarifies ethnic resistance as something to be understood in terms of the idiosyncrasies of each community. It essentializes the "Indian" into a static entity instead of exploring the ways in which state practices and ideologies inform and shape Indian identity more generally, as well as the ways in which indigenous struggles and claims have an impact on the state. Moreover, "ethnicity" is often used as a synonym for "indigenous," with no distinction between a local ethnic formation and a process of panethnic solidarity among indigenous people from different zones or regions.

Ultimately, the ethnicity-centered school's framing of indigenous concerns into a separate rationality reveals an unsettling similarity to the class-centered approach it opposes: it views Indians as limited and fixed political actors, positing their issues and concerns as defined by the isolation of a single factor. While the class-centered approach attributes the limitations of indigenous struggles to the lack of a strong class consciousness, the ethnicity-centered approach explicates indigenous people's political behavior as a natural consequence of their location in a separate, incommensurable realm.

Both of these perspectives proved inadequate in light of the 1990 uprising. The argument of an apolitical or extrapolitical ethnic rationality failed to account for both broad and issue-specific coalitions among Indians of different ethnicities or for the establishment of alliances between Indians and other national and transnational sectors that led to successful uprisings in 1990, 1992, and 1994 and significant electoral gains in 1996, 1998, and 2000. Because cultural understandings permeate state institutions, social movements, and dominant and subordinate social sectors, "Indian politics" cannot be understood apart from national politics, and the national Indian movement cannot be understood by isolating ethnographies of communities from broader historical, political, and economic processes. Both perspectives provide an insufficient basis for understanding the transition from campesino to indio politics, the development of a panethnic movement, or the changing relationships among indigenous people, civil society, and the state.

Hence, like the Zapatista movement in Chiapas, Mexico, in 1994, the 1990 Indian uprising in Ecuador caught many political activists and academics off guard. The question of how to explain this new movement and novel political identity was not only difficult empirically, but theoretically, given the intellectual and political tradition of categorizing Ecuadorian Indians' struggles as secondary and indigenous political consciousness as barely existent.

Nevertheless, the 1990 uprising also brought some closure to the class-ethnicity tension. Two things became clear: class analysis did not suffice to explain contemporary indigenous activism, and the particularities of ethnic difference had not impeded the launching of a cross-ethnic political movement. The existence and strength of the movement suggested instead that the shared subordination experienced by ethnic groups had become a basis for organizing. Scholars eager to explain this new political phenomenon and its associated actors asked a whole new set of questions, primarily regarding the cause(s) of the movement, the nature of indigenous cultural and political revitalization, and its potential effect on the polity.

Most scholars agree that land reform and rural modernization opened up sites of contestation and politicization that led to the Indian movement. Some have focused on the effects of rural modernization on the creation of organizations and organizational networks (e.g., Sylva 1986); others have explained how a decline in the hierarchical politics of the hacienda system and mestizo authority facilitated the rise of communal and intercommunal organizations (Guerrero 1993; Korokvin 1992). Still others have looked at key factors such as the role of religion in promoting resistance (Muratorio 1982), the development of a cadre of Indian intellectuals capable of spearheading the movement (Selverston 1994), and increased indigenous participation in rural development programs and internal markets (Pachano 1993). Finally, some have pointed out how changes in the political economy, specifically, how structural adjustment and economic crisis during the 1980s, produced deteriorating economic conditions, which in turn promoted more organizational self-reliance and collective action (COMUNIDEC 1992; Rosero 1990).

Most of these works have focused on the causes that prompted the politicization of activists and the emergence of a national movement. Little attention has been paid to the rearticulation of indigenous politics from class based to indianista. Hence, while contemporary scholarship after the uprising has addressed some of the social, economic, and political factors that led to this new Indian movement, none have analyzed the shift in consciousness from campesinismo to indianismo.[3] Moreover, previous analyses have used the indigenous movement primarily as a dependent variable to demonstrate how it was precipitated by macropolitical and economic changes. None addresses the micropolitics of resistance, meaning the role of consciousness in shaping movement politics, and the relationship between Indians and the state.

AN ALTERNATIVE APPROACH: THE MAKING AND CHANGING OF POLITICAL IDENTITY

The decline of a cross-racial campesinista front and the creation of an autonomous panethnic Indian movement in Ecuador provide a useful empirical basis for understanding how political identity changes. While political subjects may be identified in terms of race, class, religion, ethnicity, and gender, in specific historical conjunctures they may position themselves politically along one or two primary poles of identity. This positioning is neither a random process nor the consequence of an individualized, rational, and instrumental choice. Instead it is informed (but not determined) by both agency and structure, by the specificity of a group's insertion into society, and by the common understandings of such an insertion. In the process of making sense of relations and structures of power that determine their location in the social hierarchy, indigenous activists in Ecuador have alternatively used class, race, nation, and ethnicity as common bonds of solidarity that are the basis of political ideologies and strategies.

Political identity is distinct from social identity in that it refers to the drawing of political boundaries or frontiers around particular communities (Norval 1996, 65). Members of a community that is politically bounded have a sense of belonging to a cohesive entity that is struggling, through formal or informal means, for the attainment of power and associated resources. The construction of boundaries and of solidarity among group members is the central component of identity. Although identity formation is interwoven with economic and political processes and relations, it is analytically autonomous (Eisendstadt 1998, 246).

I argue that shifts in political identity are explained by the interaction of two main factors, macrostructural changes and consciousness formation. Structural changes consist of three components: macropolitical, macroeconomic, and macroracial factors . Consciousness formation, by contrast, is an ongoing process that involves the construction of solidarity and antagonisms in the context of movement politics.

Structural changes that have shaped the new Indian identity in post–land reform Ecuador include economic, political, and racial transformations. Political identity is intimately linked to broader societal transformations and develops through a historical and cultural process. While political identity is constructed, it cannot be merely invented outside of a specific historical context. In his discussion of the theorizing of identity within anthropology, Jonathan Hill (1990, 814) maintains:

> A constructivist epistemology, when viewed as an exclusive alternative to theoretical approaches, can become yet another form of disauthenticating discourse by reducing all cultural representations to artificial "reinventions." Discourses on power and powerlessness, no matter how imaginatively poetic or literary, must be understood in relation to social and historical processes that have real political and economic consequences, such as enslavement, poverty, or even genocide.

Consciousness formation—the interpretation, response, and creation of collective actors whose lives are deeply shaped by macrostructural factors—involves a group's awareness of a specific antagonism or difference vis-à-vis another group that may lead to political struggle. Specifically, racial consciousness stems from specific antagonisms between two groups that have been racialized and from the individual and collective recognition of power relations between the two groups (Hanchard 1994). A sense of collective consciousness is developed in the context of mobilization, as activists respond to and educate their constituencies, hold internal debates in which they air their differences, and interact with the state and other social and political actors.

My analysis of consciousness and consciousness formation draws on the work of Charles Hale and W. E. B. Du Bois. In his study of Meskitu Indians in Nicaragua, Hale (1994) explains how a specific history of social relations with British and American colonizers and their institutions was interpreted positively by Meskitu Indians. The Sandinistas and their revolution, by contrast, were associated with a history of dominant mestizo leadership and therefore rejected. This ideological affinity with Anglo colonizers, Hale claims, appears contradictory to many in the Left who believe the Meskitus' socioeconomic struggles could best be addressed by the Sandinista agenda. Contrary to some Sandinistas' views, the Meskitus were not displaying a false consciousness by rejecting the Sandinista revolution and seeking U.S.

support to obtain autonomy. Instead their position could be understood as reflecting an ethnic consciousness in which the antagonisms between Indians and mestizos outweighed potential affinities between them and led the Meskitu to develop an affinity with Anglo colonizers.

While the Ecuadorian case differs significantly from the Meskitu case, there is a crucial similarity that guides this book: the role played by mestizo forms of nationalism as well as mestizo-indigenous social relations in shaping indigenous identity and political ideologies. The historic exclusion of Indians from the "homogenous" nation-state model and the dominance of whites and mestizos in political social and economic realms has led Indians to associate most forms of nationalism with white and mestizo hegemony. Hence, while most indigenous people's economic and social needs may be compatible with a socialist agenda, their struggles are often at odds with socialist forms of nationalism that continue to reproduce mestizo hegemony. This is one of the main reasons why indigenous communities in Latin America have not always perceived an easy fit between leftist and indigenous activism. Indigenous forms of activism that may appear to reflect a false consciousness are instead the outcome of the consciousness formation process of communities that have been racially subordinate.

Du Bois (1903) provides insight into this process. In his analysis of racism and racial consciousness in the United States, he developed the notion of double consciousness. Black Americans, Du Bois, claimed, faced the contradiction of being both Negro and American. These were opposing identities because America, as a national project, was identified with the denigration and exclusion of blacks. As in the Meskitu case, a racially subordinate group's awareness of itself in opposition to others was deeply shaped by this exclusionary nationalism. This was an awareness that could not be disposed of or shed easily. Du Bois further develops the notion of double consciousness by explaining that it led blacks to see themselves as Americans saw them: they internalized a negative racial identity. The veil of color was the metaphor Du Bois used for this act of seeing oneself through the eyes of others.

Du Bois's contribution lies not only in proposing the existence of double consciousness but also in explicating the mutually constituting role of national and racial identity. One is deeply shaped by the other, and neither can be set aside. Hence, the notion of a veil of color implies more than simply stating that both race and nation have shaped the African-American political experience. It means that each one has helped to constitute and define the other. This leads to one key conclusion: any political project that seeks to empower a racially subordinate group that engages in double consciousness cannot simply eschew one form of consciousness for the other but must by necessity, involve the rearticulation of the two.

In the case of Latin America, the notion of double consciousness is rendered even more complex by the legacy of the Left. While nationalism has distinct meanings for the Left and the Right, the main premise of a mestizo, or hybrid, nation has been embraced by both. In Latin America, in contrast to the United States, the Left occupies a place of great historical importance as the main oppositional force responsible for the construction of political alternatives, via reform, revolution, guerilla warfare, student activism, or electoral politics. Leftist parties and movements sought to make states more inclusive, to expand citizenship, to redistribute wealth, and to achieve social equity. In Bolivia, Cuba, Chile, Guatemala, and Nicaragua, the Left was able to capture power and promote a socialist agenda. In most cases, however, the Left was able to obtain some electoral and policy gains. Whether in or out of power, leftist nationalism has been characterized by populism, anticapitalism, anti-imperialism, and the pursuit of a model of economic and political development that takes into account Latin American realities and does not blindly emulate Europe or the United States. That most of Latin America before the 1950s was predominantly rural meant that the countryside was an important site of political struggle and social policy. Campesinismo was the outcome of these efforts, becoming indigenous peasants' only conduit to a public identity and role as well as to a limited form of citizenship. Hence, indigenous peasants' encounter with nationalism occurs not only at the level of state institutions but also in their encounter with and political socialization by the Left.

This reality suggests a distinct alternative for inquiry. Instead of positing a model of double consciousness—Indian and Ecuadorian—I propose that the central contradiction in the Ecuadorian highlands is a campesino or peasant consciousness versus an Indian consciousness. Given the importance of the left in shaping national consciousness in the rural highlands, I claim that the campesino consciousness, infused with leftist nationalism, is the main reference point, or point of opposition, for indigenous activists seeking empowerment as Indians. In other words, campesinista politics were simultaneously a mode of struggle and a site through which many indigenous activists learned about political inequalities across the races, the exclusion of Indians from positions of power, and the prevalence of the notion of a homogeneous mestizo state.

The use of the notion of double consciousness sheds light on the politicization of Indian identity and the transition from campesinismo to indianismo in three important ways. First, it allows us to understand identity shifts as continous, dynamic processes characterized by tensions and contradictions as well as continuities. Second, it helps us to understand identity shifts as a rearticulation of the meanings and issues attached to each constituitive mode of consciousness and not as an abandonment of them. I use the notion of double consciousness to analyze how indianismo does not mean a decline in the material demands that characterized campesinismo but involves reinterpeting materiality and infusing new meanings and new politics into the quest for material gains. In contrast to previous analyses that see indigenous struggle as either a class or an ethnic struggle, or see it as both a class and an ethnic struggle, my thesis is that class, race, and ethnicity are remade by the activists in the process of political struggle.

Finally, because double consciousness occurs in the course of movement politics, it sheds light on the links between identity and mobilization. New social movement theorists have theorized the relationship between historical changes in the past thirty years and the rise of "new social movements" in which multiple forms of identity politics have superseded the traditional labor-capital opposition that characterized social movements in the first half of the century (see Melucci 1988). However, new social movement theory often assumes that identity-formation precedes political mobilization and fails to analyze how identity is reconfigured in the process of mobilization (Foweraker 1995; Haber 1996). Comparative studies of indigenous movements, by contrast, have taught us that movements are political actors that produce their own meanings. While the global dimension of indigenous struggle has stimulated local identities, Brysk (2000), maintains that it is movements that produce them. While most indigenous movements in the world share similar concepts and teminology (such as self-determination, autonomy, and pluriculturalism), these concepts' specific meaning and applications are developed in the conflicts and negotiations that accompany political resistance. Hence, political identities are as much a product of movements as a cause of them.

Understanding the creation of the new politicized Indian in Ecuador entails understanding how political identity changes. This involves moving away from false dichotomizations between class and ethnicity or rigid notions of "true" or "false" consciousness. It also requires a historically specific and politically contingent analysis that links structure and agency as well as the macropolitical and the micropolitical. In sum, it requires a theory that aims to "move" with the movement in an attempt to adequately explain the process of political change.

CHAPTER THREE

Uncertain Development

*Post–agrarian Reform Politics
and the New Racial Order*

The analysis of the origin and development of Indian political identity requires linking two important questions: how was social inequality organized and structured in contemporary Ecuadorian civil society, and how was an indianista discourse and practice that contested this inequality articulated? A pressing challenge in studies of resistance is to establish the linkages between change in economic and political structures and the production of alternative frameworks of meaning that make the construction of a collective identity possible. As subordinate groups confront and interpret the impact of broad socioeconomic developments in their everyday lives, they are also in the process of defining their collective identity(ies), developing common goals and, when mobilized, articulating forms of resistance. Although it is possible to think of cases in which collective identity has developed without leading to collective action, it is difficult to imagine a sustained movement that has not involved a process of collective identity formation.

There is a direct relationship between land reform, political modernization, and the contemporary Indian movement, as changes in relations of production contributed to the dissolution of old identities and the creation of new ones. Rural modernization in Ecuador was not a process of economic transition alone. It also entailed shifts in racial politics and in racial relations that led to the forging of a common identification among Indians of various communities and provinces. This political identity became the springboard for a national Indian movement that established cross-ethnic alliances among highland and lowland Indians of different ethnicities.

Here I explain the relationship between changes in the economic, political, and racial order and the contemporary Indian movement. Relations of production were rearticulated after land reform through the abolition of the huasipungo. The new economic order reorganized, rather than minimized, racial subordination. State-led land reform, as well as rural development and modernization policies, resulted in segmented distribution of resources in which most indigenous peasants faced increasing poverty, while middle-class and upper-class mestizo landowners benefited from policies originally targeted to assist the poor.

The public debate over land reform policy during the mid-1970s had two important consequences. First, as a power struggle between a nationalist military regime bent on social reform and landowning elites, it led to the victory of the latter in curtailing redistribution. Second, it was a site for the rearticulation of racial meaning. Debates over the social function of property and the best means of achieving rural development led to the reconstruction of the principal agents involved. Landowners were recast as efficient producers, whereas indigenous peasants were increasingly seen as inherently unproductive, resulting in a modern spin on the long-standing image of Indians as premodern. These new constructions were crucial in constraining land activism and limiting radical reform.

For most Indians, agrarian modernization marked the transition from one form of racial subordination to another. The shifts in racial politics and relations reveal the "newness" of some mestizo strategies of racial exclusion. Once Indians were displaced from the hacienda and entered the white-mestizo public sphere, socially constructed racial differences served to restructure economic and political oppression. The new transformations and their effects were understood racially because that is how they were experienced by many. Because exclusion of those perceived as racially inferior was sustained across ethnic, class, and occupational lines to remarginalize Indians in new relations of production, Indian activists were able to draw from Indians' shared experiences of racism to establish political coalitions between different indigenous groups and develop a national movement.

AGRARIAN REFORM

With the exception of Mexico, most countries in Latin America adopted some type of agrarian reform after 1950. In the Andes, the sweeping Bolivian agrarian reform of 1953 and the Peruvian reform of 1963 preceded the Ecuadorian reform of 1964. All three reforms aimed to end land tenureship, provide former tenants with access to land, and free the rural labor market. All also purported to improve rural efficiency and productivity. However, all three reforms fell short or were reversed. In this context, Ecuadorian land reform is not exceptional but rather a reflection of similar policies in the region.

The 1964 agrarian reform law introduced modernization in Ecuador, officially terminating precapitalist labor relations.[1] The huasipungo was officially abolished and former huasipungueros with a lengthy work history on a particular hacienda received the small plots of land they had worked. Agrarian modernization, defined as the joint effect of land reform and subsequent supplementary agrarian development policies, dramatically transformed the social milieu of indigenous peasants.[2] The displacement of Indians from the haciendas led to three important changes: a fundamental transformation in local power relations, as national law subverted traditional landowner power; the revival and restructuring of semiautonomous indigenous communities and local councils; and the unprecedented migration of indigenous workers to predominantly mestizo highland towns and cities.

Land reform was not a substantial threat to all highland landowners. In its first decade, most of the lands awarded were state owned. Those landowners in the northern highlands who invested in dairy production had terminated their huasipungos before reforms were implemented so as to consolidate the best grazing lands for the exclusive use of their livestock. Further, as export products became more profitable, many landowners switched from traditional domestic staples grown on highland haciendas to export products.

Nevertheless, for the vast majority of central and southern highlands landowners who depended on the huasipungo system for high profit margins, land reform was an obvious threat.[3] These landowners focused their efforts on finding ways to avoid expropriation. Some evicted huasipungueros under false pretenses or converted them into salaried workers before they could file a demand for expropriation. Once a demand was filed, landowners resorted to intimidation as well as various legal and political mechanisms to avoid unfavorable decisions. Unlike Peru, where judges who were partial to reform were selected to adjudicate lands, the court system of the Instituto Ecuatoriano de Reforma Agraria y Colonización (IERAC), the body responsible for adjudicating plot transfers, was composed mainly of official or ex-officio members of the Chambers of Agriculture and Livestock, powerful interest groups representing large landowners. This meant that many cases that merited land transfers under strict interpretation of the law did not lead to rulings that benefited former huasipungueros. The IERAC was underfunded, and like its equivalent in Bolivia, it was characterized by impropriety and corruption. Decisions were often delayed for a decade or more, and rulings were frequently appealed, ultimately favoring landowners. Another common strategy was the sale of land parcels to landowners' friends and relatives, to mestizo town dwellers, or even to "cooperative" peasants, all mechanisms that facilitated more landowner discretion over the quantity and quality of land sold. These strategies were so successful that by 1980 land reform had affected less than 15 percent of agricultural land in the country, and 68.4 percent of Indians had gained access to only 8.9 percent of land surface (Handelman 1980, 11).

As landowner tactics postponed or prevented most land reform, indigenous peasants in several highland provinces opted for more direct forms of confrontation. A direct relationship can be established between the frequency and intensity of peasant mobilizations and implementation of the law (Sylva 1986). While reform legislation created the institutional and legal framework for change, indigenous peasant struggles forced change by literally occupying the spaces landowners had so arduously protected. Through the use of land invasions, unauthorized grazing of their cattle, and unauthorized harvesting of hacienda products, Indians carried out de facto occupations of haciendas they claimed, pressuring the IERAC to rule in their favor and thus avoid their displacement. While much academic debate has questioned the role of peasants in getting the law passed, it would be extremely difficult to deny their crucial role in its implementation.[4]

Another group that became politicized was indigenous peasants from "free" communities whose need for land had not been considered by the law or pro-reform activists from the FEI. As they witnessed huasipungueros receiving lands, indigenous communities adjoining haciendas and beholden to them in looser labor arrangements demanded to be included in the reform process.

The demand for land, however, was not the only issue that prompted peasant mobilizations. Successful implementation of land reform created its own contradictions. With the abolition of servile labor, many of the landowners' former responsibilities to huasipungueros were also abolished. As huasipungueros, indigenous peasants had access to hacienda water and pasture, both crucial resources for subsistence. Although they worked in exchange for this access, there was also a common belief that it was their right. Before reform huasipungueros had relied on landowners to share their resources to ensure subsistence. After reform landowners barred former huasipungueros from any access to their land and water, punishing trespassers personally (usually by forcing them to work for free for a few days) or calling on local authorities to do so. For peasants, this denial constituted a violation of the moral economy. They responded by engaging in what Scott (1985) has called everyday forms of resistance. They would sneak into the hacienda to seize wood and water or graze their animals. While water rights were also pursued legally by some former huasipungueros, in most cases they continued to carry out these small forms of resistance.

After being excluded from these resources and having usually received the most barren and eroded hacienda parcels, the now-landed peasants realized that the sole transfer of land was no guarantee of economic survival.[5] Without access to water and pasture or credit for fertilizers, pesticides, seeds, and irrigation systems, their lands would not be able to generate the necessary income to subsist.

CONSEQUENCES OF LAND REFORM: THE EXPANSION OF CITIZENSHIP

Land reform brought at least three main consequences that transformed indigenous citizenship and redefined the relationship between Indians and the Ecuadorian state. While initial land redistribution had legitimated an unprecedented role for the national government as a supposedly neutral arbiter in peasants' confrontations with landowners and local authorities, the expansion of indigenous peasants' demands required a new role, the state-as-provider. Demands for benefits previously provided by landowners were now placed on the state, as were demands for resources to upgrade inferior plots and advance socioeconomic development: water, machinery, infrastructure, agricultural credits for the purchase of chemicals and technology, schools, community centers, and roads.[6]

The military government that seized power in 1972 addressed some of the peasant's demands in an effort to implement and direct rural development, a primary goal in its nationalist and populist agenda. This involved the creation of new institutional mechanisms. In addition to IERAC, several governmental offices were created in the Ministries of Agriculture, Work, and Social Welfare. As development projects were implemented in each highland province, the state deployed a group of experts on agrarian affairs who based their intellectual authority on their cumulative knowledge of the countryside.

However, state intervention did not necessarily mean complete state control over rural development. Unlike in Peru, where more than one thousand cooperatives were created and managed by state-appointed officials who rarely consulted with indigenous peasants, in Ecuador the cooperative model was not implemented on a broad scale. Instead individual landholders relied on local indigenous communities and intercommunal organizations to gain access to state officials and programs. This experience with the state altered the role of indigenous organizations.[7] Just as the state's knowledge of rural infrastructure grew, indigenous community leaders produced their own knowledge about state-mandated development. The presence of state bureaucrats in highland towns institutionalized unmediated exchanges between peasants and the state, in many instances legitimizing indigenous organizations as political actors. Unlike in Peru, where cooperatives were initiated and micromanaged by urban technocrats, most recipients of land reform organized into communities and intercommunal organizations that worked directly with public officials and NGOs. Participation in state-funded development projects helped local Indian activists to gain hands-on expertise in rural policy development and implementation. At the national level, local activists learned about broader political processes as they worked closely with legal representatives of national umbrella organizations such as the FEI, the FENOC, and ECUARUNARI. As this process unfolded, indigenous activists acquired valuable knowledge of the national government's structure and functions. The emerging indigenous leadership of the late 1970s and 1980s benefited from experiences their predecessors never had. Several of them had been the first in their families to complete high school. As they became involved in local organizations receiving state funds, they developed negotiating skills, gained experience in assessing, negotiating, and evaluating state proposals, and began to demand control over the planning and execution of rural development.

The second important consequence of land reform policy was the reconfiguration of local governance through the reconstitution of previous *anejos*, or annexes, into legal communities.[8] After the traditional haciendas were dissolved, indigenous peasants sidestepped the government's encouragement of state-planned cooperatives and drew on a 1937 law that established the legal and political legitimacy of Indian communities, protecting their right to land. Communities proliferated for important reasons. To qualify legally as a community, residents had to assign some land to communal use. In turn they would be protected by the law as legal communities and would have better standing in disputes with individual landowners and possible land expropriation.[9] Another reason for the growth of communities was the dissolution of traditional local power relations after the demise of the hacienda. In the Ecuadorian hacienda system, landowners, with the support of the church and local officials, had held a virtual monopoly over power, assigning local leaders or captains to mantain social control. In contrast to Peru and Bolivia, where important mining economies were prioritized over haciendas during the colonial and early national periods, Ecuador had relied primarily on haciendas as its main source of income since the seventeenth century. The long-standing dominance of the hacienda system in the rural highlands meant that political and economic power were tightly interwoven. After the 1964 reform community structures helped to reorganize power locally, replacing the power vacuum left by the hacienda's breakdown. Elected councils pursued social integration and some degree of political autonomy, using both consent and coercion to achieve community goals.

But indigenous communities also served a larger purpose. The idea of community, its survival and reproduction, lent tangible meaning to indigenous peasants' struggles, enabling the framing of what mestizo bureaucrats perceived as merely material demands into cultural claims. The joint pursuit of land for the community meant a common quest for recognition; its final acquisition signified both the end of struggle, abuse, repression, and death and the beginning of a shared, uninhibited space for cultural reproduction.[10]

The third important consequence of land reform was the spatial and economic dislocation of many indigenous peasants from the hacienda system and their insertion into a relatively new realm: town and city life. As many peasants were dismissed from hacienda duties and were confronted by new economic hardships, they increasingly sought economic opportunities in both distant cities and adjoining towns. But Indians had a tense coexistence with mestizo market intermediaries, authorities, educators, and vendors. They were excluded from many employment opportunities, as towns and cities institutionalized a labor-partitioning system that assigned them the most menial and underpaid tasks.

As they migrated and diversified their labor activities, many Indians could no longer be called peasants in the strict sense of the term. Occupational differentiation and the urban lifestyle that stemmed from it rendered their identity as peasants problematic and yet not obsolete, as their ability to function in both worlds precluded placing them in a simple worker/peasant dichotomy. Indians who still owned land or worked in agriculture were also artisans, merchants, vendors, construction workers, and professionals; and many who worked exclusively in urban jobs eventually purchased lands and returned to their communities.[11]

These three contemporaneous consequences of land reform played important roles in the formation of a collective political identity that was the basis for political action. Whether intended or not, these consequences confirm the existence of a strong relationship between modernity and the emergence of movements based on cultural and racial difference. Instead of accelerating Indians' assimilation into mestizo society, the elimination of a servile class of huasipungueros and their incorporation in state policy and urban economies actually encouraged the proliferation of "Indian" organizations that stressed cultural difference from a dominant white-mestizo society. Freed from the subjection of hacienda servitude, the children of these huasipungueros reinvented the Indian in their own modern image, reproducing ethnic identity through community living and return migration, transcending traditional spatial boundaries to promote cultural revitalization and political organization. Two crucial factors that facilitated the creation of this new emergent identity were state policies designed to incorporate former huasipungueros and changes in everyday racial relations as a consequence of economic and political modernization.

THE INDIAN AND THE STATE

State rural policies in the 1970s served to shape societal conceptions of the expected roles, rights, and duties of Indians. The ways in which the state sought to integrate Indians were made evident in public declarations concerning their role in agrarian development, the possibilities for their functional integration into the market, and their ability to advance the national development process.

Paralleling the Peruvian reform, Ecuadorian policy makers sought to reconcile the goals of equity and productivity. There were two main state approaches to the incorporation of Indians in the military regimes of the 1970s: integration through redistribution and integration through productivity. The first approach argued that integration of indigenous peasants could be achieved by simply targeting them as the beneficiaries of land distribution policies, thus freeing them to become fully incorporated in the market. It was conditioned, however, on a conceptualization of the nation as homogeneous and therefore easily able to be "guided" by a technocratic military elite. The second approach required that Indians maintain an adequate level of domestic crop productivity and occupy the place assigned to them in the agrarian structure. Although each of these approaches was initiated in different political moments to justify different policies, both still occupy an important place in contemporary political debates. While the latter has taken precedence over the former, the former has been internalized by Indian activists and remains an important component of many contemporary indigenous organizations' rhetoric.

Integration through Redistribution

The military regime that ousted President Jose María Velasco Ibarra in 1972 introduced important changes in the state's approach to rural development. Velasco owed his power to a lack of consensus between industrial and traditional agricultural elites. The military seizure of power was supported by both industrialists and landowners, who jointly believed that neither Velasco nor the populist Assad Bucaram would be able to administer the new oil revenues adequately.[12] Led by a progressive wing, the military government headed by General Guillermo Rodriguez Lara attempted to implement economic and social reforms that promoted social justice and ensured profound social change (Isaacs 1993). The Rodriguez Lara administration is comparable to the military administration of Velasco in Peru, which sought an alternative path to development that addressed the needs of popular sectors. The Ecuadorian regime's self-designation as a "nationalist" revolution reflected its desire to carve an Ecuadorian path of development that would no longer depend on or emulate first world countries. In contrast to the 1963 junta that had been unabashedly antiunion and anticommunist, the Rodriguez Lara government held a more open position toward popular organizations, occasionally seeking their support in a national development plan that hinged on fiscal and agrarian reform, import substitution industrialization, and nationalization of the petroleum industry (Bocco 1987, 155).[13]

One of the first proposals presented by Rodriguez Lara was a new land reform law designed to strengthen the 1964 law by enforcing strict limits on the amount of land one landowner could have and by extending reform to include nonhuasipunguero indigenous communities. Expanding land reform was viewed as the best means of integrating peasants into national development and of achieving legitimacy for the regime through popular support. It was also considered good for capitalist development because it was believed to enlarge the domestic market, leading to growth in industry and fuller employment of urban workers. These workers, in turn, would produce a larger demand for agricultural products, which would increase productivity and economic growth in the rural areas, integrating all the country's population. Finally, increased productivity would decrease international dependence by replacing national products for foreign ones, rendering the importation of basic staples unnecessary (Rosero 1990).

Thus land reform was considered not only socially just, and politically wise but economically expedient. Land redistribution was considered a desirable goal for its own sake, because it was judged a necessary condition for economic growth. In national addresses and declarations, the Rodriguez Lara government used a logic that intertwined economic development goals with the indigenismo of the pre-agrarian reform Left to argue for reform.[14] Proclaiming its antifeudal nature, the government made frequent allusions to preagrarian reform horrors to decry the opposition of landowners to the regime's "sincere revolutionary efforts."[15] Its attack on the hacienda system was based not only on "the degrading human relations it involves" but also on the "backwardness of its system of production."[16] The problem of land concentration was not considered an exclusively indigenous issue but a condition that hindered the entire process of agricultural development, productivity in particular. Concentration of land was blamed for slow market growth, low productivity levels, and growing inflation.[17] More specifically, it had barred peasants from economic and social integration:

"We can't go back on agrarian reform and ignore the human masses marginalized from production."[18] While increased productivity helped to justify reform to industrial elites, the main reason stressed in public forums was the regime's commitment to social justice. Publicly announcing its opposition to "groups who oppressed the dispossessed,"[19] the government claimed it would try to limit the earnings of those who "already have too many opportunities" in order to help the popular majority.[20]

The Rodriguez Lara regime's preoccupation with equity went beyond land distribution concerns to include other social benefits, such as education and health, without which, the government stated, the "marginals" could not be integrated as full citizens. Hence, this regime was the first to legitimize (if not always respond to) a number of non-land-related indigenous demands, stressing that their full participation and incorporation in national economic life was their right as citizens, not a gift or privilege (Rosero 1990, 19). Finally, this regime made the first attempts to offer legal and juridical assurance to what it called the "permanently marginalized groups," asking for their more extensive participation in the elaboration and execution of decisions that affected them (Rosero 1990, xi). Regardless of whether this new approach came out of the regime's sincere revolutionary intentions or was simply a better way of ensuring capitalist domination, its effects were profound, in terms of both policy impact and promotion of indigenous organization.[21]

What rendered the regime's approach problematic for Indians, however, was that its concept of integration was based on an ideal of a homogeneous nation that precluded the assertion of difference. While the nationalist government had used selected aspects of Indians' ethnic identity to build a national image of Ecuador that would differentiate it from foreign countries, it appropriated them as part of a mestizo myth of origin that all Ecuadorians could absorb. In this perspective, highland and lowland Indians, urban workers and rural poor, were all defined as marginals who should be integrated into the center but could not be protagonists in this process. This notion of a single national interest, defined according to urban mestizo elites' conceptions of progress and culture, was used to justify national development policies that infringed on Indians' rights and resources and excluded them from participation in decision making, in essence further marginalizing the "marginals" it purported to integrate.

One example of this occurred in the province of Pichincha, where several state-supported cooperative projects were eventually unsuccessful in satisfying indigenous peasants' expectations of reform. Although the cooperative model of rural development was not as widespread as in Peru, it took hold in Pichincha, where land transfers had been made from the state to huasipungueros. This cooperative model did not meet Indians' expectations, nor did it allow for a more democratic participation in decision making about labor practices, resource allotment, and member rights. The strict rules made former huasipungueros feel they were working for someone else. The restrictions on other employment did not allow them to pursue nonmembers' common labor strategy of working as migrants in the city and returning to work the land periodically.

In addition to the failed cooperative experiments, there were other problems with rural development. Indigenous peasants usually had no choice in determining who would be the targets of rural policies. Rural development projects organized by the Ministry of Agriculture with state and international funds often targeted areas that public officials thought were most likely to perform well because previous conditions (soil fertility, local enterprise) were already conducive to success. These projects excluded criteria based on local need and density of population and usually overlooked populations with greater financial insecurity and instability. Moreover, most important decisions about production and infrastructure were made by national or regional officials or by committees that did not include indigenous officials and rarely consulted with indigenous activists.[22]

Integration through Productivity

The Rodriguez Lara administration's pursuit of redistribution was tenuous and short lived. The premise that social equity was a necessary condition for economic growth was challenged by landed elites as soon as the government announced its intention to expand agrarian reform. The ensuing debate over the implementation of a new land reform policy in 1973 illustrates the tension between "integration through redistribution" and "integration through production" and sheds some light on the ultimate victory of the latter. As Reidinger (1993) has pointed out in his discussion of land reform in the Philippines, elite land reform debates frequently involve the idealization of landowners and the demonization of peasants, which can ultimately lead to the repression of contestation. The Ecuadorian land reform debate should also be understood as not being simply about policy implementation and land redistribution, but about the very conceptualization of Indians and their relationship to productivity and modernity.

By early 1973 the government had disclosed that the proposed law would include cases involving high demographic pressure, as well as set stricter controls on the amount of land an individual proprietor could own.[23] No details were known until a text mysteriously released to the press in July reported that the new law would expropriate the property of any landowner who was exploiting less than 80 percent of the plot (*Mensajero*, July 1973, 1).[24] Landed elites, organized in the Chamber of Agriculture of the First Zone, immediately attacked the reform plan. They initiated an intense media campaign against what they called a communist government that threatened private property and called for the removal of the IERAC's "excessive" powers. They argued that, instead of promoting the peasants' welfare, the state should be more concerned with protecting the individual right to private property of "agrarian producers," the term they reserved for themselves.

In an astute political move, elites achieved political legitimacy not by holding on to a concept of absolute property (e.g., defense of private property as a natural right to be protected at all costs) but by redefining the concept of socially functional property in public debates as well as in Ministry of Agriculture declarations and interviews. The notion of the social function of property was originally coined by the Frenchman Leon Duguast, in reaction to individualistic notions of property established in the 1789 Declaration of Man and the Citizen and the Napoleonic Code. Duguast argued that public interest and social welfare are above the interests of individuals or specific groups. In Latin American rural struggles, this notion was used to argue that it was in the public interest to prevent the concentration of property in a few hands (Muñoz and Lavadenz 1997). In Ecuador this concept was used by reform advocates to undermine the historical sanctity of absolute property rights. The main argument was that the landowners' practice of leaving significant portions of their land idle, a common phenomenon in the highlands, was detrimental to the nation's prosperity because it erased all potential for improved agrarian production. In these cases, land reform was necessary, not only because it was a just option, but also because it would advance agrarian development. It was argued that indigenous peasants in a particular area deserved the idle land because they would make use of it and increase agrarian production.

Initially a compelling rationale for reform, this argument was attacked by landed elites who claimed that the rapid modernization of agrarian technologies required new criteria for determining whether a plot of land was meeting its social function. The basis for judging cases of expropriation should no longer be the quantity of land used but the quality of cultivation, harvesting techniques, and machinery used. This meant that "producers," a new landowner term for themselves that replaced *hacendados*, could be much more productive than peasants, even when using less land. If a landowner used modern technologies that substantially improved production, the land was definitely carrying out its social function, and concerns about the amount of land remaining idle should become secondary. In addition, landowners argued that productivity could improve more easily in larger plots, not in *minifundios*, or small plots. The social function of land, therefore, should be based on the productivity and efficiency of the producer. Thus redistribution was considered detrimental to the nation's wealth because it removed resources from those most capable of carrying out the social function of land.[25]

The construction of mestizo landed elites as modern producers erased the *gamonal*, or large landowner. The disassociation from gamonalismo, now considered a defunct system of production, allowed these producers to inscribe themselves into the state's modernization initiatives, to place themselves on an equal playing field with indigenous peasants, and to accuse the government of playing favorites by placing peasant's rights above the rights of producers, thus privileging redistribution at the expense of productivity (*Mensajero*, July 1973, 3). The landed elites' campaign was successful in more ways than one. The government was put on the defensive, riddling its public declarations with contradictions as it tried to assuage landowners by presenting the policy as a reconciliation of the interests of producers and peasants. "The greatest fallacy is to say that agrarian reform will lower production: we have raised the challenge that in Ecuador it will rise," stated Minister of Agriculture Jorge Maldonando Lince (*El Comercio*, October 9, 1973, 3). Rodriguez Lara argued that peasants who benefited from reform were an aid, not a hindrance, to agrarian development: "The peasant masses will be incorporated into our national development, adding to our wealth, increasing the capital invested in agriculture and the management of efficient exploitation" (*El Comerico*, October 9, 1973, 3).

At the same time, however, the government was changing the terms of debate by incorporating the landowners' concerns in its discourse. It adopted the definition of social function proposed in landowners' arguments, as evidenced in Maldonado Lince's statement that the purpose of the new law was to "fulfill the social function of property with a criteria of efficient production." Furthermore, he reassured landowners that "the law is not an attempt against private property, since lands will only be affected if they don't fulfill their social function." In the same declaration in which he had defended peasant's rights to land, Rodriguez Lara reassured the public that the law would not infringe on producers' rights: "Land reform will not be for peasants or for landowners but for a just distribution of land" (*El Comercio*, October 9, 1973, 3).

By the time the final version of the law was decreed in November 1973, the original proposal had been considerably watered down and redistribution as a goal had taken second place behind productivity, although it included an important clause that validated demographic pressure as a valid cause for expropriation (the only aspect of the law the government was able to secure). The objective was no longer to democratize land use and distribution but to expropriate only if landowners did not comply with state-designated productivity goals. This was achieved by creating a loophole that provided landowners—with advance warning—a grace period to make their production more efficient so as to avoid expropriation. For subsequent decades, this provision served to legitimate mere reprimands in cases in which expropriation would have been historically and legally justified. It has since provided an escape valve not only for landed elites but also for subsequent administrations less sympathetic to reform. The final version of the law revealed the limitations of the nationalist revolution to popular sectors that had hoped for radical change. Pressured by landed elites and with little support from industrial elites, the Rodriguez Lara administration abandoned its progressive agenda. The political consequences of the debate could not be dismissed lightly: Maldonado Lince had been forced to step down, and a military faction that had supported landed elites' position had gained political strength, eventually taking power in 1977.

After the 1973 law productivity became the yardstick by which all state policies, as well as producers' and peasants' economic activities, were measured. Two important factors hindered peasants' ability to produce efficiently and abundantly, however. First, the government promoted urban subsidies at the expense of rural prices. Despite its expressed concern for rural poverty, the regime's import substitution model of development showed a clear urban bias by setting price ceilings on rural products, such as corn, wheat, and barley, consumed by the urban popular sector. This led to exacerbation of rural-urban inequality: between 1971 and 1983 the ratio of urban and rural wages increased from 3.31:1 to 6.49:1, while the price of industrial products Indians purchased increased substantially, producing a decrease in indigenous peasants' purchasing power (Sylva 1991). Second, peasants were excluded from most credit opportunities. Between 1973 and 1976, 75 percent of the agricultural credit was granted to producers who invested in export products or profitable domestic sectors such as dairy and livestock production, while minimum amounts were channeled to the production of staples for domestic consumption by indigenous peasants (Chiriboga 1988a).

COMPARATIVE REFLECTIONS

Land reform in Ecuador followed a path that is both similar to and different from that in Bolivia and Peru. The reforms in all three countries sought to adequately combine redistribution and productivity. All fell short on both counts. Although Bolivia instituted sweeping land reform after its 1952 revolution, it affected one zone primarily. Also, the law was used to distribute fiscal land to a small number of large producers, creating a new concentration of land and income (Muñoz and Lavadenz 1997). Although Peru was successful in attacking gamonalismo, the distribution of benefits was highly uneven. The reform distributed land only to former huasipungueros, benefiting only 400,000 of 1.4 million peasant families that were landless (Alberts 1983). In addition, as in Ecuador, many landowners had already evicted tenants and sold off their productive assets in anticipation of the reform. As De Janvry (1981) and Dorner (1992) have argued, even when large amounts of land were distributed in Latin America, other governmental policies led to reconcentration. As a consequence, most countries today have a skewed pattern of land distribution.

In all three countries, production did not increase considerably. Common factors that undermined the productivity of the minifundios were state-imposed price controls of domestic products that benefited the urban population at the expense of the rural population, inadequate infrastructure and credit, and support of larger farmers who engaged in export agriculture. In all three cases, the primary focus was on changing ownership, not necessarily on raising productivity or peasant income. Most small landholders who benefited from reform had to supplement their incomes with migrant work.

Two key distinctions of the Ecuadorian reform are relevant for this book. While the Bolivian and Peruvian reforms are considered social if not economic successes (Bolivia, for the large percentage of hectares transferred in the context of a revolution; Peru, for its ability to undermine gamonalismo if not the power of landowning families), Ecuador, by most expert accounts, was considered neither. Ecuadorian reform efforts encountered much more political opposition in their implementation, and the underfunded IERAC was not allowed to actively engage in expropriation. The basis for landowner power was not destroyed but reasserted as the hacienda reinvented itself and landed elites learned to organize the rural economy in new ways. Hence the most important social and political impact of reform was not necessarily the overturning of elite power but the politicization of indigenous peasants who began to chip away at this power to ensure the implementation of reform. The obvious need to continue the struggle to ensure implementation, even in limited ways, distinguishes the Ecuadorian post–land reform period from the other cases.

The second distinction is the limited application of the cooperative model in Ecuador, especially compared to Peru. The cooperative model was characterized by state control of production, the land market, resources, credit, and rural workers. It essentially turned former debt peons into workers for the state, assuming that these rural laborers lacked the knowledge necessary to organize their own labor and production. The cooperative was an imposed model that attempted to homogenize all rural peasants into one work model. According to Hopkins (1985), Peruvian peasants felt a loss of control over their lives that was reminiscent of the hacienda system. And according to Seligmann (1995), struggles that ensued among peasants and between the state and peasants who resented the lack of control over production opened opportunities for radical organizing, specifically, for the radical organization Sendero Luminoso. In Ecuador the state never exercised this amount of control over former huasipungueros. Although it funded selective rural development projects and aimed to integrate indigenous peasants via rural policy, it did not engage in the massive micromanagement of rural agriculture. Former huasipungueros organized their own labor and production, according to market demands. Moreover, the indigenous community and intercommunal organizations, not the cooperative, became the social and political unit that organized social and economic relations and mediated among individual producers, NGOs, and the state.

This last distinction is important, because the revitalization of communities for the purpose of implementation of land reform and other rural policies played a key role in the politicization of former huasipungueros. The relative autonomy of organization and leadership that communities offered—and cooperatives did not—allowed for the creation of networks and the building of solidarity within and across different zones of the highlands. At the very minimum, the community model offered more opportunities for cooperation by not pitting the privileged (cooperative members) against the unprivileged (nonmembers). While social differentiation in the Ecuadorian highlands has increased with changes such as land reform, migration, and the commercialization of artisan prodution, it has lacked the additional layer of cooperative membership that exacerbated interethnic and intraethnic conflict in Peru. This key difference is one important reason why a strong national indigenous movement has developed in Ecuador but not in Peru.

THE REINSCRIPTION OF RACE

The effect of the rural policies in Ecuador was the institutionalization of an agrarian production system that was organized by race, consisting of wealthy white and mestizo producers who abandoned domestic grain production for revenue-generating production, mestizo landowners of middle-sized plots who ventured into smaller-scale but still profitable production, and indigenous peasants who produced the substantially less profitable domestic grains. The latter can be divided further into a minority of petty merchants who have enough land and production to sustain themselves and sell for profit and a vast majority who have small plots and therefore must also sell their labor.

This racialization of production was maintained by constructing the Indians as unproductive. While the very design of this policy raises the question of whether it was ever intended to benefit peasants, Indian peasants were faulted for not taking advantage of reform to raise productivity and improve their socioeconomic status. The representation of gamonales as productive, efficient, mechanized, and profit-oriented producers was accompanied by the contrasting depiction of Indians as backward, primitive in their cultivation technologies, inherently lacking the capitalist spirit, and thus destined to remain at the lowest levels of production.

Here is where racial characteristics took central stage. Representations of Indianness—not peasantness—were used to justify the relegation of indigenous producers to supporting players in agrarian modernization. In this case, racial discourse, understood as the dissemination of ideas about how inherent body differences shape social realities and social relations, is expressed in economic terms. With economic modernization, economic arguments for the inferiority of Indians have intensified throughout Latin America. According to Rex (1986), racism in the region is evidenced by the fact that while many of the distinctions of the colonial caste system have disappeared as economic factors have come to the fore, racist explanations are offered for the failure of Indians to succeed in a theoretically equal society. Ideas about rural development, economic progress, and modernity are therefore loaded with racial content.

To support their position in the 1973 debate, landed elite organizations had begun circulating studies claiming that domestic agricultural production was not meeting its targets and speculating on indigenous peasants' ability to boost production. By 1976 landowners were arguing for an end to reform by denouncing what they termed the tragedy of *minifundización* (i.e., the reduction of average plot size) as the main reason for the decrease in production and the paralysis of national development. This position has a striking parallel to early nineteenth-century positivism, in which the large numbers of indigenous people and blacks were considered an impediment to national development.

Although the contemporary discussion referred to land policy instead of indigenous population per se, the strong link in the collective imagination between indigenous peasants and low productivity infused this debate with racial meaning, as reform was viewed as a threat to humanity. On March 9, 1978, *El Comercio*, one of Ecuador's two major newspapers, published an editorial describing agrarian reform as antiproductive, anti-Ecuadorian, antisocial and antihuman. It was judged antihuman because it was blamed for the decline in productivity and a general economic decline in the rural sector. Through the late 1970s and the 1980s, landowners denounced the displacement (however limited) of "producers" from land that in their view had brought a shift from a mythical pre–land reform prosperity to poverty and misery. In their view, Ecuadorian development had been stifled because of land reform. By 1983, for example, when the government was addressing the agrarian "problem" once again, the Chambers of Agriculture and Livestock of the highlands and lowlands denounced a new agrarian code proposal:

> This law attempts to reactivate and deepen agrarian reform, which has brought the destruction of efficient units of production, the scarcity of food, and to the so-called beneficiaries of reform has brought unemployment and more poverty.[26]

Reviewing a clause that proposed the strengthening of communal and cooperative property rights, the chamber found it unacceptable that article 17 supported the transfer of private lands to the public domain:

> [T]his is not a positive thing, since it has led to a grave deficiency of production and to the destruction of important economic units that are today in a lamentable state of abandonment and deterioration.[27]

The notion of abandoned land that had been used by land reform advocates to obtain reform in cases of sociodemographic pressure was now being applied by the former landowners to indigenous producers. Furthermore, the notion of deterioration suggests, once again, the existence of a previously prosperous highland countryside. By the late 1980s and early 1990s (particularly after the 1990 uprising), the Chambers of Agriculture and Livestock were hiring foreign experts to confirm their claims about the positive correlation between land reform and economic decline. Completing the reversal of roles, chamber representatives in one meeting I attended called the Indians the *terratenientes*, or real landowners, because they now owned a majority of the land.[28] The "terratenientes'" lack of skills, their cultural distinction from white and mestizo society, and their traditionalism were blamed for the decline in productivity.

The Second Military Government: Colonization, Repression, and the Decline of Reform

In addition to the consolidation of racialized production and the decline in agrarian reform implementation, two other state practices ensured the subordination of Indians: the project of lowland colonization and the legal sanctioning of the repression of peasants who were involved in land struggles. Colonization of the Amazonian lowlands, initiated by the Rodriguez Lara regime and consolidated by the 1977 military triumvirate, was posited as a way to address peasant organizations' land claims.

Colonization provided for state adjudication of "empty" lowland plots to peasants willing to leave the highlands and settle in the rainforest region. Posing the Amazonian region, or *oriente*, as a "no-man's land" enabled the state to declare that there actually was enough land for all those who needed it, even if the redistribution issue in the highlands remained unresolved. The omission of lowland peoples from the national imaginary can be explained in part by the dominant representation of lowland Indians as savages, whereby Indians are viewed as an extension of nature and not as a part of civilization (Muratorio 1994). While colonization was initially promoted as a support policy for redistribution in the highlands, in its implementation it became a replacement for it. When the Instituto Ecuatoriano de Colonización y Reforma Agraria (INCRAE) was created in 1977, IERAC's budget was slashed by 55 percent, as funds were redirected to the colonization of lowlands.

The repression of Indians who were active in land struggles was another mechanism of control. The reform law created the necessary legal framework for land adjudication, but most transfers were finally implemented because of organizational pressures, such as land invasions, animal kidnappings, and de facto occupation of the hacienda. Until 1979 these acts were not always considered illegal. Depending on the case, the state had considerable discretion in whether to intervene or let an incident slip by. As peasant unions proliferated, however, landowners felt more threatened and lobbied successfully for a law that would prohibit and punish violations.

The systematic, state-enforced prohibition of invasions was not secured, however, until the military triumvirate decreed the Agrarian Development Promotion Law in 1979, months before the democratically elected president, Jaime Roldós, was to be inaugurated. In a process that excluded the participation of peasant organizations, the Chambers of Agriculture and Livestock negotiated extensively with the triumvirate to obtain the stated goal of promoting export production and lowering the domestic production deficit. The law implemented a series of protections for "producers" and restricted peasants' access to agrarian reform benefits.

Another important component of the law, article 37, called for the punishment of all land invaders, disqualifying all those who participated in an invasion from receiving any of the land finally adjudicated. This policy greatly increased the risks attached to land invasion by ensuring state retaliation and facilitating landowners' use of police and military forces to remove peasants from lands in dispute. Through the 1970s and early 1980s, many methods of repression and abuse were used against Indians who organized, including paramilitary forces, death threats, imprisonment under real or false charges, and torture. Although few activists were actually killed, harassment, physical violence, and beatings were routine.

Two notable examples are the conflict of the Llinllín hacienda, in Chimborazo province, and Quinchuquí, in Imbabura province. In Llinllín, the owners, the Davalos Donoso family, had turned the hacienda into a company in 1979 and hired the former huasipungueros as wage workers, a common tactic used to avoid expropriation. The peasants organized to obtain back payments for years of labor, asking for land parcels and houses as minimum demands. The landowners' failure to meet these demands led to a labor strike in October. In response, forty-five police occupied the hacienda residence. When the land court found in favor of the peasants, police repression intensified, and police officers attacked, imprisoned, and tortured several of them (*Nueva* 62 [February 1980]: 21).

In Quinchuquí indigenous peasants had lodged a demand for land expropriation in 1975. In December 1977 there was an initial police intervention, and in 1978 the landowner Carlos Montufar, secured a permanent police patrol. In addition, military personnel started gun "training" on hacienda grounds. Police persecution, imprisonment, and torture intensified and continued until 1981, when the Ecumenical Committee for Human Rights secured the withdrawal of police. Repression was both selective (four founding members of the cooperative were imprisoned and tortured in August 1979) and random, designed to intimidate. All members of the nine communities in the area were at risk. A nineteen-year-old peasant woman described her encounter with the police:

> I was getting on the bus that goes to Otavalo when in that instant the police grabbed me, made me get off the bus, and hit me right on the street. Then they took me to the hacienda and beat me there, and then they took me to the Otavalo jail. The next day three policemen hit me:

one threw gas at me, one held me by the arm, and another one hit me with sticks and a rock. They hit me as much as they wanted.[29]

Another woman described her experience with the police in her community:

> I was arrested almost a month ago. I was not saying or doing anything. I was sick and only stood there to watch. I am not a man, so how would I hit? All the people ran up the hill when they saw the police. The police were throwing those things ... what are they called ... those bombs [tear gas] ... [T]hey threw them up the hill and the people kept running. I told them "Don't run. We're only women standing here, we are not doing anything." And when they caught some of them [men] the women would tell them, "Don't hit them too much sir." And then they started calling us dirty Indian woman, Indian this and Indian that ... here ... here ... and they started hitting us with a stick. Even though I was sick they hit me a lot and they took me to prison and I still can't get better.[30]

When the National Planning Development Corporation handed down a judgment favorable to the peasants, Montufar organized a cooperative of his own, offering to sell the land to three hundred mestizos, *chicha* (alcoholic drink) vendors, and Indians who had never worked on the hacienda, instigating them to seize the lands and attack the peasant workers. Members of the peasant cooperative visited the IERAC office in the governor's office earlier that day to request protection from an imminent attack, but none was given. Later that day three hundred of Montufar's people attacked one hundred peasants, and twenty Indians were hospitalized in serious condition.[31]

Article 37 of the Agrarian Development Law did not call for the use of violence in land conflicts, but it facilitated and legitimized landowners' use of the police. Landowners' ability to use force even when cases had been decided in favor of the peasants and the lack of protection for indigenous citizens who filed (and eventually won) legal claims reflected the new environment created by the law.

That this law was passed just a few months before Roldós's inauguration is not coincidental. It guaranteed certain transition to a democratic regime in which integration through redistribution had been eliminated as a development option, landed elites' privileges could once again be guaranteed, and peasant activism would be controlled. If the contradictions between redistribution and productivity had been tensely negotiated in the Rodriguez Lara administration, the institutionalization of rural reform that meant increased productivity and colonization was finally and undeniably secured under the military triumvirate.

The New Racial Relations: The Maltrato and Its Implications

The indigenous activist Alberto Taxco staged a public trial in Cotopaxi province during the Indian uprising of 1990, holding local authorities responsible for the *maltrato*, or mistreatment, of Indians. He received an enthusiastic response from all those present as well as the thousands of highland indigenous people who heard of it. Although he made specific reference to the responsibility of Cotopaxi's governor and city councilmen for the abuse and exclusion of Indians in the province, he could have been referring to any of the highland towns in which similar mestizo-Indian relationships prevail. In addressing particularly common racial incidents, he was referring to the everyday set of inequities facing Indians: abuse by public authorities, unequal exchanges with mestizo merchants and intermediaries, and ostracism of town dwellers.

In Ecuador and most of Latin America, far from dissapearing, race has become more salient with modernity, facilitating the creation of an imagined community of different ethnic groups who share a similar socioeconomic location in multiracial countries. The homogenization of all pre-Colombian groups into one naturalized Indian category began in the colonial period and has been maintained and rearticulated in subsequent periods. It has been reiterated in Latin American scholarship on the Indian throughout the nineteenth and twentieth centuries that had been read widely on the continent and understood to apply to all Indians in the Americas. If cultural and language differences facilitated the racialization of the Indians on the continent (Todorov 1992), the long-standing generic categorization of indigenous peoples of many ethnic groups has generated its own dynamics, enabling whites and mestizos to make distinctions between themselves and other ethnic groups, as well as enabling those classified as Indians to identify among themselves as a group distinct from white and mestizo others.

Like many colonial regimes, those in Latin America were characterized by a rigid caste structure that legitimized colonization, repression, and slavery. By the late colonial and early national periods, however, intermarriage and the concomitant increase in racially mixed populations along with post-independence nationalist ideologies of mestizaje and indigenismo had a distinct effect on Latin American national identities. The nation-state model created in the nineteenth and twentieth centuries valued integration and homogeneity over plurality and heterogeneity. Becoming mestizo characterized the new hybrid citizen, embodying simultaneously the supposed disappearance of racial divisions and the inheritance of a grand precolonial past. The erasure of distinction was emphasized, difference was considered problematic, and hybridity represented the future.(Vasconcelos 1948).

Taxco's public discussion of contemporary post–land reform racism takes on particular resonance in a region characterized by racial exceptionalism, or the notion that Latin America, compared to the United States, had somehow freed itself from racism (Hanchard 1994; Skidmore 1992). Racial exceptionalism is the coexistence of a myth of racial harmony and a reality of "strong racist sentiments and discriminatory practices" (Hanchard 1994, 44).

Whereas in the colonial caste structure racism is acknowledged, after the elimination of slavery and debt peonage and the insertion of free blacks and Indians into the labor market intellectuals considered class, not race, the central organizer of difference in the Americas. Hence the indigenous activists now highlighting the salience of racial discrimination against Indians were not only faced with the "surprise" of mestizo officials who denied racism but also were accused of being racists themselves.

The appeal of Taxco's message almost thirty years after land reform challenges racial exceptionalism by pointing to the existence of everyday racism, despite land reform and rural modernization. Land disputes were not the sole cause of confrontation between Indians and mestizos and were absent in communities with no hacienda tradition. The dissolution of the hacienda led to a reshuffling of local economic boundaries, which raised the stakes in interracial competition between mestizos and Indians for state and non-state resources. Once Indians were displaced from the bounded realm of the hacienda and entered the spatial, political, and social terrain of the mestizos, the latter asserted their dominance in everyday practices where, as Escobar (1992, 75) states, the interests of the dominant elites are contested, and the social practice of difference is played out. Before land reform, huasipungueros had been relatively isolated from town mestizos. Bound geographically and socially by the hacienda, they rarely visited adjoining towns except to make selected purchases (those not available in hacienda -managed stores) and to attend church or religious festivals. The hacienda supervised the resources and expenditures of peasants and even oversaw their leisurely activities. Priests, tenientes políticos, and merchants who wanted access to Indians had to negotiate with the hacendado before taking any action.[32]

Land reform brought significant transformations both in indigenous communities and in adjoining towns. Within indigenous communities, new relationships were established between Indians and mestizos. Former huasipungueros established a more direct relationship with mestizo parish dwellers to negotiate the new aspects of posthacienda life, such as tax issues, contracts, and land conflicts.[33] Because it was difficult for them to command the attention and respect of local authorities without the intervention of the landowner or overseer, they increasingly relied on mestizo town dwellers to act as mediators with local authorities (Salamea 1980). As their dependence on mestizo intermediaries grew, Indians became more vulnerable to mestizo exploitation of their limited knowledge of Ecuadorian law and politics. In addition, Indians became more vulnerable to mestizos' encroachment into their communities. Without the presence of the hacendado, communities were much more vulnerable to the growing presence of chicheros (vendors of chicha, a fermented corn drink popular in the Andean highlands), chulqueros (moneylenders), and others targeting the communities. Local indigenous leaders increasingly perceived mestizo vendors, particularly chicheros, as a threat to their way of life and initiated early efforts to defend their communities by organizing campaigns to eject them. Hence many early attempts to organize involved issues of defense of the community against encroachment and exploitation by outsiders.

Interracial relations became increasingly complex as many Indians who were economically displaced by reform sought work in the adjoining towns and cities as market carriers, construction workers, and food vendors. More dynamic than their small populations may suggest, pueblos are frequently mini-centers of ceremonial events, commercial activities, and administrative functions. For Indians, the pueblos represent an intermediary space—not necessarily a place of transition between rural and urban life but a permanent in-between. Pueblos are the symbolic and ceremonial center of the rural highlands (Pachano 1986, 55). Surrounded by several indigenous communities, they are the site of encounters between the community and the nation-state, the Indian and the mestizo. It is in the pueblos that most of the post–land reform generations of Indians first encountered mestizo power as they attended school, sought jobs, and carried out commercial transactions in local markets.

Just as the pueblos were the site for new forms of material reproduction, they were the location of new, specifically urban practices of racial domination. Faced with the threat of indigenous newcomers, mestizo townspeople struggled to preserve their economic and political control in a number of ways. In some cases, mestizo notables organized committees of town *fuerzas vivas*, or live forces, which relied on claims of the pueblo's historical tradition and identity to exclude Indians from positions of power, often in the name of preserving hygiene, morality, and sobriety. Generally, however, this was not necessary. Exclusion was secured through a complex of everyday practices, most notably segregation and de facto discrimination in schools, workplaces, public offices, and local markets.[34] These relations were not a mere remnant of pre–land reform behavior but the product of a rearticulation of racial subordination that affected all highland provinces. As late as ten years after reform, in the pueblos the spatial domain of Indians and mestizos was clearly demarcated in public offices, public transportation, employment, education, the market, and the street.

Public facilities were racialized and privatized. Indians could not occupy specific public places, which could include certain sidewalks, churches, parks, and plazas (Burgos Guevara 1977). Waiting rooms in hospitals and public offices, for example, were out of bounds. These practices were sustained through the notion that Indians were dirty, smelly, and flea-infested. Having them wait outside offices while mestizos waited inside was considered a necessary sanitary measure. A local activist in Guamote, Riobamba, refers to these practices:

> Guamote is a pueblo that is very racist. We could say that they treat the Indians as if they were anybody and it is very rare to see them giving service to an Indian in a public office, regardless of whether the Indian is from the town or the country. They insult them tremendously. They call them *rocotos*. "You are sitting in the chairs, rocotos, how dare you, *verdugos* [executioners]." Well they are very strong and hard insults, threatening ones. And if the Indian responds, they [mestizos] call him arrogant, abusive, aggressive.[35]

Another activist from Chimborazo province remarked:

> When an Indian goes to the civil registry to request a document, if she [the office worker] sees that it is an Indian, she continues to paint her nails—"Wait a moment, I'm busy"—and she continues on with her business, commenting on the intimate details of her personal life to her coworker. But if she sees a mestizo coming: "How are you, how have you been, rest, how can I help you?"[36]

Manuel Paca, president of Inca Atahualpa in Tixán, Chimborazo, mentioned problems in the public offices as a major concern of his organization. Specifically, he referred to the custom of charging Indians for services that were their rights:

> When we created the organization we had a fight with the parish and canton authorities, because before, to get a birth certificate you had to pay between 3,000 and 5,000 sucres. And then we talked to knowledgeable people and they told us that we should not be paying anything, that the people working in those offices have a salary. Based on that, we gathered several people and we went to ask them why they were charging us 4,000 or 5,000 sucres. And it's not only with money that they have hurt us. They also asked us to take them hens, eggs, milk. And in the civil registry... if an Indian went to get a paper in order to marry, they would ask him his name. If one of the last names was wrong, then it wasn't only 5,000 sucres, but 60,000, 70,000, and even 100,000 sucres, and what could people do but sell their animals.[37]

In buses, one of the few sites where mestizos were obliged to share a space with them, Indians were expected to stand or sit in the back. As one interviewer explained,

> In a bus, some twenty-three years ago, if an Indian got on and sat in front, even if the car was empty, the driver would send him to the back, to the last seat, insulting him. That was a daily experience, and people would prefer to sit in the back to avoid conflict. For example, in a bus if an Indian was sitting down and a mestizo arrived, and there were no more seats available, not only the driver but all the mestizos would say "Hey, hey, get up," and they would be furious. And that was terrible because one could not answer back. I remember in my case in a bus in Quito. I was standing in a space, and then a man came along and he took over my space without any consideration, as

if nobody had been there. So I reacted by not letting him push me, and then he immediately pushed me and started insulting me. And I responded, saying, "You started it." And all the people defended him, and they threw me out of the bus, accusing me of being a thief.[38]

There were other abuses that Indians would experience while riding on a bus that mirrored common hacienda practices such as removal of one's clothes as punishment or payment:

The car wouldn't stop for you, or you would be pushed around inside, or they would remove a piece of your clothing if a coin was missing.[39]

When Indians sought employment, they were hired only to perform the most menial tasks as domestic servants, market carriers, and construction workers. They were usually excluded from service sector positions that require exchanges with mestizos. With the exception of successful self-employed indigenous merchants, this pattern has not changed significantly in the last two decades, despite a substantial increase in the numbers of educated and professional Indians.[40] Gladys, a young activist in the Movimiento Indígena de Chimborazo (MICH) who is a high school graduate and an assistant in a medical office, commented:

If they [mestizos] see an Indian working in a medical office, they won't speak to the Indian, they look for a nurse with a skirt [a mestiza], no matter how illiterate, but she should wear a skirt. No matter how much the Indian knows, they simply ignore her.[41]

Gladys added that she had been able to obtain some respect in the medical office but that the doctor lost ten patients as a result of hiring her.

Young Indians faced difficult experiences in the rural education system. Most activists interviewed said they first faced discrimination in mestizo-administered schools and in encounters with mestizo students as well as teachers and administrators. Mestizo administrators and teachers frequently punished indigenous children for speaking Quichua in the schools or for wearing traditional clothes. Indigenous children's intellectual capacities were usually not taken seriously by their teachers, and they were frequently ostracized and humiliated in public by mestizo peers. A migrant worker from Chimborazo now working in Quito remembers that in his attempt to get an education he was reminded of his "place":

A school that was far away was only for them [mestizos]. They did not want to even give poor peasants a desk. "This Indian should sit over there," they would say in the school. "Why is this Indian studying, he should go herd the sheep, he should go plant, not study." And that is why, until recently I only knew how to sign my name.[42]

Segundo Andrango, an activist and engineer from Cotacachi, discussed his school experience in the late 1960s:

I studied in the elementary school of the city [Cotacachi]. Of thirty kids, two of us were Indians. In the country we were normal children, but over there [in school] we had to be quiet all the time because the mestizo kids would get angry if we laughed too loud. We had to be very submissive people, and then they would say that we were alright. . . . For example, all the mestizos would call us *tu, vos* [informal second person]. But for us it was impossible to call them *tu*. We had to call them *usted* [formal second person]. It was an unequal relationship. And the teacher observed all that and never said anything. That is what makes me angry about the teachers. And we would wear a white shirt, white pants, and in those times they used ink with a special pen that had a metal [tube] in which one placed the ink in order to write. They would grab the ink and throw it on our pants that were white. And so we suffered a lot, those of us who studied in the urban school. Terrible, terrible. It was a suffering made of terror.[43]

Local law enforcement authorities (all mestizo) were responsible for some of the most blatant forms of maltrato; repeated instances of unwarranted arrests, police brutality, torture, and other forms of inhumane treatment were common. Local courts were notorious for their unjustified delays in processing Indians' cases, an obvious partiality to mestizos in cases involving mestizo-Indian disputes, and excessive penalties and sentences in cases involving Indians.

Another important site of interracial tensions was the local market, where indigenous participation as vendors and purchasers increased considerably during the 1970s (Pachano 1986, 73). Mestizo intermediaries exploited indigenous producers in several ways. They took advantage of Indians' scarce resources by purchasing Indians' crops months before harvest for prices much lower than they would have eventually obtained in the market. Racial allegiance was used effectively to maintain mestizo control over product prices, as evidenced in the common practice of price-fixing. In this process all mestizo intermediaries purchasing products in rural markets would agree to offer only an excessively low price for indigenous products. When Indians arrived in town, they would not be able to sell for more than this price. Finally, the "snatching," or *arranche*, still remains a common problem in many highland markets. Instead of asking for the price of a particular product, a mestizo first snatches it from the grasp of Indian producers and then pays whichever amount he or she considers adequate. The arranche is especially important because of its racial overtones. Although the economic exploitation of vendors by intermediaries occurs among mestizos throughout the country, the seizure of products and the lack of basic respect it embodies are a specific feature of interracial relations in the highlands. Whereas unfair pricing mechanisms are also used against poor mestizo peasants in predominantly mestizo provinces such as Carchi, the arranche is one of many practices that portray the Indian as the mestizo's servant.

The idea that Indians are servants is reflected in a number of racist practices originally enforced in haciendas and later reproduced in urban environments. Removing an Indian's garment in mockery or as punishment, forcing Indians to do unpaid chores, and enforcing strict norms on how an Indian should greet a mestizo were "reminders" of the Indian's place in sites outside of the hacienda:

> Here, some fifteen years ago, the municipal police would take clothes from Indians in the communities. They would take your hat, your pants, and make you work on the sewer system, install street posts, or make sidewalks [to get the clothes back]. So the cities have been built entirely by *mingas* [forced labor]. . . . [O]n Sundays, as we went to mass, if there was some damage the police would grab a piece of clothing. . . . [I]f there was some damage, we were the ones who had to work and repair it. So I think that in that sense, they have used us as workhorses.[44]

The reconstruction of servile relations suggests a transposition of racial knowledge that had served to exploit Indians in a previous time and that would also become a focal point of contestation in the history of indigenous resistance.[45] Some practices were not entirely new, such as the arranche and bus-seating arrangements. What makes them so distinctive, however, is that the number of people affected was much greater after huasipungueros were freed from the hacienda. Incidents were not only more frequent, but they involved many more indigenous peasants, whose commercial, religious, and governmental transactions had previously been restricted to the hacienda. They also involved new sites, particularly schools and public offices, which had previously been rarely attended or visited by hacienda Indians without mestizo intermediaries.

In addition, there was increasing public awareness and discussion of the maltrato after reform, as indigenous peasants had obtained new experiences of citizenship and a new awareness of their rights. Maltrato practices were increasingly considered unacceptable and became the focus of early activism of the 1970s. It was this sense of shared discrimination, more than any common tradition, that became one of the strongest bases for common identification. Forced labor, the arranche, public taunting, bus-seating arrangements, and discrimination in the schools were experiences shared by all indigenous groups throughout the highlands, free community members or former huasipungueros. Ethnic distinctions among Indians did not allow any of them to escape the maltrato or minimize the effects of racial subordination.

All of these practices share a common trait: the use of material dispossession. Excessive charges at public offices, spoiled pants, removed clothes, forced labor—all were perceived to deprive and rob Indians of something. In addition to depriving them of material goods, these practices reinforced Indians' sense of difference from mestizos. The white or mestizo was not only viewed as the attacker of the Indian but as the beneficiary of those rights and goods that were being taken from or denied to Indians. If newly forming indigenous organizations were just beginning to affirm a more positive identity, a sense of who they were and who they wanted to be, this negative identity, or sense of who they were not and who they were against (and who was responsible for their subordination), was already understood. As the Cotacachi activist Pedro de la Cruz stated:

> Before there was no one, no one who would say these [Indians] are worth something.... [A]ll that was Indian was useless.... [F]or example, they would call the little dog "an Indian's dog" or the [small] hen "an Indian hen." What I mean is that everything that was little, all that was negative belonged to the Indian, and all that was positive, that was developed, belonged to the mestizo... so much influence. In the schools they would say, "Quichua is useless." Now our grandparents say, "*Llanga shimi* Quichua." *Llanga* means useless, that it had

no use; shimi means language. That is what our grandparents and parents would say, "Llanga shimi."[46]

Together, these interweaving daily practices of segregation, exclusion, discrimination, and labor segmentation reveal a complex pattern of post–land reform domination in which discrimination against Indians was increasingly viewed as operating outside the boundaries of any one ethnic group. As Indians became an important part of town life and its institutions, their racial identity—their Indianess—came increasingly into focus as a set of apparently unchangeable physical and cultural traits that made them unsuited for contemporary urban life or modern rural development. While broader state constructions emphasized their backwardness, unproductiveness, and potential for violence, town mestizos focused on their lack of cleanliness and their servile nature.

The existence of maltrato in the post–land reform period may have alternative explanations. If one assumes that changes in relations of production should have mitigated or ended racial discrimination, one could conceive of a lag theory, which would argue that racial relations and racial politics were a couple of decades behind reform and that they would eventually be redefined in a more equitable manner. But without significant resistance, these changes did not take place. Moreover, the relationship between the new economic order and the institutional and everyday racism is not coincidental. There is, however, a very different assumption: racism can not only persist but can be reinvented in the process of building a new economic order. Thus race played a key role in the formation of a new class system, and the new economic order was characterized by constructions of racial difference that were used at different points in the policy process to justify specific distributive arrangements.

In highlands Ecuador, exclusion was rearticulated after reform by a new and intense competition for political resources during the reorganization of relations of production. Competition between mestizos and Indians, landowners and peasants, old merchants and new ones, led to the more heightened relevance of race, in terms of both the reorganization of the economic and political order and the organization of resistance to the new order.

Since everyday rural racism was located in these specific forms of maltrato, their elimination became an important goal for Indian activists. The abuses of local public and police authorities, for example, led ECUARUNARI, the first regional Indian organization in the highlands, to make demands no peasant organization had ever made before, such as lobbying for the appointment of Indian tenientes políticos and for state-funded indigenous teachers. Eventually, when the vote was expanded to illiterates, Indians would run for and capture local offices. While other, more complex patterns such as the arranche and other forms of servitude were often not specifically addressed in broader organization campaigns, they were extremely important in the process of consciousness raising that took place initially in small groups whose members eventually formed organizations. As chapter 7 illustrates, young Indian intellectuals and national activists used these discussions to describe, analyze, and problematize the mestizo-Indian power differential, to draw distinctions between peasant and Indian identity, and to assert the need for Indian organization and resistance.

CONCLUSION

The indigenous experience in Ecuadorian agrarian modernization challenges views of race as a superstructural or merely ideological phenomenon whose survival depends on the survival of specific relations of production. Former huasipungueros were not automatically integrated as equals in a modernizing society. In theory, new rural development programs presented opportunities for all producers, Indian and non-Indian, wealthy and poor. The exclusion of Indians as unproductive and therefore noncredible participants in the agrarian transformation allowed non-Indian producers and former landowners to benefit from rural development programs.

Economic restructuring went hand in hand with the development of a new racial formation in which some forms of subordination persisted, some became defunct, others were reconstructed, and new ones were invented to organize inequality in entirely new situations. Constructed racial differences were used as political tools in the organization of the labor market, the production market, and the distribution of goods and services by local and national governments. Contemporary power relations were not "deracialized" as a consequence of land reform but were taken out of the more private realm of the hacienda and the local teniente político and into the realm of public policy and discourse.

Post–agrarian reform racial subordination involved the reinvention of the Indian both as an object of domination and as a subject of resistance. In the economic and political reorganization of rural society, mestizo privilege was maintained through social hierarchies based on racial difference. Despite the egalitarian rhetoric of the first military administration, Indians were relegated to a second-class position in an agrarian development model they played no role in defining. The subordinate role assigned to them in the postreform development model is evidenced in their inferior socioeconomic position, their secondary role in a segmented agrarian production, and the persistent construction and reconstruction of everyday forms of discrimination against them all, regardless of occupation, ethnicity, or place of origin. Indians were fully aware that despite agrarian reform, or more precisely, because of it, the stigma of being Indian seemed inescapable.

How, then, do we explain the racial and political connection between this post–land reform period and the development of a collective indianista identity that has played such an important role in the formation of a national Indian movement? On a basic level, the creation and proliferation of Indian organizations precisely in this period could be viewed as a problem of unmet expectations. Borrowing from Gurr's (1970) relative deprivation theory, one could posit that indigenous mobilization stemmed from the gap between indigenous expectations of reform and what they actually received. Clearly, some contradictions existed between a state discourse of equal citizenship and integration, on the one hand, and a policy that sustained inequality and promoted diversification and segmentation of production, on the other. Furthermore, the limited redistribution model was depleted by the late 1970s and then discarded after the 1981 debt crisis exhausted the possibilities of the original development model (Rosero 1990). But beyond the broken promises lies a bigger issue. State rural development policies designed for a homogeneous nation by definition seemed to exclude the majority of indigenous peasants from participation, which facilitated the reproduction of subordination. As Warren (1978) concludes in her study of Indian identity in Guatemala, despite democratic rhetoric, there are informal mechanisms in the labor market and political realm that, in practice, ensure the separation of Indian and Ladino spheres and impede democratic access to institutions. As the experience of liberalism in the United States has shown, universal rights are often far from universal. The nonrecognition of difference often leads to the prevalence of the interests and beliefs of some groups and the total absence of others. The contradictions inherent in Ecuador's plan for rural development led Indians not only to question the effects and implication of state-designed development but also to question their lack of representation in the polity and their absence as political actors. Lacking any presence in decision-making bodies or elected office, they had little or no say in shaping policies and debates. This lack of voice and access was by no means the only reason for racial subordination, but it became an important factor in the organization of resistance. As the next two chapters on local movements illustrate, the changing relations with mestizo authorities and town dwellers and the new relationship with the state led to the development of new Indian demands that traditional peasant unions had not addressed.

CHAPTER FOUR

REPRESENTING THE RURAL POOR

Citizenship and Political Identity in Cotacachi

> *Just because we are indigenous, don't we have the right to be politicians and participate in political life? Comrades, we have the full right, as Ecuadorians that we are, to participate in politics and to create great political activity, and that is why the UNORCIC will never stop participating in politics.*
>
> Former UNORCIC president and twice councilman
> ALBERTO ANDRANGO,
> Speech at Artistic Festival, March 31, 1991

The massive mobilizations throughout Ecuador have demonstrated that the national Indian movement has broad roots in hundreds of communal and intercommunal local organizations. Indigenous activists have become mobilized in different ways at the grassroots level, developing different types of organizations, political strategies, and local identities. Indianismo, as a broad ideological and political construct that frames indigenous politics, both informs and is informed by local movements. The study of the politicization of Indianness, therefore, would not be complete without an understanding of the organizational forms, ideologies, and strategies of resistance deployed by local organizations.

The increasing autonomy of indigenous politics and the concern for more direct participation in the policy-making process paradoxically, in the age of postcampesinismo, has required coalitions with parties of the Left. In the highland provinces collectively organized indigenous electoral participation usually has been the product of alliances between indigenous organizations and the Left, most notably the Frente Amplio de Izquierda (FADI), the PSE, and the Movimiento Popular Democrático (MPD).

The UNORCIC in Cotacachi, a small city located in the northern highland province of Imbabura, is an excellent example. Since its creation in 1977, the UNORCIC has maintained a relationship with the Left, both in its affiliation with a national syndicalist organization, the FENOC, and in its alliance with non-Indian Socialist Party activists in the competition for public office. From a national perspective, the UNORCIC is considered the oldest and most successful case of extended indigenous representation in a city council. This representation has been almost continuous since its cofounder and first president, Alberto Andrango, was elected to the city council in 1979.

Like other organizations, such as the Unión Campesina del Azuay (UNASAY), and Pichincha Riccharimui, the UNORCIC has remained committed to traditional class rhetoric and class strategies. It has retained its campesinista politics while simultaneously cooperating with CONAIE in national events and embracing most of the national Indian movement rhetoric. Most important, it established an electoral coalition with socialists that lasted from 1980 to 1996. Despite the UNORCIC's use of explicit class language in its organizational affairs, its origin, rhetoric, and use of symbology incorporates an appeal to racial identity in the carrying out of its everyday politics. The act of belonging to the polity and of becoming citizens has involved both the creation and deployment of class-based and race-based strategies.

As the UNORCIC extended its involvement in the local electoral process, it increasingly depended on alliances with nonindigenous members of leftist parties to create governing coalitions and obtain significant policy gains. This process, however, is not devoid of problems. The UNORCIC's attempts to unite mestizos and indigenous activists under a broader umbrella of class politics have met with difficulties. Coalition failures on the local level, the national Indian uprising in 1990, and the subsequent consolidation of the Indian movement as a significant political force have brought important challenges to the practice of interracial alliances.

THE UNORCIC: HISTORY AND BACKGROUND

Imbabura province is the headquarters of the UNORCIC, which represents twenty-nine indigenous communities located in the large canton of Cotacachi, whose capital has the same name. The total population is 33,250, divided into an urban population of 6,051 (of which 4,685 reside in Cotacachi city) or 18.1 percent, and a rural population of 27,200 or 81.8 percent.[1] The rural population, in turn, is composed of approximately 12,500 mestizos (45.96 percent) and 14,700 Indians (54.04 percent) (Zamosc 1995, 80).[2] In addition to the Cotacachi municipality, there are eight parishes: Apuela (1,616), García Moreno (2,836), Imantag (2,637), Peñaherrera (1,838), Plaza Gutierrez, (457), Quiroga (3,576), Cuellaje (1,232), and Vacas Galindo (781). Of these parishes, the Cotacachi city periphery, which includes the indigenous Sagrario and San Francisco zones, Imantag, and Quiroga are predominantly indigenous, whereas the remaining parishes, collectively called Intag, are predominantly mestizo.[3]

Most of the communities adjoining Cotacachi city are exclusively indigenous, and a few of those closest to the metropolitan area are mixed, with a mestizo minority. The indigenous parishes are relatively close to the city, whereas Intag parishes are farther away and less articulated with the city's economy. Although the urban population in Cotacachi city is predominantly mestizo, the indigenous population in proportion to the mestizo population has become more significant, as Indians from neighboring communities have migrated to seek educational and labor opportunities. An increasing number of urban Indians work solely in the city or in nearby Otavalo and Ibarra, but most of them still own and work land in rural communities. Many whites and mestizos are involved in agricultural production, commerce, or leather manufacturing for the national and international tourist market. By the late 1970s Cotacachi was prosperous, with its main source of income the manufacture and sale of leather goods, an exclusively mestizo enterprise.[4]

The majority of the people represented by the UNORCIC are poor, but socioeconomic differentiation has increased significantly with the growing migrant labor force and the commercialization of handicraft production.[5] Because few haciendas in the area were directly involved in litigation associated with the 1964 land reform, there was little state-mandated redistribution of land.[6] Instead most haciendas modernized by engaging in commercial endeavors that required concentrating their land. Those who benefited from reform were left with small plots of land that barely allowed for subsistence. Former huasipungueros and their descendants were forced to diversify their domestic economies, generating a family income from a

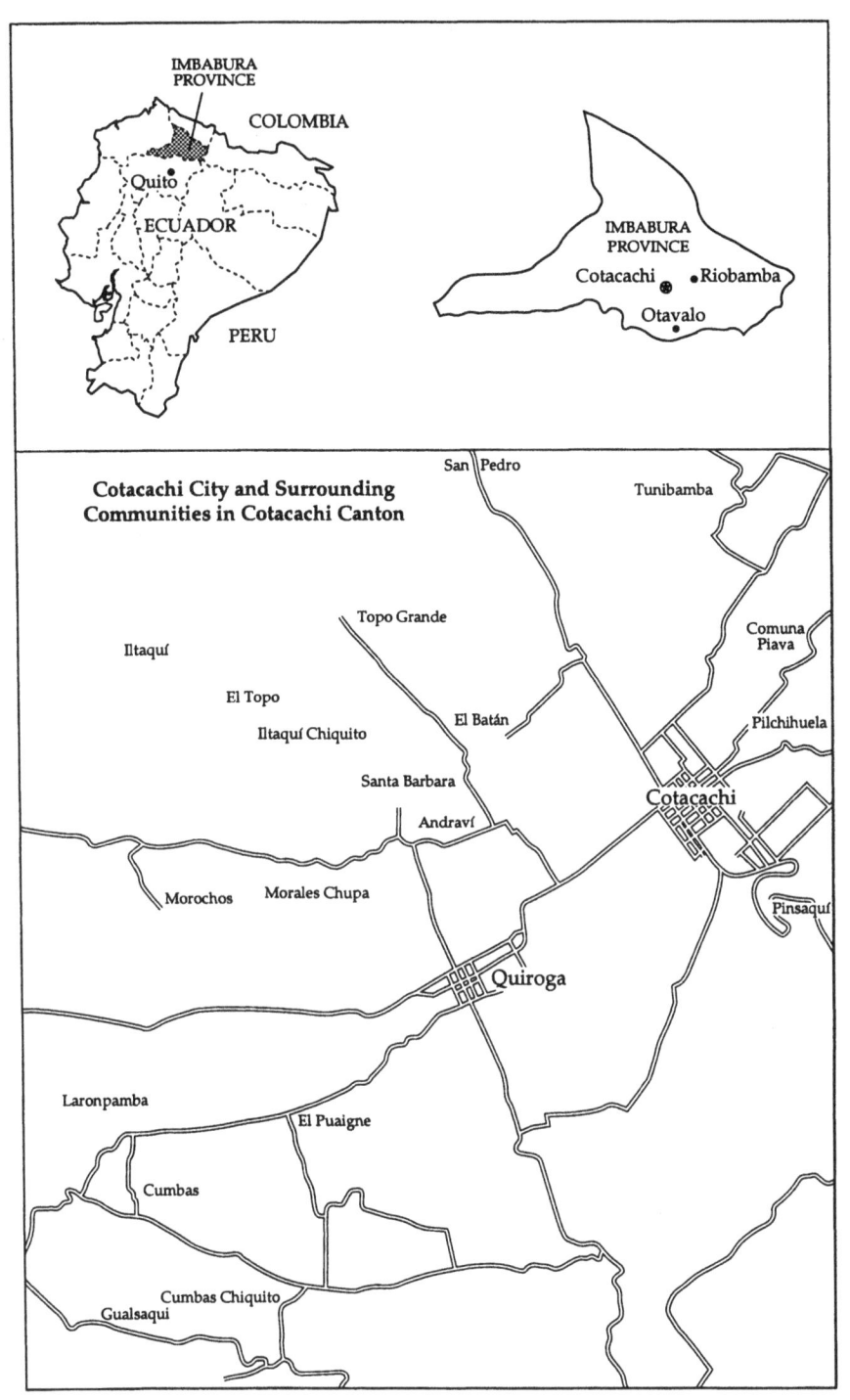

Cotachi City and Surrounding Communities in Cotachi Canton, Imbabura Province.

combination of subsistence agriculture, sale of agricultural products, and migrant work. According to one study of 2,764 landowning indigenous families inhabiting thirty-nine communities represented by the UNORCIC, 88 percent own less than 1 hectare, 13 percent own 1- to 5-hectare plots, only 2.6 percent own 10 to 50 hectares, and no one owns more than 50 hectares (FODERUMA 1988). Thirty years after the reform, 91.5 percent of the population owns a mere 23 percent of the land, revealing a dominant pattern of land concentration in commercial enterprises owned by non-Indians, such as export flower production.[7]

Origins: Maltrato and Police Abuse

In 1972 some students in Cotacachi organized a sports and cultural club to unite area communities through the revival of traditional music, dance, and sports. Accused by the church of being communists, the young students were eventually expelled from the club by members who felt they were too radical and were tainting the cultural activities with politics.

Many of these young people went on to political work in rural communities in the mid-1970s. In community meetings they discussed the maltrato, the mistreatment of Indians by urban mestizos. In addition to racial discrimination, community dwellers complained of the general lack of respect by authorities, neglect by public officials, and manipulation of their vote by political parties that disregarded their needs after the elections. The activists' desire to address these collective concerns led them to join other community leaders and provincial activists and create the Federación Indígena y Campesina de Imbabura (FICI). A provincial-level organization, FICI was originally founded in Cotacachi but was later transferred to neighboring Otavalo. A serious disagreement between Cotacachi activists and FICI leadership led to a split in the FICI. Cotacachi activists felt excluded from the leadership cadre and the decision-making process and decided to create a separate organization that would represent solely the communities surrounding the Cotacachi canton. In April 1979 they founded the Unión de Organizaciones Campesinas de Cotacachi (UNORCAC), whose name would eventually be changed to the Unión de Organizaciones Indígenas de Cotacachi (UNORCIC).

While land was not a central demand of UNORCIC founders and their followers, obtaining *respeto*, or respect, was. Respeto entailed the treatment of Indians as equals in all aspects of social life. Activists felt that gaining respeto required a comprehensive approach that tackled poverty, lack of public services, lack of political representation, and everyday forms of maltrato. Perceptions of racial discrimination in multiple realms of everyday life generated feelings of indignation and powerlessness that became a source of common identification among various communities.[8]

"Maltrato" refers not only to the contemporary practices of landowners—who insisted on pursuing indentured labor despite new land reform law—but also to interpersonal and institutional forms of discrimination practiced against Indians by Cotacachi authorities and mestizo locals.

As in other highland parishes, Indians were used as sources of unpaid labor by local authorities. One activist whose life span covers both the pre- and the post–land reform periods discussed his experience of forced labor. He remembered the pre–land reform situation:

> It was most of all the abuses of the representatives of the state who for us are the white-mestizo people, and also the abuses of the mestizo people here in the towns who were very linked to the hacienda.... There were too many abuses. For example, among the ones I witnessed as a child, there were municipal police, we call them chapas. On Sundays they would go to downtown Cotacachi. Without any explanation, they would grab our parents who went to the city.... [T]hey would grab them by their braid and they wouldn't ask, "Look, we're recruiting people for the city," nothing. They just grabbed them and put them in a car. Then they would take them to do some mingas. They [those seized] would return in three days.[9]

These were specifically racial practices: poor mestizos were never targeted. These practices, however, did not end immediately after the 1964 land reform. The transition from peons to wage workers was not easy for Indians, as they were prevented access to previously accessible and "free" resources such as water and land for grazing their animals. These resources were now monopolized by the haciendas, which forced Indians to work in exchange for them. Indians now "freed" by land reform had become more vulnerable to the imposition of forced labor as payment for economic transactions. If Indians did not comply as day laborers they were threatened with fines:

> We worked in haciendas and they did not pay us in time. When we crossed through haciendas to get water we feared getting caught by

the patron who would seize our water and remove our poncho, for any reason. When we were in the center of Cotacachi, they would imprison us for two days and make us pay fines, and when we went to church on Sundays the municipal police would remove our hats and ponchos to force us to work in any public drainage or street repair and cleaning.[10]

Ironically, the much awaited transition from a huasipungo system to a wage labor system served to deprive local peasants of certain protections from the law that the hacienda had guaranteed. The hacienda system had not only restricted Indians' travel to urban spaces and access to urban bars, it had also acted as a buffer between rural peasants and urban mestizos, and between peasants and local police. Once the custodial role of the hacendados was undermined, the confrontation between Indians and the agents of local power became more direct. Increased urbanization of Cotacachi and increased indigenous contact with Cotacachi after land reform led to the exclusion of Indians from certain urban economic sectors. When indigenous migrants attempted to penetrate mestizo labor and retail markets, they faced mestizo intermediaries who wanted to retain control over most retail activities. In this context, the new "enemies" were the police, mestizo urban elites, and local public institutions that, absent the traditional "protection" of the landowners, had failed to recognize the Indians as citizens with equal rights.

For those who remained in the communities, the situation was not much better. As the economic expansion caused by the oil boom produced an increase in municipal funds and urban infrastructure projects, indigenous community leaders and activists became increasingly aware of the neglect of the rural sector. All public funds were targeted for projects in the city of Cotacachi and the smaller mestizo towns. Although indigenous communities contained the majority of the population in the canton, they did not benefit from basic services accessible to city dwellers, such as potable water and electricity. Also, in the communities there were few elementary schools, no high schools, high illiteracy rates, and low levels of high school graduates as a proportion of the general population (see table 2). Finally, Indians were not represented in local public offices, and no Indian had ever held a public position in municipal or provincial government.

A more precise analysis of racial discrimination in Cotacachi requires drawing the distinction between rural Indians or community dwellers and

TABLE 2.
A Comparison of Illiteracy Rates between Mestizo and Indian Parishes, 1974

	ILLITERATE	TOTAL POPULATION	ILLITERATE AS PERCENTAGE OF POPULATION
Entire Cotacachi Canton	9,836	20,497	47%
PREDOMINANTLY INDIAN PARISHES			
Sagrario	3,033	3,703	82%
Imantag	1,626	2,197	74%
San Francisco	349	648	54%
Quiroga	1,471	3,122	47%
PREDOMINANTLY MESTIZO PARISHES			
Apuela	715	1,651	43%
García Moreno	617	1,978	31%
Peñaherrera	539	1,399	29%
Cuellaje	408	1,074	38%
Vacas Galindo	336	807	42%

SOURCE: *III Censo de Población y Vivienda: Imbabura* (Quito: INEC, 1974), 401–402.

urban Indians, migrants in the towns and small cities as well as the residents of communities that are extremely close to the city. Urban Indians are differentiated from rural Indians not only because of their physical location and involvement in the urban economy but also because of their greater access to education. Many of the UNORCIC founders were young Indians who lived in Cotacachi or in Topo Chico, a nearby community. Urban Indians were situated between urban mestizos and rural Indians. Some had achieved middle-class status; they benefited from many of the urban resources available to them but encountered glass ceilings and rejection in the urban sphere. There were two types of reaction to this rejection. Some urban Indians sought to improve their status by distancing themselves from rural Indians, a vertical movement that involved abandoning Indian dress, language and traditions. Others, confronting discrimination in the school and the workplace, became active in cultural revival (learning or relearning Quichua, returning to Indian dress, founding cultural clubs, reproducing traditional dance and music) and political resistance (organizing communities and creating the UNORCIC). Many young urban Indians sought connections with rural Indians; they visited communities (some for the first time), appealed to a common bond of Indianness, and underscored the salience of racial discrimination and its role in keeping Indians socioeconomically subordinate.[11]

If urban Indians confronted differing levels of marginalization, rural Indians faced total exclusion and the stigma of criminality. Indigenous visitors from rural communities were rejected at public offices and hospitals. Cotacachi residents felt that rural visitors did not conform to urban hygiene standards and dirtied the city. Indians were ostracized when they walked on the sidewalks or ventured too close to mestizos in the city park. In fact, they were discouraged from crossing the central plaza.

Public officials and mestizo citizens also argued that Indians caused the moral decay of the citizenry. By 1970 the city and the *jefe político* (political chief) were involved in a public campaign against drinking that specifically targeted Indians. The police imprisoned several vendors of *guarapo*, a popular indigenous drink, and also closed or fined several city bars and *chicherías*, claiming that drinking promoted juvenile delinquency and street fights.[12] This was accompanied by a discourse that reflected concern for maintening local morality, which appeared threatened by Indians. Also, according to authorities, Indians had to be saved from themselves, as they were spending their money on drinks instead of agricultural production, exacerbating their socioeconomic condition. One jefe político of the canton reported:[13]

> As concerns the well-being of the citizens, there has been no novelty except for the uncontrolled way in which the indigenous peoples have become depraved, dedicating themselves to drinking every day of the week, [a situation] that created an ill feeling among the citizens, who, irate, would go to authorities, who despite their prudent efforts achieved nothing, until the governorship of Imbabura, conscious of its duty to watch over the interests of its people and the citizens' well-being, dictated a specific order to eradicate this habit, which implemented by this authority together with the national police is obtaining good results.... If achieved [stopping alcoholism], Indians will gain self-confidence and economic recuperation, as the profits from small agricultural production [not spent in alcohol] will provide better nutrition. It will also prevent their inclination to thievery and delinquency.[14]

Thus, Indians were considered a threat to public morality and a criminal menace. Moreover, as the above report clearly demonstrates, their behavior was considered the greatest threat to the peace and stability of "citizens," a category used to refer strictly to the non-Indians. While most Indians were not citizens until the illiterate gained the franchise in 1979, this letter demonstrates how specific behaviors, such as public drunkenness, became important markers of the distinctions between citizens and indigenous noncitizens. Several subsequent reports in the 1970s on the closing of indigenous drinking holes reveal a central concern with curbing the indigenous presence in the city and preventing what was considered an endemic problem.[15]

The purportedly immoral drinking habits of Indians were also considered a principal reason behind escalating reports of indigenous "crime." A review of archives of the office of Cotacachi's jefe político reveals an increase in the number of reports on indigenous violence as a police problem and massive arrests in the 1970s.[16] The reports' narrow focus on alcohol and public disorder masks the fact that many of these "criminal" encounters were racially charged instances in which urban as well as rural Indians participated. Some of the conflicts among Indians escalated because of mestizo police intervention; many others involved disputes between mestizos and Indians in which the former were rarely arrested or prosecuted.[17]

In fact, indigenous "deviance" was frequently a response to racial ostracism from town mestizos and police. In the decade after land reform, the entrance of Indians into new realms was characterized by increasing mestizo hostility toward them and young Indians' growing impatience with the status quo. All this led to an increase in interracial tensions during the late 1960s and early 1970s. Indigenous responses ranged from minor acts of everyday resistance to more violent methods. One activist describes the first type of incident:

> Slowly it [resistance] grew, and it was not only here in Cotacachi but at a national level. Since the hacienda was in crisis, that allowed a new space for us. Because the hacienda was weakening, we had quite a few confrontations here. In the streets it was common to see, in a street full of Indians, the hacendados would pass through it very quickly with their trucks. And we would maybe not insult him but start coughing really loud. But he would realize that we were answering

> back to him, so he would pass almost running over us. In some cases he would get out of the car and insult us. We logically would have to deny it and tell him we weren't saying anything.[18]

Whereas exchanges with former landowners and current employers called for some restraint, confrontations with urban mestizos were more open and direct, quite revealing of the increasing mestizo discomfort with and rejection of the indigenous presence.

> There were some of us who would always answer [when insulted] with some word or some gesture to not let ourselves be dragged down. Then we would enter into direct violence. They [mestizos] would kick us and insult us and hit us. So many of our youth began to react like that. More direct violence appeared, more strongly, because the young people started answering back, reacting. The violence would become more intense. Violence, in part, became acceptable to us, mostly to resist, to overcome, to prevent things from becoming worse. It was not because we were all in agreement [to act in this way], but maybe because we thought the world wasn't going to change. It was one of those reactions that are somewhat suicidal.[19]

Given their lack of legal or institutional recourse in the face of discrimination, Indian activists in Cotacachi sought to alter power relations by creating the UNORCIC and addressing the principal grievances. Simultaneously, many Indians were opting for violence as a response to the perceived unfairness of the system, facing as a consequence massive arrests, heavy fines, and police brutality. These two paths, organization and individualized resistance, were distinct but not unrelated. It was the intensification of the latter that would finally grant legitimacy to the former.

"Long Live Rafael Perugachi":
Racial Politics and the Legitimization of the UNORCIC

An incident of police brutality became an important catalyst for the legitimacy and growth of the UNORCIC: the death of Rafael Perugachi. On November 2, 1977, seven months after the organization's creation, Perugachi, a founding member and a migrant worker, was sitting in a restaurant when he witnessed a police officer beating an Indian who had been involved in a conflict with another Indian. Perugachi intervened.[20] The officer subsequently attacked him, beating him continuously, after which the officer literally dragged him to jail and repeatedly beat and tortured him. On the following day, the police allowed Perugachi's relatives to transport him to the local hospital where he died a few days later.

The Perugachi incident elicited strong popular reaction because it symbolized the collective mistreatment of all Indians in Cotacachi canton. Police brutality directed at Indians was a common experience and a fear shared by members of different communities. Communities that had previously hesitated to join the organization were now willing to engage in intercommunal organizing and demanded that UNORCIC leaders have the police officer punished. In addition, Perugachi's death carved out a role for the organization as a representative and defender of Indians in a society whose legal and public institutions had proved threatening to Indians' personal security. By the end of 1979 several communities had joined the UNORCIC as a direct consequence of the Perugachi incident. Andrango remembers:

> The death of Perugachi was a great commotion here in Cotacachi, both among people of the city and among Indians. Then Indians realized that the police were always abusing, exploiting, mistreating them. The police always looked for a pretext, the minimum pretext to take our youth to jail. And besides hitting us, they charged us fines of 240 sucres, which in 1977 was a lot of money. So Indians were always against the police. We considered them our enemies, and once we had the federation, the police could no longer grab us, because we were already organized, there was already someone to defend Indians. It's possible that when Perugachi died, with no need to go recruit the indigenous *compañeros*, saying "Come join us," is when Indians automatically affiliated, saying, "We agree with you. Your struggle is good. We are Indians, we are mistreated, exploited, and we join you." That is how the organization continues to mature, without having declared anything, without having invited anyone. I always say: on the one hand, we lost a great compañero, but on the other hand his death served the purpose of making communities unite.[21]

After Perugachi's death, there was consensus among community leaders and activists concerning the role of the UNORCIC as their representative. As Indians they had faced similar experiences of subordination, exclusion, and discrimination in Cotacachi in the decade after land reform. Hence, the goal of the UNORCIC was clearly interpreted by all parties involved as the defense of Indians from whites and mestizos who threatened their livelihood and security and undermined their rights as citizens. The organization's struggle to punish those responsible led to the local support of more moderate town mestizos as well as to internal police reforms to prevent its reoccurrence. The policeman was punished and spent a brief period in jail.

In addition to validating the organization as a necessary mechanism for ensuring respect for Indians' civil rights, the Perugachi incident had a larger significance: it politicized race, leading community leaders for the first time to publicly denounce the abuses they suffered at the hands of mestizo townspeople and authorities. This antiracism is a defining characteristic of indianista organizations. The issues that came to the fore—mistreatment by authorities, mistreatment in public offices, and interracial relations—were ones that had been exacerbated after land reform and modernization.

During its first years, the UNORCIC waged a strong antiracist campaign. For an entire decade the organization staged Rafael Perugachi anniversary commemorations in which racism was openly denounced. The incident was retold orally and reproduced in organizational materials, with an emphasis on his solidarity with others and martyrdom. Differences among mestizos seemed largely irrelevant in this early stage of consolidation. Differences among Indians were also overlooked, as urban or semiurban educated leaders helped to organize the rural illiterate poor by underscoring a common racial identification that overrode class, regional, and status distinctions.

CLASS RHETORIC AND RACIAL CONSCIOUSNESS

The racial origin of the UNORCIC did not lead to an explicitly indianista platform. Like many organizations of its kind, the UNORCIC sought to confront and combat racial discrimination, achieve some degree of political autonomy, and promote socioeconomic development through government- and NGO-sponsored agricultural credit and infrastructure projects.[22] Unlike other intercommunal organizations developed in the late 1970s and early 1980s, however, the UNORCIC explicitly adopted a model of campesinismo that emphasized class issues, focusing on the general condition of rural poverty that affected most indigenous community dwellers. Although racial discrimination had sparked the creation of the organization, what was considered most important politically was their poverty. When the UNORCIC's leaders referred to their struggle, they spoke of it as the struggle of the poor against the rich.

The "Indianization of poverty," or the equation of rural poverty with "Indianness" in political rhetoric and policy served several purposes. First, it facilitated the erasure of class difference among Indians. The discourse of poverty created a new opposition: Indians (always understood as poor) versus the rich. Because, according to this perspective, a rich Indian was an impossibility, mestizoness was always implicit in the definition of relative wealth. When specifically mentioned, racial discrimination was considered a direct consequence of the behavior of the wealthy and therefore an effect of class exploitation. By its fourth congress, the UNORCIC's executive committee reviewed its history as follows:

> Our indigenous organization is born as the product of our identification with our reality of exploitation, racism, and migration. . . . [T]he lack of attention of the authorities was one of the principal problems. . . . [I]n these circumstances it was necessary to create an organization that would make us notice the needs we should address and enable us to protest against the forms of domination imposed by the rich.[23]

The "we" in this passage is by definition poor and Indian. This reflects the conflation of race and class, which frequently has characterized racial politics in Ecuador and the region. It interchanges Indians and the poor, making them practical equivalents. It does not, however, refer to a double exploitation, or two levels of consciousness, as poor and as Indians. In this first phase of UNORCIC's development, indigenous distinction from the mestizo poor was not theorized, problematized, or even mentioned in public speeches or organizational documents.

Although the official rhetoric of the organization did not sound much different from the language of other nonindigenous organizations, the UNORCIC's specificity as an indigenous organization that focuses on indigenous identity was evident in its actions. Official documents and speeches since the early 1980s may underscore the primacy of class consciousness and call for organizing as a peasant class, but explicitly racial discourse and practices were present in three distinctive sites. These sites reveal a deeply embedded racial consciousness that is not exclusively cultural (as activists at times sustained in political discourse) but has important material dimensions.

First, the most formalized and obvious stage for the promotion of a common Indian identity was the creation of organization-sponsored cultural festivals and anniversaries, which usually involved dance and music competitions. Unlike the traditional fiestas held during the harvest period in June, these were events created by the UNORCIC to promote the maintenance or revival of traditional cultural expressions, commonly called a *recuperación*, or a recovering. Recovering included the learning and performance of dances that had not been performed in years, as well as the creation of the Sara Ñusta, a beauty contest that honored the goddess of corn and required that contestants embody the qualities of a traditional indigenous homemaker. Many of these events involved the participation and attendance of community members, and some were held in indigenous communities instead of the city. They served to underscore the distinctiveness of indigenous peoples vis-à-vis mestizos. The Sara Ñusta, for example, was distinct from mestizo contests in two ways: first, it valued the beauty of indigenous women, who were often excluded from serious consideration in local beauty competitions; and second, it emphasized criteria by which an indigenous woman would be valued, as opposed to mestiza women in other competitions. Contestants, for example, could not wear makeup, considered a practice of mestiza women, and they were judged by their ability to prepare corn.

The second site where Indianness was promoted was the bilingual education program in which UNORCIC activists had participated extensively. Most UNORCIC activists were or had been bilingual educators, and the organization arranged workshops to train literacy and bilingual education teachers. The appeal to cultural and more specifically racial consciousness was also evident in school debates over the use of Indian dress by Indian students in schools and popular marches and events in which Indianess was emphasized both symbolically and literally. In a June 25, 1986, letter to Rodrigo Guzmán, provincial director of education and culture, Alberto Andrango, then president of the UNORCIC, discussed the growing enrollment of indigenous children in the Modesto Peñaherrera elementary school.

> Yet they [mestizo school officials] have not respected their traditions, their cultural values, and their special costume. We ask that white clothes [indigenous garb] be allowed as well as *alpargatas* [Indian sandals], and that you don't make them wear shoes, ties, and colored

pants. We hope for your intervention so that in this year's Cotacachi festivities, the children will not have to march like [they did] in previous years.[24]

By 1993 the annual school parade held in the city reflected these demands, as indigenous children marched with their own outfits or, more commonly, combined some mestizo elements with indigenous clothes. The role of clothes as a marker of cultural identity has gained political salience in the highlands, particularly in Imbabura province. With the emergence of indianismo and cultural revitalization, activists who had earlier adopted mestizo dress shifted to traditional garb. Furthermore, sports clubs and other youth activities were created with the specific purpose of preventing migrant youth from losing their cultural identity in the cities.

In addition to these examples, racial politics and ethnic symbols were often contained in class discourse, either located in symbolic sites that appeared to be simply cultural or "coded" in campaign speeches as well as in debates about the strategies and ideologies involved in political organizing. The concomitant use of class and race identities as principles of social organization and determinants of popular consciousness would in fact be the modus operandi of the UNORCIC during the 1980s.

Indigenous-Mestizo Alliances

In its effort to seek further empowerent in a zone with a large mestizo population, the UNORCIC developed a number of strategies to obtain mestizo support. To obtain more electoral and organizational power, it sought to develop a mestizo constituency and establish electoral coalitions with mestizo leftists. The UNORCIC affiliated with three organizations—the national peasant federation FENOC, FADI (a multiple-party coalition of the Left) and later the PSE—in an effort to win municipal elections.[25]

After Perugachi's death, the UNORCIC established a relationship with the FENOC. The FENOC, a national campesinista institution that was on solid economic ground and funded by several international foundations, was able to offer the UNORCIC legal assistance as well as public attention to the Perugachi case. This assistance, however, was contingent on the UNORCIC's affiliation. For the UNORCIC this seemed the logical choice, particularly considering that Ecuarunari, the other alternative, was an unlikely candidate given its long-standing relationship with FICI's leadership.[26] This initial support developed into an institutionalized relationship in which the FENOC sponsored several health and rural development projects, used its national political clout and legal council to assist the UNORCIC on specific political issues, and trained UNORCIC and community leaders in *concientización* (consciousness-raising) and "national reality" workshops.

The latter were important in ensuring that FENOC's ideological perspectives were disseminated among Cotacachi activists. Lessons on the political system, national reality, and strategies of struggle held during these workshops underscored the primacy of "peasant politics," syndicalism, and the national peasant-worker alliance. Indigenous participants were often encouraged to think of themselves as peasants first and to view their socioeconomic concerns as an agenda they shared with poor peasants throughout the country.

After the 1978 redemocratization process and the granting of the vote to illiterates, the Ecuadorian Left targeted the rural highlands, either directly or through syndicalist organizations such as the FENOC, to gain support from Indians. Because the FENOC maintained a strong link with the leftist FADI, and later the PSE, many of the workshops' instructors were members of these parties who advocated a campesinista perspective and underscored the overlap between indigenous concerns and a socialist agenda. Hence, despite the lack of an explicit discussion of Indian rights in their party platforms, the FADI and later the PSE articulated policy demands that included an intensification of land reform, rural health insurance, higher wages and better working conditions for laborers, increased state support for social policy, and credit programs for the popular sectors. In the past few elections, the rural highland vote has been usually distributed between the Center-Left (Izquierda Democrática, Democracia Popular), the populists (Partido Roldosista Ecuatoriano), and the Left, followed by a Right that has occupied a marginal position in relation to its proportional representation in the rest of the country.[27]

The national alliance with the FENOC, however, was not the sole expression of cross-racial campesinismo. Another goal that preoccupied UNORCIC activists was unity of all rural community dwellers in the canton, a proposition that required incorporating the communities in the zone of Intag, composed of several parishes that have a predominantly mestizo population. At first glance, the UNORCIC's desire to incorporate Intag may seem perplexing. It was already a strong and resourceful intercommunal organization representing almost thirty communities, while Intag communities had not yet developed into a second-degree organization. In addition, the UNORCIC had established relationships with several NGOs involved in rural development projects, as well as state-funded credit programs, while Intag communities had not even begun to establish these connections. Clearly, Intag communities had more to gain by UNORCIC's programs. Nevertheless, UNORCIC activists believed they could benefit from a coalition with Intag in a number of ways. First, the increase in the number of communities meant they would be the sole rural organization in the canton, controlling most of the resources destined for the region. Second, they could elicit more extensive support from state funds and NGOs. Third, incorporating Intag communities would enable UNORCIC activists to gather additional electoral support and develop governing coalitions with Intag representatives.

The incorporation of Intag peasants took two directions—making them member communities of the UNORCIC and developing electoral coalitions in which Intag activists would also run for elections with the UNORCIC's party of choice. Given that Cotacachi council seats are at-large positions, the UNORCIC was willing to campaign for Intag candidates in indigenous communities and assumed that Intag voters, in exchange for organizational affiliation and electoral support, would do the same. UNORCIC activists assumed that if they supported mestizo candidates, these candidates would in turn bring in mestizo votes for indigenous candidates, support indigenous communities on key issues, and would, together with indigenous councilmen, be able to develop a governing coalition.[28] This would not be the case. Intag's affiliation with UNORCIC was a brief and conflictual affair that ended with the mestizo communities' withdrawal from the UNORCIC. While Intag representatives resented UNORCIC activists' control over the agenda and decision making, UNORCIC activists felt that they were only being used by Intag to have access to project funds and that Intag communities were riding on the UNORCIC's coattails without offering any significant political allegiance in return.

With the exception of their relationship with the FENOC, by the late 1980s the institutional basis for campesinismo had begun to erode. If the affiliation of Intag communities with the UNORCIC was brief, other coalitions with mestizos had been sporadic, restricted to occasional cosponsorship of marches with students or leather workers' unions. Labor segmentation that excluded most Indians from transportation, retail, and leather craft opportunities meant little or no interaction between mestizos and Indians in labor unions. Popular efforts to cross ethnic and racial boundaries were extremely rare, and the only remaining source of cross-racial unity was in the relationships between UNORCIC activists and urban socialists in electoral coalitions.

The Politics of Electoral Coalitions

The establishment of electoral coalitions with mestizos led UNORCIC to pursue a different discourse. Electoral politics entailed the building of a long-term relationship between UNORCIC activists and mestizo urban socialists from the early 1980s through the mid-1990s. Since its inception, UNORCIC sought to procure indigenous empowerment through an electoral strategy that would ensure at least one organization representative in the municipal council of Cotacachi. UNORCIC activists and members believed in the importance of the representation of Indians by Indians on the council, a novel concept in a country where Indians, even when they were the majority, were almost never elected or nominated as public officials. Hence the UNORCIC is one of the first organizations to successfully enter into municipal electoral politics after redemocratization, and one of the few to be consistently successful at it.[29]

After the decision to participate in elections was made by a majority of community leaders in an intercommunal meeting held in Tunibamba in 1978, the UNORCIC decided to support its president, Alberto Andrango, as a candidate for city council. Running for office entailed working with a political party willing to support indigenous candidates. In the 1980 elections, the UNORCIC associated with FADI, a national leftist front that in turn joined other parties of the Left to create the Unión Democratica Popular (UDP). This did not imply the conversion of voters but only the strategic affiliation of the candidates who were running for office. Moreover, even the decision to affiliate with the FADI was understood, on the part of indigenous activists at least, as a negotiated support that could be renewed or changed every four years. On this one occasion, no real negotiation with local mestizos was involved, as the FADI label only required the consent of the national FADI leadership. There was no FADI representation on the local level and therefore no mestizo competition for places on the ballot. In an unusual occurrence, all the local FADI candidates were Indians who were active in or associated with the UNORCIC.[30]

During Andrango's campaign, Indianness returned as a central component of political identity. While the FADI's platform lacked any substantial discussion of Indian specificity, the UNORCIC's campaign in 1979 was full of racial imagery. Indigenous candidates primarily targeted rural communities, using antiracist rhetoric and stressing the need for Indian representatives who would understand and address indigenous demands.

The campaign stressed the "different" nature of the UNORCIC founder Alberto Andrango. The campaign emphasized that, in contrast to a mestizo candidate, only he could understand the Indian experience. Andrango's campaign constantly highlighted the historical "abandonment" of indigenous communities, pointing out that mestizo candidates, not being Indian or able to understand the "Indian" problem, had simply neglected them.[31] Along with the basic promises of helping Indians gain access to land, light, and water services during his term in the council, Andrango said he would address the problem of mestizos' lack of respect for them.

In the 1980 elections Andrango received 863 votes, making him the third top vote getter after the Popular Democracy Party (DP) and the Izquierda Democrática (ID) candidates.[32] He was therefore able to capture one of the three spots in the council, becoming the first indigenous councilman in Cotacachi history and the first in Imbabura province.[33] When Andrango's election showed the viability of the Left in Cotacachi, the monopoly of UNORCIC activists on the ballot list was lost, as mestizos established a local branch of the party after his election. Subsequent elections required the negotiation of nominations with urban mestizos from the FADI and later the PSE, as well as with rural mestizos from Intag.

At this point, the discourse and campaign of UNORCIC activists and electoral candidates took on a decidedly different character. Whereas the conflation of Indianness and poverty and the equation of indigenous peoples with the poor had been the prevalent model, the new approach involved the separation and distinction of the two dimensions of exploitation of Indians, as poor people and as Indians. In campaign speeches and organization rallies and festivals, activists focused on the conditions of poverty that they faced as a separate analytic category. Whereas earlier discussion of the maltrato and the lack of respeto had seemed sufficient reasons to justify their struggle, UNORCIC activists now felt the need to separate the two.

Andrango stated:

> As Indians we organize with peculiar interests, for our interests, such as the respect that we want them to give us. We want them [mestizos] to be conscious of our situation, of our traditions, of our culture . . . but our UNORCIC also unites with the Left to work together with the mestizo peasants, Indians, [and] the popular sectors. . . . [T]o organize as an Indian party is not convenient because it means only organizing as a race. We would be isolated in this way, and the struggle is not only to obtain indigenous people's objectives. We must realize that we are in a class struggle. We must unite with the poor without forgetting that we are Indians.[34]

Why did the UNORCIC change its political rhetoric? On the one hand, while not formally affiliated with the CONAIE, UNORCIC leaders were following national activists' debates about Indianness versus peasantness. In the 1980s the highland organizations ECUARUNARI and CONACNIE, the national network that predated CONAIE, were having frequent encounters and meetings with the purpose of discussing who Indians were, what Indian politics were, and how their politics should be distinct from peasant politics. An important outcome of this debate was the resolution that Indians did not have to be either one or the other but could be both. The notion of a double dimension or double layer of exploitation, which distinguished the specifics of peasantness and Indianness, was becoming an important focus of political analysis and component of political platforms.

The double layer thesis proved quite versatile for UNORCIC leaders, who were able to use it in different ways in encounters with national leaders in the FENOC, mestizo politicians, and its grassroots constituency. With FENOC's leaders, UNORCIC activists focused on their indigenous specificity to pressure for more power within the national organization and to broaden the organization's agenda. At the local level, this double layer discourse simultaneously established a bridge between Indians and mestizos (who together could organize as the poor) and created a separate, autonomous space that mestizos could not easily access, much less claim. This last point distinguishes the UNORCIC from other campesinista organizations in which the political lines between Indians and mestizos were blurred or nonexistent. As Andrango explains above, it also allowed Indians to be viewed by themselves and others as citizens who were concerned about all the disadvantaged population, not merely Indians.

Most important, the double layer thesis constitutes a response to the constituency's fears and hesitations about working with mestizo politicians in a time in which most indigenous organizations throughout the highlands were emphasizing indigenous political autonomy. Andrango's statement about the disadvantages of organizing solely as Indians is clearly a response to constituents' request that they organize a separate, indigenous party. This was a constituency, after all, that had become accustomed to the equation of Indians with the poor and mestizos with the rich. By sustaining a dual layer thesis, UNORCIC activists were able to emphasize Indianness when indigenous candidates were running and poverty and inclusiveness of all the poor when mestizo candidates were running. In addition, separating poverty from Indianness allowed for a broader definition of Indian, by linking Indians who were peasants with migrant workers, merchants, and urban professionals.

It also established commonalities between Indians and mestizos, linking Indians with non-Indian peasants from Intag and other popular and labor sectors. This involved making distinctions among mestizos, which the previous discourse had dismissed. Declarations during the UNORCIC's first years draw little or no distinction between mestizos of different classes and often refer to all mestizos as rich. By the mid-1980s UNORCIC activists begin to make distinctions among mestizos, in particular, highlighting the existence of working-class mestizos and blacks (from the neighboring Chota Valley in Imbabura province) as popular classes who were the Indians' brethren and shared their experience of exploitation and sense of powerlessness. Furthermore, as mestizo candidates began to run on ballots with UNORCIC candidates on the party lists, UNORCIC leaders would signal that they too were capable of understanding Indians' issues, because they shared that second level of class exploitation.

The UNORCIC's effort to generate a cross-racial appeal, urban mestizo socialists' pressures to share in the powerholding positions, and the perceived lack of eligible and willing indigenous candidates were three important factors that led to a long-term mestizo-Indian alliance. The UNORCIC became active in political work with a small cadre of urban mestizos from the Socialist Party as well as with a selected group of Intag activists. When these mestizos joined indigenous activists in the bid for electoral positions, UNORCIC activists campaigned for them among indigenous communities, assuring their audiences that these mestizo *compañeros*, or comrades, had proven worthy of their trust and warning that any rejection of them would be considered an act of racism. Furthermore, because these mestizos were affiliated with the UNORCIC's party of choice, they were characterized as part of the Indian ticket. Therefore, their success would not only be considered an electoral success for Indians, but would enable the development of a socialist governing bloc that would work for policies that benefited indigenous communities.

In 1986, when the UNORCIC disaffiliated from the umbrella party FADI and joined the PSE, Andrango campaigned in indigenous communities, stressing the dual dimension of their exploitation.[35] In a study in contrasts, he first urged Indians to vote for indigenous candidates, drawing important distinctions between them and mestizo candidates, who, by his own definition, were incapable of understanding the indigenous situation. While he first explained why Indian candidates were a better choice, Andrango followed this with one qualification: PSE's mestizo candidates were an exception.

> Look, here is the difference. Not only are they [indigenous candidates] our candidates, but above anything they are our leaders, who, whether campaigning or not, are permanently, every day, leading us, representing us. That is why the triumph will belong to all the communities of our federation, and we don't even have to be thinking about [nominating] other people whom we don't even know and who have no feeling for our life in the country, our suffering, they do not know what it is like to be peasants, Indians, they do not know what is poverty, hunger, our work, our tradition. You are wrong if you believe that because a candidate is a white-mestizo from the city, he is more capable, more intelligent. . . . But compañeros, let's not be confused, there are the white-mestizo compañeros who struggle for the poor. We can trust them because they are our compañeros, they are with us, because you do know that the federation was not created to promote the struggle of Indians against whites but to promote the struggle of the poor—in which we find ourselves—against the rich who threaten our lives, so then compañeros, let's look well, let's not fall into the trap, let's not support electoral candidates of the parties of the rich who speak very beautifully and offer marvels.[36]

The first section of this speech provides the rationale for voting for indigenous candidates while simultaneously evoking racial unity, vilifying those nonindigenous candidates who "don't know" or "don't understand." The second part constructs a category of mestizo candidates who can be trusted and who "struggle for the poor." This provides an opening, an inclusion of mestizos in a more broadly drawn definition of the poor. Although the internal contradiction is evident, the logic followed by Andrango is coherent insofar as it presents no alternative options to indigenous voters: however it may pain some voters "as indigenous peoples" to vote for nonindigenous candidates, "as the poor" they must put their confidence in those mestizos who struggle for them. In the process Andrango rewrites the origins of the UNORCIC, claiming the struggle against poverty as the sole force behind the movement. Further, the speech reveals the electoral benefits of separating the indigenous and the poor dimension, as it offers the voters a next best identity to choose from when indigenous candidates are not available. More important, this passage underscores the specific form of citizenship that Indians should exercise. Indigenous citizenship has two dimensions, along class and ethnic lines, and to be full and responsible citizens, Andrango indicates that they must consider both dimensions and participate as both Indians and poor people.

However, UNORCIC leaders remained focused on the importance of class organizing and avoiding the perils of organizing primarily as Indians. In this way, the UNORCIC clearly stands apart from other indigenous organizations that were emphasizing Indianness as the main axis of political identity. Pedro de la Cruz, a UNORCIC leader, argued that an exclusive focus on indigenous concerns was not only potentially divisive and unproductive but also racist:

> There are pros and cons to working either way [as Indians or as the poor]. Why do I say this? Because with only Indians in the struggle of course there are many benefits, there is an integration among us, we know each other, there is a cultural attraction. But by doing that we are creating a bit of racism, the Indians only here, the mestizos over there, the blacks the same. For a cultural struggle that [behavior] is convenient. But for general things, for example, land for who works it, if we are all separated the government or congressmen will not listen to us. *There is not much that is specifically indigenous*, there are many things that are general and apply to all, because most peasants are poor.[37]

This comment underscores the two levels and also illustrates the secondary importance assigned to the "indigenous," as a rather restricted category or realm, and the questioning of the breadth and depth of the indigenous agenda. In a careful statement, de la Cruz is not eschewing the indigenous struggle but creating a separation between "the cultural struggle" and the general good, which he suggests could be undermined if the cultural struggle was taken too far, leading to separatism. The danger for him lies not in forgetting the indigenous dimension but in overemphasizing it at the expense of a broader cross-racial peasant solidarity, instigating a form of separatism in the process.

Electoral Disappointments: The Limitations of the Cross-Racial Alliance

The UNORCIC's new discourse proved successful in obtaining some important electoral gains. Since 1988 at least three mestizo PSE candidates have won with substantial support from indigenous communities. The goal of obtaining at least two representatives was achieved in 1990, when then UNORCIC president Pedro de la Cruz and mestizo Alejo Guzman won city council elections, capturing together the highest percentage of votes in the canton. In 1992 Alberto Andrango, who was once again elected to the city council, joined them.

However, while the strategy of combining Indian and non-Indian candidates on a common ticket was successful electorally, the actual experience of governing with mestizos proved disappointing to many UNORCIC supporters and to the activists themselves. There was some consensus that Andrango and de la Cruz had been productive and benefited UNORCIC communities, but many UNORCIC members were disappointed with the tenure of the mestizo candidates, claiming that once in power they were more prone to developing alliances with mestizos of other parties than with indigenous councilmen and to ignoring their indigenous constituency.

A review of the city council minutes between 1988 and 1992 confirms this view. The records of three mestizo council members who received UNORCIC support reveal a consistent preoccupation with the needs of the mestizo communities, and a dearth of proposals designed to address the needs of indigenous communities. By contrast, Andrango and de la Cruz are the sole councilmen who consistently request public works for indigenous communities. While mestizo leftists occasionally supported some of these policies, they did not initiate any policy or carry out a programmatic effort to address indigenous demands in a comprehensive manner.[38]

For example, one mestiza council member, Carmen Aros, was elected by the Socialist Party in the late 1980s and catered mainly to the Intag population. While in office, she switched to another party, an act that UNORCIC activists considered a betrayal. One UNORCIC activist recounted how she and other mestizo activists' used their city council positions to separate themselves from the UNORCIC:

> We nominated Carmen Aros who campaigned with us, with the Socialist Party. Well, she won and she started her term at city council, because the UNORCIC supported her candidacy, but once she was in power she started to betray the Socialist Party, and she was strengthening, organizing another party. So that was a betrayal to indigenous people. The UNORCIC didn't think this was correct, and what's more, she did absolutely nothing, nothing, nothing to benefit the communities. Nothing. We named her our candidate because she had a friendship with the UNORCIC, but she really didn't do anything, rather she identified with ... of course since she is from the city, with people from the city, she worked with other councilmen for works in the city, but not for the communities.... [T]his made people distrust white-mestizo people who have done nothing despite being supported by the UNORCIC. That was also the case of the compañero who made an organization of communities in Intag, the mestizo section. He replaced an indigenous councilman when he left for a scholarship. He did absolutely nothing for the communities of the UNORCIC, and instead he worked for that other party, and since then the Cuellaje [Intag] Union has no relationship with us. Second negative experience with a white-mestizo. Then we had a third compañero. He also didn't do anything for the communities.... So there have been three councilmen who received UNORCIC's support, but did no works.[39]

In an interview with me, Aros stated that she did not feel in any way beholden to the UNORCIC or its constituency. Moreover, she felt she had maintained positive relations with members of Indian communities without using the mediation of the UNORCIC.[40] This absence of a sense of accountability to the organization suggests that unlike indigenous candidates, mestizo candidates who have received indigenous support have frequently separated themselves and their municipal positions from the organization's agenda once in office. Their ability or tendency to do this suggests that in the case of interracial alliance, electoral coalitions have rarely been able to become governing coalitions, a fact that constrains Indian representatives as well.

By the mid-1990s UNORCIC leaders were disappointed with the outcomes of these coalitions and were confronted with constituents' demands that these alliances be questioned if not terminated. The organization was at risk that the disappointment with coalition politics would also lead to disappointment in the organization and a sense of betrayal. Because the UNORCIC had won the role of guarantor of Indian empowerment, constituents and member communities had agreed to elect unknown mestizos to office. They had assumed that coalitions with mestizo organizations and politicians would be a two-way street and that these new relationships would not resemble previous relationships in which Indians had felt used and manipulated. In addition to these local disappointments, one other crucial factor was leading Cotacachi Indians to question the UNORCIC's political strategy: the development of an indianista national movement.

POST-1990 POLITICS:
THE RISE OF INDIANISMO AND PARTY CONFLICT

The UNORCIC grassroots participated in the June 1990 national uprising called by the CONAIE, despite the fact that its main leaders were away at a conference in Europe during that time and that the FENOC did not participate. Cotacachi Indians also responded to CONAIE's calls for activism in 1991, 1993, and 1994. Cotacachi's participation in a 1991 uprising was extensive and took an interesting local twist: on the night of June 10 four hundred Indians occupied the city council and asked for resolution of a long-pending land case in the Tunibamba hacienda, forestation in certain eroded land tracts, and expropriation of lands. In Ibarra, the capital of Imbabura province, Indians occupied the governor's palace for twenty hours, presenting the *Mandato Provincial por la Vida y el Desarrollo de Imbabura* (Provincial Mandate for Life and the Development of Imbabura Province), which had twelve major demands. After being kidnapped in the gubernatorial palace, Imbabura's governor Mauricio Larrea signed an act of commitment to nine of the twelve points.

Pedro de la Cruz, who was both UNORCIC president and city councilman at that time, spearheaded the occupation. One of UNORCIC's demands concerned the "better treatment of the indigenous councilman" at a time when de la Cruz had complained about being disrespected by several members of the council and administrative staff. That de la Cruz would lead a movement against the very institution he was part of suggests that the formal acquisition of power through the representation of Indians in the council did not necessarily entail equity within the institution. This pattern of joint electoral participation and disruption remains characteristic of Indian politics on the national level as well. De la Cruz's act was an attempt to highlight that the patterns of racial inequality of Ecuadorians were being reproduced in the council and that the possibility of internal transformation was limited. It placed the indigenous/nonindigenous opposition at the center of the UNORCIC's struggle. It suggested that despite years of indigenous participation in "formal power" in the council, informally power was still used to exclude Indians.

De la Cruz's ability to place himself as an outsider and to use protest politics as a resource to confront the unwritten rules of power differential between Indians and non-Indians was effective in obtaining some concessions and in reminding UNORCIC members where UNORCIC leadership "really" stood, despite years of membership in the city council. De la Cruz himself has conceptualized his role as one that combined formal and legal mechanisms with confrontation and would, in the ultimate instance, rely on the power of protest to gain attention for indigenous demands:

> There is value in having an indigenous representative because it means there is a source of support for everyone else. Now they [Indians] can say "We have a compañero there, the organizations now pay attention to us, we can go to them and complain." And that is how it has occurred. So here one can personally complain or one can send a letter. If that doesn't work, we threaten with staging an uprising. Then yes, even despite themselves, they yield. What's important is that they do yield, that they yield, or they are screwed.[41]

The occupation of the municipality must also be understood in the context of a culture and practice of indigenous opposition in which the threat of protest and mobilization are central (and not merely replaced by electoral politics). While many Cotacachi Indians sympathized with indianista sentiments and perspectives represented in CONAIE, they were embedded in an institutional setting that competed with CONAIE. The UNORCIC was affiliated with the FENOC, which was ambivalent about the Indian movement during the first year after the uprising and remained opposed to some of its basic indianista perspectives. Instead of critiquing a national party system and political structure that excluded Indians (as did CONAIE and many of its affiliates until 1996), the UNORCIC had developed coalitions with nonindigenous socialists to found and support the Socialist Party and had elected local representatives to city council. However, despite the absence of a more formal indianista rhetoric, the method of protest served to legitimize Cotacachi activists as advocates of the new, more radical Indianess embodied by CONAIE.

Nevertheless, the contradictions between contemporary indianista discourse and practice, on one side, and the affiliation with the FENOC and the Socialist Party, on the other, generated a questioning of the purpose and effects of the UNORCIC's affiliations and political coalitions with non-Indians. Moreover, as indigenous politicians tried to increase their decision-making power in the party and in the council, they confronted great resistance from mestizo members of the PSE. This resistance revealed the limitations and perhaps the exhaustion of the cross-racial coalition. While mestizo socialists had been willing to share electoral platforms with Indians, their cooperation was usually limited to campaigns, and there was little cooperation outside the electoral sphere or within city councils. Mestizo socialists, on the other hand, thought that UNORCIC candidates were openly beholden to the organization rather than to the party.

In 1992 these conflicts came to the surface in a dispute between indigenous and mestizo socialists over the selection of the PSE nominee for council president. After fifteen years of electing city councilmen and galvanized by the growing strength of the Indian movement, UNORCIC activists had grown weary of the fact that there was no increase in political power within the council itself. They proposed that an Indian be nominated by the party for the presidency of the council in the upcoming elections. Mestizo socialists, were vehemently opposed, however, and instead proposed a list that included, as usual, one indigenous candidate for city council and a mestizo for council president. UNORCIC activists protested and rejected the plan. Mestizo socialists first refused to budge, accusing the Indian activists of corruption and private enrichment and questioning their socialist credentials and loyalty to the party. In protest, they withdrew all their candidates at the last minute, leaving UNORCIC activists a few hours to come up with an ad hoc list of names of indigenous people, few of whom had any desire to run or chance of winning. This resulted in the sole victory of Alberto Andrango for city council and the defeat of all the other indigenous candidates. Relations between indigenous and mestizo socialists remained tense through the early 1990s.

The 1992 Congress

Conflict with the socialists was considered by many local indigenous activists an act of sabotage and a public humiliation and was one of the main topics of discussion in the UNORCIC's 1992 congress.[42] Every aspect of the organization's relationship with the party was questioned, as was the UNORCIC's participation in city council elections and its affiliation with the FENOC.[43] Although there was no significant change in UNORCIC policy, this was the first time the UNORCIC's affiliations were openly contested. The UNORCIC decided to mantain its affiliation with the party, albeit with the understanding that it hinged on the communities' continued commitment to the coalition:

> We can renew it [our relationship with the party], depending on the situation. But if you ask them [mestizo socialists] they tell you that no, the organization is ideologically with us, we belong to their base, and we are going to participate. Pedro de la Cruz and Alberto Andrango are affiliated because they have to be to run for office, . . . but if at a certain moment we decide that we don't want anything [to do] with the party, they will be prohibited from working for the party.[44]

Meanwhile, mestizo socialists were claiming that the party was losing prestige by associating with Indians who expected the party to serve the organization.[45] Mestizo socialists' ability to break with the UNORCIC, however, was limited by their dependence on indigenous voting power to have a local presence. Furthermore, national Socialist Party leaders had developed a close relationship with both the FENOC and the UNORCIC and were more concerned with cultivating that relationship (which delivered votes and legitimized the party's general identification with the indigenous cause) than with the support of a handful of urban socialists.

Another affiliation that was questioned at the 1992 congress was the FENOC-UNORCIC connection. Institutionally, the FENOC had lost much of its resources and was no longer able to offer the UNORCIC the legal assistance and rural programming that it had in the past. Most important, although since 1986 it had made some concessions to the UNORCIC's demands of incorporating Indians (including adding "Indian" to its name, nominating Indians like Andrango and de la Cruz to high positions in the national hierarchy, and including cultural demands in its agenda), the FENOC had rejected indianista demands for autonomy and multinationalism, suggesting frequently that these were racist positions.[46]

According to Sidney Tarrow (1994), social movements are an amalgam of organizations that are connected through institutional networks and cultural solidarity or common meaning. On this front, the UNORCIC seemed bifurcated. While the UNORCIC's institutional affiliation was with the FENOC, it shared the cultural meanings of the CONAIE and its affiliates. The FENOC's unwillingness to adopt indianismo and its ambiguous relationship with the CONAIE, which it saw as a competitor and at times an opponent, began to contrast sharply with the position of local activists who had blocked the roads and participated in marches during the uprisings.

As UNORCIC activists continued to participate in uprisings, disseminating and sharing the symbols and common understandings of the movement, many became somewhat detached from the FENOC's ideological and political goals and less willing to participate in its usual May Day and cost-of-living marches. At the 1992 congress, there was a clear split between those who wanted to continue with the PSE and the FENOC and those who wanted to switch to CONAIE. Misgivings about continuing the relationship with the FENOC were frequently expressed to me by community and intercommunal activists. For example:

> For ten years they helped us quite a bit, but today the relationship with the FENOC is a little false. In the last congress we said by majority vote that we would agree to keep belonging to the FENOC, but in the next congress it remains to be seen if we will continue with it or not, because the FENOC has carried out a more urban classist struggle, and Cotacachi's participation seems a little forced. Cotacachi has a tremendous sympathy for CONAIE and its proposals, but because of past relationships we continued tied to the FENOC. And if the FENOC does not update itself, does not modernize, surely Cotacachi

will unlink itself. It all depends on the future, and that future restructuring depends on how participation is granted to the indigenous world as an indigenous world, not as proletarians and peasants or any of that. The FENOC lacks that, and we are demanding that it change, They [FENOC] are worried that if they continue like this there could be a threat that Cotacachi becomes autonomous and possibly becomes part of CONAIE.[47]

Thus there has been a transition from a simple sharing of cultural meanings between the UNORCIC and CONAIE to one in which networks have been reproduced if on an "informal" basis. In the early 1990s CONAIE national activists, at the request of the UNORCIC, were holding political workshops in indigenous communities in Cotacachi. Even those who still support the affiliation with the FENOC admit that the CONAIE is better able at this point to deal with specifically indigenous issues, which are no longer considered secondary:

With the CONAIE we have a direct relationship, a mostly direct relationship as Indians, because the CONAIE is struggling specifically for us. Despite the fact that the FENOC-I has practically the same platform of struggle, but the relationship is more *de manos* [practical]. But that doesn't mean we are with the CONAIE more [than with the FENOC]. We go when we have to converse about that which is ours, but we are more with the FENOC.[48]

The Reconfiguration of Local Politics

By 1998 three important developments had taken place. First, in response to the national indianista movement and the demands of its constituents, the FENOC had attempted to use indianista rhetoric, organizing workshops on multiculturalism, joining the CONAIE and other indigenous and peasant national organizations to work in state-supported institutions, and allying with the CONAIE to form a united political front on land reform and modernization issues and to secure development projects. Second, while the UNORCIC remained affiliated with the FENOC, it was also informally linked with the CONAIE. The possibility of working more directly with the CONAIE is something that may not be institutionalized formally, but it already exists in practice. As the CONAIE has gained resources and institutional and political legitimacy as the main voice of Indians nationwide, it has worked more closely with the UNORCIC in the resolution of land disputes, particularly in the final phase of the Tunibamba community hacienda case (which was at a standstill until it was included in the negotiations between activists and the state after the 1990 uprising), and a land case in the community of La Calera in 1993. In La Calera, the CONAIE president, Luis Macas, visited the Cotacachi municipality (at the request of an activist from the community) and negotiated the declaration of that hacienda as public property, thus enabling its expropriation.

The third key development occurred in 1996, when indigenous activists followed the Cotacachi example and participated in electoral politics in a coalition with mestizo activists. The CONAIE joined a coalition of social movements to create a new political party, Pachakutik–Nuevo País. Departing from its previous policy of nonparticipation in elections, national and provincial indigenous activists organized national and local ballots that had significant indigenous representation. In Cotacachi this led to a definitive break between the UNORCIC and the Socialist Party and to the nomination of UNORCIC and UNORCIC-supported local candidates under the banner of Pachakutik–Nuevo País. Also in 1996, the first indigenous mayor of Cotacachi, Auqui Tituaña, was elected with substantial indigenous and mestizo support (see table 3). Although Tituaña is from the city, he was not a leader of the UNORCIC (though he had established a long-standing relationship with it as a consultant). Instead, he had been a national officer of the CONAIE for several years. With the UNORCIC's support, Tituaña ran under the newly created Pachakutik–Nuevo País Party affiliation. As table 3 shows, the vote in indigenous communities was consistently supportive of Pachakutik–Nuevo País, with almost equal levels of support in the mayoral and city council races. With the exception of Quiroga, Tituaña won in all the indigenous parishes. The city council vote was more contested, as the DP-UDC won overwhelmingly in Quiroga parish and the populist Partido Roldosista Ecuatoriano (PRE) had a slight advantage over the city council position in San Francisco. These figures also show, however, that Tituaña did have significant support in mestizo parishes, often running second after the PRE candidate. Further, the small but important discrepancies between the mayoral vote and the city council vote in the mestizo parishes show that Tituaña had an appeal to mestizos that extended beyond his party.

TABLE 3.
1996 Cotacachi Elections, Support for Pachakutik–Nuevo País

	Mayor	City Council
Indigenous Parishes		
Imantag	29.45%	27.13
Quiroga*	16.64%	15.70
San Francisco	27.90%	22.29
El Sagrario	31.75%	25.9
Mestizo Parishes		
Apuela	16.29%	14.78
Garcia Moreno	6.87%	6.97
Peñaherrera	16.75%	12.05
Plaza Gutierrez	16.20%	11.33
6 de Julio	22.94%	19.8
Vacas Galindo	10.56%	6.88

Source: Tribunal Supremo Electoral: Tribunal Provincial de Imbabura
*Quiroga is the only indigenous parish that did not deliver a plurality of its votes to Tituaña; 28.68 percent of the mayoral vote went to the SP–UDC. All the mestizo parties preferred the PRE candidate.

On the one hand, Tituaña's election appears to mark an alternative path for the election of indigenous candidates, without the need of the PSE. Every local indigenous activist who has run for city council since 1996 has done so under the Pachakutik–Nuevo País, which now has a formal relationship with the UNORCIC. On the other hand, the reliance on mestizo electoral support (which was crucial for Tituaña in a close election) means that Tituaña does not focus primarily on an indigenous agenda, nor does he embody the organization as de la Cruz or Andrango did.[49] That he was elected with significant mestizo support has led him to be involved with developing projects for mestizos as well as for indigenous communities and with the promotion of urban tourism and infrastructure projects that some organization activists claim detract from indigenous demands.

There are two conclusions to be drawn from this change in electoral politics. First, while the creation and development of Pachakutik–Nuevo

País has the potential to increase and strengthen indigenous representation, it has not necessarily led to an increase in the representation of UNORCIC leadership. In fact, UNORCIC activists' ability to win city council seats has declined. For example, in the 1998 elections, the mestiza candidate for Pachackutik–Nuevo País, Martha Sarzosa, obtained more votes than the two organization leaders, Cornelio Orbe and Miguel Robalino, even in overwhelmingly indigenous parishes. All these factors have led to a decline in the UNORCIC's electoral power precisely at a moment when most outside observers would consider an indigenous mayorship an exceptional coup for all of Cotacachi's Indians. While this decline may be attributed to several causes, including the loss of popular leaders Andrango and de la Cruz to national positions in the FENOC and the concomitant decline in available young leadership, it could also be concluded that the legitimacy granted by Pachakutik–Nuevo País to indigenous candidates who have not been UNORCIC leaders (such as Tituaña) has undermined the UNORCIC's monopoly over indigenous candidates and thus diminished (but not entirely undermined) its role as an electoral mechanism.

Second, despite being a self-proclaimed indigenous party, Pachakutik–Nuevo País may not be such a departure from previous coalition politics. The primary distinction between it and the UNORCIC-PSE coalition is that mestizo candidates in the former from the outset have understood that the mestizo-indigenous alliance is the constitutional basis of the party and are therefore more open to negotiation with indigenous candidates. Indigenous voters, in turn, associate the party with the CONAIE and indianismo and are less likely to be suspicious of mestizo candidates and more likely to give them their vote. Nevertheless, this modus operandi has meant that decisions about candidacies and nominations are no longer made exclusively by the UNORCIC, in negotiation with the Left, but by Pachakutik–Nuevo País leaders as well. Hence, it is possible that this coalition party, defined by its interracial component, may lead to a loss of organizational autonomy and decision-making capability for local indigenous organizations. This is why it is precisely when Cotacachi Indians have apparently made more gains in electoral representation, with an indigenous mayor and the replacement of the PSE by a partially indigenous party, that the role of the organization that started it all may no longer be viable.

CONCLUSIONS

In June 1993 an ordinary citizen, Julio Cabascango, was killed by an unmarked truck during a political march organized by the UNORCIC. The next week his funeral was held in the main plaza of the city where the CONAIE president, Luis Macas, the FENOC president, Mesias Tatamues, and the UNORCIC president, Pedro de la Cruz, stood together during the eulogy, each giving a speech on the importance of the indigenous struggle.

The image of these three leaders together was a revealing expression of the contemporary political environment in Cotacachi. The leaders of the CONAIE and the FENOC, once bitter rivals, came together to join one of the strongest intercommunal organizations in the country in a massive event attended by journalists and activists from throughout the country. Both the CONAIE and the FENOC were claiming Cabascango as one of the movement's martyrs. The FENOC's presence alone would not have attracted the media or galvanized an audience whose members included several visitors from other provinces and the capital. De la Cruz invited both leaders and catered to both, placing himself, as the embodiment of the UNORCIC, at the intersection of both. Although there are no official ties with the CONAIE, de la Cruz understood the importance of a common cultural framework shared by the UNORCIC and the CONAIE and its members. The "movement" crosses the boundaries of institutional affiliation and relies on a network of informal solidarity that informs the political action of local movements.

This solidarity in the agendas of the UNORCIC and the CONAIE can be understood as an expression of the politicization of race. The coexistence of class and racial politics as a component of citizenship is evident in UNORCIC's politics. While the UNORCIC fought racial discrimination, its readiness to disregard race in its official political rhetoric appeared to indicate transition from racial consciousness to class consciousness (something some Latin American Marxists such as Anibal Quijano [1979] would view as a transition from the prepolitical to the political). According to Quijano (1979, 8), peasant movements become political once they attempt to address structural change (and not small conflicts) and once they have a clear position on who the enemy (defined along class lines) is. In this sense, the UNORCIC appeared to be going against the national trend.

However, despite the leadership's efforts, race never disappeared from the political agenda; in fact, it was used quite consciously by UNORCIC leaders to generate support for their campesinista goals. Unlike the earlier indianization of poverty thesis, the double layer thesis allowed the organization to both create and justify coalitions with mestizos and maintain a separate source of solidarity among Indians. Racial issues were often coded in class terms, and symbolic elements, ceremonies, anniversaries, and everyday practices were also used to reinforce racial affirmation. Moreover, the politics of massive disruption and protest came to be associated with indianista politics, and the UNORCIC's participation in them helped to legitimize and reproduce indianista politics despite the existence of a more explicit campesinista agenda.

After the Indian uprising of 1990 and the eruption of a broader Indian movement on the national scene, however, the "success" of this type of politics began to decline as older UNORCIC activists began to participate in the national movement and stage local uprisings to secure local changes that they had not been able to achieve through formal channels. In addition, as local coalitions with Intag mestizos and mestizo socialists broke down, younger activists began to question the campesinista strategy, pushing for a disaffiliation from the FENOC and the PSE. Although the affiliation was maintained by the 1992 congress, the UNORCIC had become increasingly close to the CONAIE and its activists, at times very openly suggesting that the CONAIE's agenda was its own.

However, by 2002 this formal affiliation had not happened, and the UNORCIC remains campesinista in name but indianista in practice. While indianismo as an ideological construct was not embraced explicitly by the UNORCIC, it resonates in local circles, constituting an important ideological resource for local activists. In the CONAIE and its affiliates and allies (such as the Catholic church, human rights organizations, and other social movements working closely with the CONAIE), the UNORCIC has a new network of possible allies from which to generate human and material resources. Moreover, one of the main distinctions between indianismo and campesinismo that had made some UNORCIC leaders weary of CONAIE, participation in electoral politics, had collapsed.

In the immediate future, the UNORCIC is likely to maintain this bifurcated status, as growing Cotacachi mobilization and pressure has led the FENOC to grant Cotacachi activists increasing power in its national leadership. Former Cotacachi president and city councilman, Alberto Andrango, for example, has become president of the FENOC, and former president

Pedro de la Cruz has succeeded him as the current president. More interesting, the FENOC itself has begun to participate in national indianista politics with the CONAIE in recent mobilizations. Moreover, the UNORCIC's official affiliation with Pachakutik–Nuevo País has provided a nexus with the CONAIE's national activism and national-level electoral support, thus strengthening the indirect relationship with the CONAIE and the concomitant ideological affinities without requiring formal affiliation.

The CONAIE's political perspectives have gained a hold in Cotacachi, not because socioeconomic issues have become less important, but because indianismo has reinterpreted the commonsense understandings of poverty and the racial nature of indigenous subordination. The racial origin of the UNORCIC, the presence of race in local electoral "class" politics, and the fact that race was often encoded in class language show that racial meanings were already present and politically important, if tacitly so, and that power differentials had been understood racially. In this sense, the UNORCIC's sympathy and attachment to the CONAIE and its move away from campesinismo cannot be understood as merely instrumental but as a reflection of a common cultural framework shared with the CONAIE and its affiliates, which has led to a recognition of common interests that can be maintained despite official association with the FENOC.

CHAPTER FIVE

Our Own Teniente Político

Gaining Indigenous Autonomy in Cacha

Between small everyday acts of resistance and revolution lie forms of local resistance that can lead to dramatic breaks from one social order to another without subverting all dominant norms and practices. Unlike weapons of the weak, which require no formal organization and tinker at the margins of hierarchical relations, grassroots movements that dramatically break with the past involve a collective and open critique and reinterpretation of dominant understandings, requiring more direct confrontation and higher political risk. Unlike revolutionary movements, however, collective goals do not usually call for replacing the state.

In this chapter I examine contemporary indigenous resistance in Cacha, Chimborazo province, to address two key questions. First, why and how did a dramatic and relatively rapid break in local power relations occur? Second, what are the long-term consequences of such a break? In other words, how does the social construction of resistance shape and reconstitute power relations? The case of contemporary Cacha involved a dramatic break from domination and labor control to political, religious, and legal autonomy. The Cachas were able to discover a common past, create a common semantic, symbolic, and physical space, and pursue political autonomy as a parish. Together, these factors facilitated the invention of a common Cacha ethnic identity that served to confront racial subordination and formed the basis for a distinct and separate political entity. Conversely, Cacha also exemplifies the complex ways in which resistance, as a social construction, can simultaneously legitimize subversion and reinforce dominant norms and practices.

The why and how of this type of resistance is better understood by first analyzing acquiescence. To explain resistance it becomes important to explain the lack of resistance as a particular state (or stage) that must be problematized. In his discussion of the Meskitu in Nicaragua, Hale (1994) argues that populations that fail to rebel are not passive but are containing resistance through negotiation or adjustment. This idea of adjustment or negotiation of power relations is reminiscent of James Scott's (1985) work on everyday forms of resistance by South Asian peasants.

However, although concepts such as small acts of resistance, appropriation, and negotiation correctly undermine the notion of a passive peasantry, they do not adequately capture the broad range of possibilities contained in acquiescence. While in some situations the very possibility of negotiation requires awareness of alternatives, in more rigid situations these so-called alternatives are not even visible to social actors. The analysis of these situations can be facilitated by applying Pierre Bourdieu's concept of doxa, defined as a realm in which social arrangements are not questioned. Doxa involves a strict correspondence between social structure and mental structures. It is a situation in which the relation of order that structures both the real world and the thought world is accepted as self-evident (Bourdieu 1984, 471). Doxa is that which goes without saying and is therefore unquestioned because there is a quasi-perfect correspondence between the objective order and the subjective principles of organization (Bourdieu 1977, 166).

This analysis applies the concept of doxa to the Cacha case to explain why existing power relations were unquestioned and to explore the specific ways in which domination was rendered natural. This does not suggest a complete state of subordination but the existence of a realm in which many everyday practices and religious rituals reinforced domination and made acts of resistance rare, isolated, and difficult. The Cachas actively and willingly participated in practices that, despite their exploitative nature, were the only ones considered possible. Instead of seeing acquiescence and resistance as binary categories, we should focus on the broad continuum of possibilities contained in the realm of acquiescence. What Hale calls negotiation, for example, occurs in a state of partial acquiescence, a qualitatively different stage in which power relations are questioned and to a certain extent altered (albeit without open confrontation). The stage of negotiation and adjustment seems qualitatively different from the stage of doxa, for example, because it implies a preexisting separation between objective conditions and subjective interpretations of these conditions. In a stage of doxa, however, this separation is not evident.

The transition from doxa to what Bourdieu (1977) calls heterodoxy (in which alternatives are visible) involves a transformation of meanings such that the natural order of dominance and subordination is questioned. Alternatives that were not previously visible require, according to Bourdieu, both an objective change or crisis and the transformation of subjective perceptions of reality. The dominated must have both the material and the symbolic means for social classifications to become the object of struggle.

The second question addressed here, the long-term consequences of dramatic breaks, is best understood by positing resistance as a social construction as well as a social act. In dramatic breaks from one form of social organization to another, the construction of resistance itself—including the types, sites, and agents of resistance that have been established as legitimate, the alliances and oppositions created in the acts of resistance themselves, and the assumptions embedded in critiques of a previous order and common understandings of a new one—both generates new realities and new subjective conditions and frames power relations. These three factors are the key elements of the social construction of resistance. As a social construction, resistance can play as important a role as the acts of resistance themselves, generating new narratives and myths as well as placing new limits and constraints on future social actions. In the process, what is considered acceptable or unacceptable, possible or impossible, is altered, often in unexpected ways. For example, the subversive and the conventional may be simultaneously embraced, or the conventional may become subversive. The shift can be so great that the past may become almost incomprehensible to those socialized in the new social order. However, the new order produced by this act and construction of resistance can also generate new modes of domination from which it becomes almost impossible to escape. The heterodoxy achieved after resistance may indeed contain the seeds of a new doxa.

CONSENT AND COERCION: THE STRUCTURE OF SOCIAL CONTROL

Contemporary Cacha is a group of approximately twenty-three indigenous communities located in a mountainous region surrounding the small town

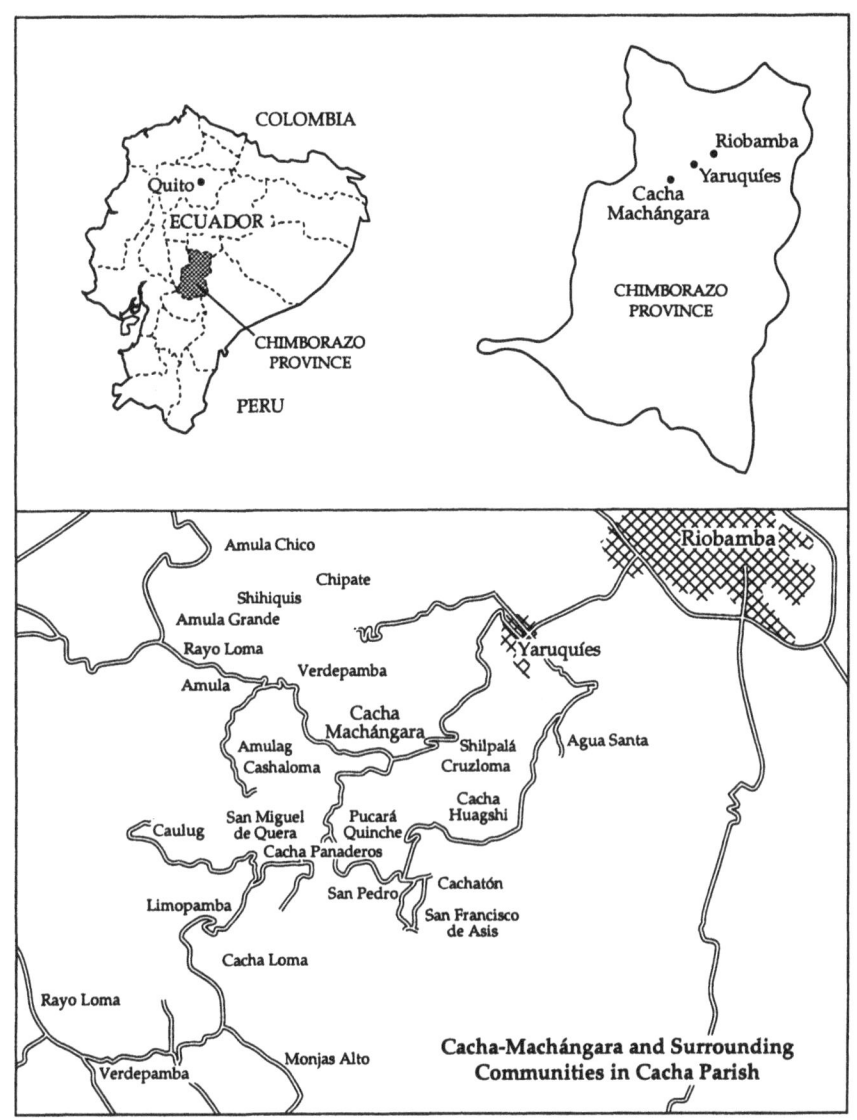

Cacha-Machángara and Surrounding Communities in Chimborazo Province Affiliated with FECAIPAC.

of Yaruquíes. Until the 1970s what is today known as Cacha consisted of three distinct anejos of the Yaruquíes parish: Cacha, Amulag, and Querag. The most important sources of income today are migrant work and commerce, and needlework and agriculture are important profit-making activities in a few communities (Arrieta 1984; FEPP 1993). Yaruquíes is directly in the path between Cacha and Riobamba, which is the political and economic center of the province of Chimborazo. Until 1981 the only form of transportation to Yaruquíes and therefore to Riobamba was by foot or donkey and could take several hours. As all the small trails required crossing Yaruquíes to get to Riobamba, Yaruquíes was a necessary rest stop.

The white-mestizo Yaruquíes dwellers' domination of the indigenous Cachas was secured through the obligatory use of Yaruquíes space for indigenous cultural and material reproduction and socioeconomic survival. The town of Yaruquíes and the roads that connected it to the indigenous communities were, literally and symbolically, sites of racial domination and confrontation. The Cachas' visits to Yaruquíes were of two general types: those that involved passing through on the way to Riobamba and those in which the town was the object of the visit. The indigenous Cacha had to pass through Yaruquíes to reach the city of Riobamba, site of the weekly major *feria*, or market, where they could buy and sell agricultural goods, look for work, or catch a bus to work in other cities. Whenever they passed by Yaruquíes, they were pressured to engage in commercial exchange in the town instead of the city. The Cachas' distance from Riobamba and the lack of a road suitable for automobile transportation directly to the city led to dependence on Yaruquíes vendors and moneylenders. Given the nearly total absence of large haciendas in the area, the mestizo economy hinged on the Cachas' demand for Yaruquíes goods as well as on mestizos' routine use of Indian forced labor for public works. The second type of visit, an exclusive trip to Yaruquíes, was usually made on Sundays and religious holidays. These visits were necessary because Yaruquíes was the ceremonial center as well as the center of local government.

In both types of visits indigenous deference to white-mestizos was expected. Although indigenous people constituted approximately 93 percent of the population by 1982, they were a political minority. Until 1960 Yaruquíes was a *parroquia* with complete political authority over Cacha, and until the late 1960s and early 1970s Yaruquíes exercised political and economic control over the entire Cacha zone. Hence, Cachas were beholden to mestizo powerholders and public officials from the town. They registered their marriages, births, and deaths in the Yaruquíes civil registry. They were also under the authority of the town's teniente político, the local policing authority with a mandate to settle disputes and ensure order.

The Cachas' communities in the periphery framed the whiteness of Yaruquíes at the center. The physical distance and difference in altitude served as markers of an existing racial barrier. The ritualization of racial interaction and the maintenance of physical barriers promoted social distance. In this rigid geographic arrangement, mestizaje and assimilation were not achieved by increased contact but by leaving Cacha. Those in Yaruquíes were white while those in Cacha were Indian, and the social barriers were rigid. In the racialized social hierarchy Indians had an ascribed status that was not only characterized or embodied in cultural difference but also underscored by prevalent understandings of their racial inferiority. Indians were considered ignorant, childlike beings incapable of defending their own interests and therefore in need of protection from the laws and institutions of the state by the local white-mestizo elites. Drunkenness, laziness, and stupidity were attributes commonly used by the town mestizos to describe the Cachas. At the same time, however, Cachas were forced to confront this barrier by passing through; and they could even symbolically transgress it during the religious fiestas that were celebrated in the town. These exchanges were ritualized and controlled, however, involving contact that was limited to certain times of the year and specific public places. These ritualized uses of space, with a simultaneous exclusion from them in everyday life, deepened the dependence of the Cachas on Yaruquíes.

This unequal relationship between Indians and mestizos in many free communities of the highlands was maintained with the assistance of a cacique system of local rule, derived from the pre-Inca Karaku system. In the colonial period, caciques were Indians of noble lineage who became partners with the Spaniards, securing Indian tribute and allegiance to the crown in exchange for land concessions and dispensation from forced labor activities. By the mid-twentieth century the cacique persisted in name in many areas of the province, but there had been dramatic changes in their ethnic identity as well as in the role they played in local administration. While most were the mestizo descendants of original caciques who had intermarried, some were mestizos of humbler origins who had gained status in the towns and consequently assumed the role of caciques. Their former monopoly of power had given way to greater dependence on the teniente político's ability to make Indians comply. In early-twentieth-century Yaruquíes, one cacique oversaw the local administration of one annex considered to be under his exclusive control. The cacique did not rule directly but appointed indigenous *alcaldes*, or mayors, who supervised communities. Cacha Indians complied with the caciques' orders in exchange for their protection within the town limits and intercession with mestizo authorities when necessary. When conflicts could not be resolved within a community or family, the Cachas would rely on the cacique to lecture, admonish, and punish the guilty party.

As in many experiences of social domination, the naturalization of hierarchical relations in Cacha was achieved through a combination of consent and coercion. The coexistence of violence and domination with what Jimenez (1989) calls a close identification between the dominant and the subordinate characterized social relations in Cacha. The caciques had authority because they were vested with authority by Indians, who identified closely and personally with them and to this day refer to them as *mi cacique* (my cacique). The Cachas' consent and participation in this social order was possible because of a profound and culturally reinforced intertwining of their own livelihoods and those of caciques and other mestizo notables. Cacha Indians' sphere of prestige relied very heavily on their relationship with town mestizos. Unlike hacienda communities, where one's standing with the landowner was primarily a determinant of social status among families, in free communities status hinged on one's acceptance by mestizo authorities, merchants, and other town notables. One's compliance with town and cacique authority and friendships with mestizos of status became yardsticks with which Indians measured their own positions in their communities.

Close identifications were made through interpersonal relationships, and these were reinforced in religious *fiestas*,[1] which acted as agents of socialization and domination. The match between the subjective and objective structures that characterizes doxa was most evident during these celebrations. During the fiestas, indigenous resources were literally "redistributed" to the pueblo and its inhabitants. Every January 1, in a ceremony called "the passing of the baton," Yaruquíes caciques appointed several indigenous men to the position of alcalde, responsible for coordinating the fiestas. The *alcalde de doctrina or ordinario* was the highest position and oversaw all the fiestas. In addition, an alcalde was appointed for each of the three annexes. These appointments, which were accorded high status in the communities, were usually prearranged, and were given to men who had demonstrated great generosity as *priostes*, or captains, in previous fiestas. Most of those designated alcaldes had given the caciques and teniente político sizable gifts beforehand. The alcaldes in turn appointed those who would be priostes in each annex. A prioste was responsible for sharing the financial responsibility for the fiestas. Being selected a prioste was considered an honor and tested a community member's capacity for leadership as well as his generosity to the caciques, the pueblo, and other communities. Those nominated were obliged to accept this responsibility, as a refusal to participate was perceived by others as an indicator of low social status (Arrieta 1984, 150). While coercion occasionally played a role in the acceptance of these appointments, on most occasions societal and familial expectations were sufficient sources of pressure.[2] There was little room for refusal. Because compliance with caciques and alcaldes established status in the community, family expectations were that one would fulfill this duty. "To have said no would have been a shame and [carried] a stigma of despising one's community and one's own family" (Arrieta 1984, 151). As Manuel Janeta explained,

> They would say, "Now compadritos you are already married, you have to be a prioste, you have to do [the fiesta of] Easter." After that they would say, "You have to be an alcalde." Then our parents would say, "Well, alright." [otherwise] they will say, "Because they have no money they don't participate. They will speak, gossip." This forced our parents more, so we had to do it.[3]

"They will speak [or] gossip" suggests that there were no alternatives and little room for refusal, given community expectations. That there was no fundamental contradiction between family expectations and those of Yaruquíes authorities suggests a tight fit between the mentality of some of the Cachas and the objective structure that reinforced their domination by the mestizos. Doxa was maintained by the societal pressure of one and all, as each community member constrained and imposed on others in the same way he or she was constrained.

The costs of being a prioste were significant. He was responsible for providing three days' food and drink in proportions sufficient to feed the entire town of Yaruquíes and the Indians visiting from the communities. Because the position served as a marker of status and differentiation, priostes were competitive among themselves. Instead of sharing the expenses of a band, for example, each prioste paid for a different one. In their effort to establish a good name and outdo each other, they would purchase large quantities of foods from Yaruquíes mestizo vendors as well as barrels of chicha from mestizo chicheros.[4] The need for money led to frequent borrowing from chulqueros, who would provide cash at high interest. The Cachas were often forced to offer their land or harvest as collateral, and not infrequently they would lose their land because they were unable to pay fiesta debts.

Procuring large quantities of food was not enough. Because these celebrations catered to the cacique, the teniente político, and governor, the food was expected to be of an "acceptable" quality, that is, expensive food that Indians did not produce on their lands and could not afford to purchase for themselves. Hence they could not rely on barter or on their own production but were forced to spend cash. As an informant explained,

> The fiesta of the Virgin of the Rosary had sixty to eighty captains who would come down from Friday to Monday. One had to work hard, raise animals, pigs, fatten them, sell them. In the fiesta they were well received because the caciques were well served, with prepared food, guinea pigs, chickens, fish, habas, and hominy.[5]

Fiestas can often act as equalizers, by eliminating economic surplus and the individualistic values that may be associated with it. But they can also be a differentiating force, creating distinctions among community members by assigning prestige and status. In Cacha both processes were at work. In communities with minimal class difference, fiestas served to allot prestige, power, and distinction. But in the repeated act of the fiesta, any possibility that an economic surplus would stay in Cacha was eliminated, because most potential wealth was transferred to Yaruquíes vendors. The fiesta reproduced power inequalities between mestizos and Indians, preventing the creation of political alternatives. While the fiestas created nonmonetary distinctions among Indians, they perpetuated their subordination by widening their distance from town mestizos. The purported "ideal" intent of the fiesta—redistribution among community members—was counteracted by a very real outcome: the continuous and ritualized transfer of resources from Cacha to Yaruquíes.

The reality of this transfer of income raises the question of how this was made sense of by indigenous fiesta participants. Why and how did Indians consider this an advantageous process, or how, in Bourdieu's terms, was necessity made a virtue? The fiestas were particularly powerful mechanisms of domination because they were considered the creation of the

Indians, events they organized and controlled.⁶ Even though the mestizos determined who would be alcaldes, what food would be served, which bars Indians would stop at and purchase chicha from, and which saints would be revered, the fiestas were considered by all an exclusively indigenous, not a mestizo, cultural production. The participation of mestizos in their construction and re-creation is often underemphasized. That they are considered primarily an Indian production has contributed to contemporary Cacha inhabitants' bafflement at their ancestors' willingness to participate in them. Looking back, they usually attribute it to ignorance, mystification, self-deception, or some form of false consciousness that kept them ignorant of the real objectives of the fiesta.

But the fact that the fiestas made sense underscores the existence of a realm of doxa, in which the objective and the subjective are so deeply intertwined that they cannot be easily separated or questioned. There were three important ways in which the fiesta made sense. First, although Indians were excluded from most realms of mestizo social and political life, the effect was mitigated by interracial relations in which indigenous community notions of equality, reciprocity, communal obligation, and respect were reinforced. The most crucial equalizing mechanism was the *compadrazgo*, the process by which an indigenous parent would have a Yaruquíes mestizo be the godparent of his child. Through the compadrazgo an important bond was established between Indian and mestizo adults. The mestizo became part of the Indians' social circle as *compadres*, mediators, advisers, and friends. In this context, fiestas were an opportunity to rejoice with mestizo power brokers and compadres, to celebrate, reinforce, and display to other Cachas the interpersonal relationships between Indians and mestizos.

Second, religious festivities made sense because of the conflation of religious and political authority. Indigenous alcaldes were also responsible for governing their particular annexes all year, controlling community issues, settling disputes, and ensuring that Indians fulfilled forced labor obligations and other duties in the town of Yaruquíes. The alcalde system enabled the teniente político to maintain control without entering into the communities. Since the alcalde's authority rested on the authority of the teniente político and the cacique, he had the power to make Indians submit to town rule. He watched over the morality of the communities, resolved problems of inheritance and neighbors' fights, organized large mingas for public maintenance of the streets, the cemetery, and the church, and organized the fiestas in the annexes.[7]

Third, the fiesta reinforced and legitimized more formal relations of dependence on the white-mestizos of the town, who served as intermediaries between Indians and public officials. For Indians, interactions with the state were complex and difficult, both because of language difference—most Cachas spoke primarily or only Quichua—and because of the authorities' routine abuse. Public offices were notorious for serving mestizos before Indians, making the latter wait, or refusing them altogether. Since Spanish alone is spoken in Ecuadorian public offices, language was the main barrier monolingual Cachas had to confront. Even Indians who spoke Spanish were not likely to be literate[8] or to have the bureaucratic sophistication needed to defend one's interests adequately in the official realm.

Thus Indians never approached authorities directly but routinely relied on intermediaries, or *quishqueros* (translators) to intervene for them in public offices as well as in church for the arrangement of marriages, deaths, or legal disputes.[9] These intermediaries could be caciques themselves, chulqueros or chicheros, or members of the wealthiest Yaruquíes families who also employed several Indians as field workers and house servants. All religious ceremonies such as funerals, special masses, and baptisms always required a previous "donation" of livestock, eggs, or some other product. Indians paid twice: once extraofficially to public officials or the priest who performed the service and once to the quishquero. The use of quishqueros, however, was by no means a guarantee that the issue would be resolved fairly. In Indian-mestizo land disputes, for example, mistranslation and miscommunication (many purposely so) could lead to a Cacha's loss of land to mestizo speculators. This made the careful selection and pleasing of quishqueros a central preoccupation for the Cachas.

Whereas Indians' consent and participation in the reproduction of mestizo power was prevalent in the fiestas, it was lacking in other areas. This is exemplified in many Cachas' aversion to and rejection of forced labor. Yaruquíes authorities believed the Cachas owed them servile labor of both a public and a private nature. Caciques, the teniente político, the governor, who assisted the teniente político, and the priest used their public authority to make arrangements that provided them with an "extra hand." As a condition for marriage, for example, indigenous brides and grooms were first obliged to do menial tasks in the house of the teniente político and the priest for a period of two weeks:

> Until the 1970s they made the grooms work. I worked two weeks in 1966 with the commissioner and the priest, one week with each one was the requirement in order to get married. They would teach us any old Our Father, and the rest of the time I spent cutting grass, weeding, filling pitchers.[10]

Indian labor was also used for the maintenance of public grounds, city parks, and streets. It was considered a way of earning the privilege to use town facilities. As a condition for attending mass, for example, Indians were expected to sweep the floors of the church and clean the church square.

> The authorities, police, always treated us as if we had committed a crime. In the early morning they would take us in a pickup to work. To attend mass one first had to take the broom and sweep the floors. After mass we had to pass the cacique's house to greet him or they would say we weren't worth anything.[11]

These practices were not only considered humiliating, they caused economic hardships by depriving the Cachas of their labor power and time. In some cases they led to job loss when employers became impatient with unexpected absences. They were racialized practices, affecting only Indians. The use of Indians for forced labor was a widespread practice in the Ecuadorian highlands that stemmed from Spanish appropriation of the mita, a form of public, collective labor used in the Inca empire. The Spaniards had used Indians for public works in exchange for protection. After independence, Indians continued to be used as mitayos by hacienda owners in hacienda zones and by public officials and priests in free communities. Poor mestizos, regardless of their low socioeconomic status, were not called on to participate in these activities.

The use of coercion to ensure compliance was common. When the alcaldes failed to secure labor in the communities because of Indians' reluctance, Indians were punished by jail or by forcing their family members to work instead. There was an alternative way of ensuring compliance. The forced passage of Indians through Yaruquíes on their way to jobs in Riobamba or other cities brought about unexpected "encounters" with the teniente político. When headed toward Yaruquíes in the small hours of the morning to leave for migrant work sites, they would often be stopped by the teniente político and held for a day or more to perform forced labor. When Cachas changed their schedules to avoid the teniente político's ambush, the official would eventually catch on and surprise them at the most unexpected hour. While the white-mestizos interviewed claimed the Indians "offered" their services, the Cachas' oral accounts suggest something entirely different: a routine and planned use of force.

> The teniente político of Yaruquíes would pick up people to pave the Riobamba-Yaruquíes road. He would get money from the municipality to fix the public road but would never even give [us] a glass of water. We would rise at 1:00 or 2:00 in the morning to [go] work in the city, and he would spy on us with two policemen and would grab one or two. I was so scared when I found him at 2:00 A.M. in the entrance to Yaruquíes. [He said], "Aha, *longo*[12] son of the great bitch, finally you're in my hands." He grabbed eight that night. From 1:00 A.M. until 5:00 P.M. we cleaned a pool, and we had only bread and water. I asked myself then, what kind of authority is this?[13]

> They used to grab you and force you to work when you were going down to Riobamba or going to mass. [We would say] "Please, please, mister teniente político, we haven't eaten, how are we going to work? We have no money, we have nothing, what will we eat?" He would damn us, saying, "Jesus these damn . . ."[14]

Coercion was also used in daily interactions and commercial exchange. Cachas transporting livestock and produce to Riobamba were often stopped by townspeople who would practice el arranche, the common practice of seizing a product first and then paying the owner an undervalued amount. In this way, Cachas who preferred to sell in the larger market of Riobamba were prevented from doing so and town mestizos had access to goods below market price.

In both cases of coercion and consent, the Cachas' literal distance from Yaruquíes justified subservience but also reproduced it. In the late 1960s the Cachas were ruled by white-mestizo Yaruquíes in virtually every aspect of their economic, social, and political lives. In contrast to even the poorest of town mestizos, Indians had to undergo coerced labor, obey cacique rule, and pay extraordinarily, in kind, for public services. Yaruquíes housed the Cacha dead and ruled over the living. The Yaruquíes civil register recorded

Cacha births, marriages, and deaths; the teniente político controlled their movements and had the power to punish or imprison them to obtain their labor. Relationships that were considered reciprocal, of fair exchange, were actually skewed toward mestizo vendors. Yaruquíes caciques appointed fiesta organizers, and Yaruquíes vendors profited greatly from these ventures. Indians, in contrast, spent resources they did not have to repeatedly engage in the fiesta as public spectacle. In doing so, ironically, they were made responsible for what mestizos called the moral degradation of the town, which during the fiesta became contaminated, as mestizos claimed, by Indian drunkards engaged in mindless celebration, racialized as simultaneously childlike and threatening, proving beyond a doubt their need to be protected and controlled. In the political and administrative realm, Yaruquíes quishqueros "mediated" for Indians, their very existence dependent on the maintenance of rigid boundaries between mestizo and Indian worlds and on the perpetuation of Indian ignorance.[15] In the words of one mestizo informant, it was not an improvised system.[16]

LEAVING YARUQUÍES: RESISTANCE AND THE QUEST FOR AUTONOMY

In his discussion of doxa, Bourdieu refers to a moment of crisis in which objective relations are transformed and a critique establishes the route for new alternatives (Bourdieu 1977, 169). At this moment, the match between objective structures and mental structures that characterized doxa is undermined. Cacha experienced such a break and crisis after several developments disrupted the preexisting order. Although the 1964 and 1973 national land reform laws did not restructure landownership patterns in Yaruquíes or Cacha, agrarian modernization played a significant role in the political and economic transformation of the zone. By the late 1960s and early 1970s, the rural modernization that accompanied land reform had led to an institutionalized state presence in the rural highlands, which included the free communities. As it began to expand rural resources and institutions and implement development policies, the state became more receptive to indigenous communities' claims, encouraging them to become legalized communities so as to present their demands. It was also more capable of meeting their demands through its recently acquired rights to repossess land and control all water sources in the country.

Economic changes restructured the economic and political role of Riobamba in the nation as well as in the region. The freeing of labor and subsequent massive migration to the coast, particularly to the coastal city of Guayaquil, had two important effects. First, it provided many Cachas with more labor opportunities outside of Yaruquíes, which decreased dependence on seasonal agricultural labor arrangements with Yaruquíes landowners and exposed many Cachas to labor organizing experiences in the cities, experiences that would help them to organize their communities on their return. Second, the dramatic growth of Guayaquil as a consequence of this migration gave Riobamba an increasingly important role as a food supplier for the city. As it grew, Riobamba consolidated its resources and annexed adjoining Yaruquíes in 1960, changing its status from a rural to an urban parish. The outcome of this annexation was the abolition of the Yaruquíes civil registry and the teniente político's office in the 1970s, as these offices were granted only to rural parishes. Yaruquíes fell under the authority of the Riobamba police commissioner and civil registry for larger and distant offices, thus freeing the Cachas from the grip of the local offices and marking the beginning of a dramatic breakdown in local authority, ultimately diminishing the power of the local mestizos.

The teniente político's departure in the early 1970s, more than a decade after the official abolition of the Yaruquíes parish, facilitated the legal development of indigenous communities as well as eventual intercommunal activism. Without fear of reprisal, young activists were free to develop a political alternative, a reorganization of the social and political order that would lead to self rule within a decade. Absent the tight control of the teniente político, the traditional handling of local conflicts progressively eroded. The communities in various annexes began to circumvent alcalde authority and organize in defense of their socioeconomic rights by applying for the status of legalized communities[17] and presenting demands directly to the national government.

Disregarding or replacing the traditional public authorities, the alcaldes, these new communities began to focus on other needs such as schools, community centers, and irrigation. They also began to target state agencies and international NGOs to fund these projects. These were the first leaders not selected through the fiesta process. Most of the activists were elected presidents or officials in their communities, and by the late 1970s they were joined by several literacy coordinators, creating a cadre of activists who did not owe their power to the dutiful fulfillment of fiesta rituals. They began holding roundtables to discuss their socioeconomic needs and political strategies.[18]

Despite these developments on the political front, the Yaruquíes caciques still expected subordinate behavior through the fiesta. Deprived of the policing power of the teniente político, mestizos in the new urban parroquia had increasingly relied on the ideological control of the church to ensure the continuation of religious rituals that benefited them financially. By the mid-1970s, however, the last legitimating source of the eroding order was overturned by Catholic activism. Liberation theology had become prevalent in many areas of Chimborazo, spearheaded by then Monsignor Leonidas Proaño, who promoted Christian pastorals throughout the province. This new church was represented for the first time at the local level by Father Modesto Arrieta, who began working in the town in 1972. Arrieta opposed white-mestizo domination in the town and was a key source of support during the water conflict in the communities of Obraje and Shilpalá. He urged activists to travel to Quito and secure their legal water rights by seeking an ally in the national government. His relatively modest campaign addressing the educational needs of indigenous people was vehemently rejected by local white-mestizos, most notably those intermediaries and small landowners who depended on the subservience of Indians.

Using a methodology designed to raise consciousness, Arrieta began to promote the open discussion of Cacha's needs in a religious context. Cacha participants analyzed their own socioeconomic subordination, focusing particularly on the unjust and un-Christian nature of the fiestas and on their abuse at the hands of the authorities. A common conclusion reported in the minutes of these meetings was that the fiestas were a form of exploitation and should be eliminated (Arrieta 1984). Arrieta joined organized communities that were already campaigning to end the fiestas and encouraged them to air their complaints to Monsignor Proaño and higher religious authorities.[19]

In 1975 Arrieta decided to suppress the baton ceremony, which undermined the authority of the caciques by eliminating their last remaining function: the appointment of alcaldes. He was able to do this because this ceremony had been traditionally sponsored by the church and celebrated at Sunday Mass, with the priest's blessing. The initial effect was complete disarray, as many communities had depended on alcaldes for internal organization. In communities that still relied on traditional authorities, this change left a noticeable power vacuum. The tight control of the alcaldes became evident after their demise, as communities could no longer rely on members to attend meetings or heed notices and work citations; and the few community governments that were in place barely functioned (Arrieta 1984, 174).

With the withdrawal of church support, the match between the social and the normal or natural was broken. Absent the cultural and religious authority that provided the institutional support for the fiestas, the economic hardship they entailed was no longer buttressed by religious ideology. Gradually, even in the most traditional communities, popularly elected cabildos began to assume the roles and responsibilities previously carried out by the alcaldes and his assistants. Although the fiestas continued, their implementation lost much of its previous significance, as local power and the social status necessary to get it were no longer linked to the adequate fulfillment of fiesta obligations.

Arrieta's activities in the town also threatened to undermine the well-established organization of space. He planned to build, in Yaruquíes, a center for teaching handicrafts and manual manufacturing techniques to the indigenous people and the mestizo poor. In doing so, he was tinkering with the well-established barriers that separated the town from the indigenous communities. This was a threat to many Yaruquíes townspeople who felt this was an unsolicited use of their town space, an "invasion" by Indians. Vendors, chulqueros, chicheros, and a few prominent landowners organized into groups called the Concerned Citizens of Yaruquíes. They opposed the handicraft center, claiming that Arrieta was favoring the Indians at the expense of the "citizens" of Yaruquíes.

Soon after the money for the handicraft project was secured from the Catholic church, Arrieta was accused of stealing sacred figures and selling them to fund projects for the Indians.[20] A group of Yaruquíes notables moved to have Arrieta removed from the town, calling for an investigation into the alleged pilfering of the church. Addressing the diocese of Riobamba, one hundred thirty people, claiming to represent the entire town, signed a letter that stated "the priest is causing much damage to the tranquillity of the Yaruqueño family" (Arrieta 1984, 188). Finally, when their written appeals failed, the organized townspeople expelled Arrieta by force on January 30, 1977. Arrieta's warning that he was not abandoning the cause but merely relocating to Cacha angered townspeople who believed he was the only one responsible for "opening the eyes of the *verdugos.*"[21] After Arrieta moved to Cacha, Monsignor Proaño punished the town by closing the Yaruquíes church for several years and not replacing him. For many years, Arrieta was publicly harassed and prohibited from even passing through the town.

Ironically, Yaruquíes's opposition to the cancellation of the fiestas and the opposition to the handicraft center for Indians were simultaneous campaigns. Not coincidentally, the expulsion of Arrieta occurred exactly eight days after a group of Indians asked the bishop in Quito to end the fiestas. The Yaruqueños were not necessarily opposed to an Indian presence per se, as the town benefited greatly from the managed presence of the fiestas, but to an Indian presence that was outside their control and did not provide a profit opportunity. The handicraft school was barred before it was opened. Until this time, Indians' presence and absence had been preordained and regulated by Yaruquíes mestizos and had served specific purposes. Arrieta, the organized indigenous Catholics supporting him, and the newly organized communities were threatening this order. The rejection of Arrieta's presence in Yaruquíes symbolized the rejection of any change in interracial relations. His persecution was both retribution for threatening the old forms of control and a deterrence against any further "opening of the eyes." Once Arrieta moved into community territory, the lines of conflict were spatially demarcated: Arrieta and his supporters, as well as indigenous activists, belonged in Cacha; mestizos belonged in town.

What the Yaruqueños did not anticipate was how this demarcation would be used by Cachas to separate themselves more fully than the Yaruqueños had imagined possible, much less desired. By the time Arrieta arrived in Cacha, leaders of the most recently politicized and legalized communities, young activists involved in education and literacy projects, and migrant workers with organizing experience in the cities had created a federation of communities. They had decided that intercommunal unity was necessary to promote social and economic development and undermine dependence on Yaruquíes. They attended several communities' elections, where they spoke about the importance of creating a broader organization. They began to create networks of supporters in various communities. This Pre-Federation of Cabildos of Cacha, later FECAIPAC, had the empowerment of communities, autonomy from Yaruquíes, and the creation of their own parish as its main goals. Initially created with fourteen communities, each of which had a representative in the federation, by 1994 it had twenty-three affiliated communities. Together, Arrieta and the new activists planned a transformation of power relations in three steps: construction of a highway leading directly to the city of Riobamba, elimination of fiestas, and establishment of Cacha as an autonomous parish.

As Yaruquíes was now perceived by many Cachas as a place of bondage, activists decided that one way to achieve racial liberation was to divest the act of crossing Yaruquíes of its importance. Because racial hierarchies in Cacha were spatially configured, activists believed that the power relationship could be transformed by altering the use of space. Cacha activists soon found that although it was not possible to avoid crossing through Yaruquíes, the act could be divested of its previous significance. Hence the first project was the completion of a highway that would connect Cacha to Yaruquíes. This allowed the Cachas to pass quickly through Yaruquíes on their way to Riobamba, instead of encountering chicheros and other Yaruquíes merchants. The plan was attacked by the Yaruqueños. They accused the FECAIPAC of destroying individual property, told their Indian compadres that it was all a hoax, and blocked the road when indigenous workers were scheduled to work.

The Yaruqueños were unsuccessful in blocking the construction, but they were correct in seeing its larger significance: it would deprive them of commercial control over the zone. The direct transportation to Riobamba led to the proliferation of stores in Cacha and to its eventual commercial independence from Yaruquíes, changing the meaning of "going down."

> Before, we used to go down for holy mass. On the roads, people [from town] would sell chicha, liquor, only for us to drink and waste money. Thankfully, we now have cars [that come] here. If they want to go down, they don't have to go down to Yaruquíes.[22]

By 1977 Arrieta had built a religious parish center in the community of Cacha-Machángara, which would allow all sacraments to be conducted in Cacha. Most important, however, was the elimination of the fiestas held in Yaruquíes. By the late 1970s some organized communities, such as Obraje, had already received permission from national church authorities to suspend their fiestas. After the suppression of the baton ceremony, the fiestas were continuously questioned and gradually banned. Fearing reprisal, activists decided to first reduce the amount of time they devoted to fiestas.

On one occasion, they did not arrive in Yaruquíes until the morning of the fiesta, depriving the town of the liquor and chicha profits traditionally obtained from indigenous consumption on the eve of the celebration. On another occasion, approximately eighty priostes and hundreds of indigenous people held a procession to a hill just outside Yaruquíes, where they could be seen by the townspeople.

> We did not go down to the town, but until San Francisco, we ate foods and then we went back up. They [Yaruquíes dwellers] wanted to kill each one of us and they chased us. They would threaten to kill the leaders, saying that they [the leaders] were against the caciques and the town of Yaruquíes. . . . They would say, these longos, these verdugos, who open the eyes of our people, our servants, they don't even have the grace of God. They would not accept [the fact] that there was no fiesta, especially chulqueros would say there must be a fiesta.[23]

Retribution against the Cachas was difficult. Several physical confrontations with Cachas kept Yaruqueños away from the communities. Instead they attempted to punish the Cachas by barring them from their usual activities, exacerbating interracial tensions. For example, Cachas were prevented from using the town cemetery to bury their dead. If the live Cachas would not bother to come down for the fiesta from which they had profited, they were not going to allow them to bury their ancestors. This issue was finally resolved with the construction of three cemeteries in the Cacha zone, but until this occurred, there were several confrontations between Indians carrying bodies and mestizos who physically blocked their way to the burial grounds.

The final objective of the federation was to create its own rural parish with Indian authorities, an unprecedented move in Ecuadorian history. FECAIPAC activists believed this would ensure political autonomy and legitimize their territorial independence. While being serviced by offices in the city had freed them from the arbitrary power of the Yaruquíes teniente político, it did not eliminate the problem of mestizo intermediaries and Riobamba authorities' neglect of indigenous affairs. In February 1980 the FECAIPAC asked the mayor of Riobamba to establish the political parish of Cacha with its own civil registry and teniente político.

There was opposition from Yaruquíes and in Cacha. In part, the Cachas were influenced by the opinions so freely shared by their Yaruqueño compadres, who falsely claimed that they would have to pay more taxes if Cacha was made a parish. Others feared that when Cacha became a parish, white-mestizos would be able to control them more directly and effectively, to the point of seizing Indians' lands and houses (Arrieta 1984, 60). But a more powerful reason for opposition rested in the negative valuation of Indians; they were deeply convinced that Cachas lacked the ability to govern themselves. An alternative order in which Cachas could rule Cachas and gain complete autonomy from the Yaruquíes mestizos was not even imaginable. When they heard that Pedro Morocho might be nominated as the first teniente político, they complained.

> Morocho is like us, he knows nothing. It's better for us to have white authorities. (Arrieta 1984, 131)

> The people would laugh in their [the organizers'] face. They did not believe in creating a parish. . . . [I]ncredulous, they did not believe that a parish could be created in Cacha itself, and they did not believe that its leaders were going to be indigenous people.[24]

While the activists' goal provoked the ire of local townspeople, it appealed to the national government's neoindigenista policy. The Cachas targeted their project by identifying with the new democratic government's rhetoric of respect for ethnic patrimony and multiculturalism, claiming that a Cacha parish would fulfill this new goal perfectly. When making their case to political and civil authorities, they used cultural difference as the main reason for wanting a separate parish with its own teniente político and civil registry. They argued that having their own parish would enable the Cachas to preserve their cultural legacy and facilitate their incorporation into the state. Furthermore, the former was posited as a necessary condition for the latter. In a letter to provincial authorities they stated, "Not just our language, but our sociocultural conditions are so different and distinct, that we need a separate service, preferably [carried out] by an indigenous peasant" (Arrieta 1984, 57).

By 1980, despite their many efforts to block the project, Yaruqueños could do nothing more to prevent it. Cacha was declared a parish on August 19, 1980, by the cantonal council of Riobamba in a document that emphasized ethnic and cultural values. Inauguration of the parish took place in April 1981, attended by then president Jaime Roldós, who arrived in Cacha by helicopter. In one of his last public acts before his tragic death, Roldós delivered an emotional speech in which he lauded the Cachas for preserving their customs and cultural identity and referred to the historical importance of the zone.

With the establishment of the parish, Cacha was freed from all formal dependence on Yaruquíes. Since 1980 Cacha has operated its own institutions, managed all civil procedures, and resolved most local disputes, permanently eliminating the white-mestizo intermediary in commercial transactions as well as public affairs. The inauguration of the parish was soon followed by the creation of a new indigenous civil registry and Indian teniente político.[25] The teniente and federation officials were elected at the same time. For this purpose, the FECAIPAC organized an electoral college in which all the communities and twenty adult education centers sent representatives to express the will of their constituencies (Arrieta 1984, 129).

The creation of the parish, however, did not immediately end the Cachas' use of Yaruquíes. Many Cachas continued to bury their dead there. Paradoxically, some Yaruqueños, incensed by the new parish, began to impede indigenous use of the town. This led to an escalation of conflict and to incidents that the activists considered humiliating, including fights between the Cachas who insisted on using Yaruqueño burial grounds and the Yaruqueños who were trying to block them. In reaction, federation members and the new teniente político implemented sanctions to punish Cachas who went down to the Yaruquíes church or cemetery or insisted on continuing the fiestas. The sanctions consisted of fees or, in rare cases, incarceration. In addition, the FECAIPAC was able to obtain a governmental order that did not recognize marriages and birth registrations held outside Cacha.

The breaking of old habits was so difficult for some that the organization, like the Yaruquíes authorities of the past, ultimately relied on coercion as well as consent. These measures were able to decrease the number of ceremonies held outside the parish. To this day, however, there are "deviant" Cachas who in great secrecy, at risk of being discovered, hold their ceremonies outside the parish. However, after the imposition of sanctions, the power differential shifted dramatically. The FECAIPAC was in control of the Cachas' behavior, and Yaruqueños who dissented risked sanctions by religious and provincial authorities for disturbing the new parish.

SUBJECTIVE CONDITIONS:
ETHNIC IDENTITY AND THE POLITICIZATION OF HISTORY

The break between the remnants of the old system and the present one is so great that is often difficult for young Cachas today to understand how their ancestors could ever have participated in such an exploitive system. When thinking back on the old system, Cachas try to explain it by attributing it to ignorance and a lack of education, which impeded their forebears' understanding and justified an imputed false consciousness:

> Even I went [to a fiesta]. But those people [the elders] didn't know. The elders did not know much. Now, with schools, we know more. Now there are people who have studied, who finish school, now even the poor know.[26]
>
> We did not realize, we did not realize.[27]

It is not only formal education that explains the difference between Cachas then and now but a particular knowledge of something that was previously amiss. What did Cachas not realize back then? What do they know now? What does the knowledge consist of and how was it acquired? This realization was not a sudden opening of the eyes, to cite one of the church's favorite expressions, but a complex change in consciousness and action.

In this transition, the recuperation of history, the transformation of the meaning of space, and the implementation of a new indigenous local administration played key roles. Activists relied on the "recovery" of pre-Columbian and colonial histories of noble grandeur and ethnic resistance to achieve changes in the status quo. New attention was paid to Cacha history as unique and distinctive, giving Cachas a sense of pride. In 1980 a number of activists joined Arrieta's efforts to organize workshops to familiarize Cachas with the history of the Cacha dynasty, which played a central role in the creation of the Ecuadorian Inca lineage.[28] The workshops also gave Cachas a sense of Cacha as a spatial unity. In nightly sessions, Arrieta and local activists held discussions on what was unique about Cachas, such as the Cacha dynasty and the Daquilema rebellion, which lent historical importance to Cacha as a zone of rebellion. Paralleling the history of many other nationalist groups that have undergone a similar process of historical education, the Cachas were posited as a distinct and distinctive ethnic group with an important tradition of resistance. After these workshops were held, activists and community members shared this knowledge in informal meetings and organizational workshops. Today, this history is known and shared by all, and it is becoming incorporated into oral tradition.

The effect of this teaching and learning of history was the legitimization of the FECAIPAC's activities and the promotion of the new parish. Activists agree that before the workshops were held, most Indians had no knowledge of Cacha history. No one "remembered" the Duchicela dynasty, nor did they speak of Daquilema and his rebellion. New activists discovered that the absence of memory, however, did not necessarily impede this recuperation; perhaps it facilitated it. The absence of memory allowed for selective representations of historical moments, representations that might reflect myth more than historical reality but that underscored important connections between the Cachas of the past and of the present: a shared geography, a shared oppression, and a shared struggle to resist oppression.

Unexpectedly, the Duchicela dynasty was soon given a contemporary life. In the mid-1980s Cacha was visited for the first time by alleged descendants of the last Inca emperor, Atahualpa. They were a family who had emigrated to the United States a generation earlier and were now in Cacha to bury their father. While they had never been in Cacha and actually had trouble finding it, they were soon declared Cacha royalty; Felipe was crowned and his sister was married in Cacha-Machángara.[29] Many people attended the ceremonies, which were an important symbol of the historical and cultural heritage of Cacha.[30]

Another important effect of culture and historical education was the concept that the entire area of indigenous communities had once been one political entity called Cacha. Before the workshops most Cachas throughout the zone consisted of three annexes of Yaruquíes: Querag, Amulag, and Cacha. Now they learned that Cacha had once been a heavily populated political and geographic entity in its own right, until an earthquake destroyed it in 1640, while Yaruquíes, ironically, had been a mere appendix. According to Arrieta, it was this knowledge that encouraged Cacha activists to propose the idea that the three annexes should become one political parish. He reminded Cachas that in doing so they were not breaking away from tradition but continuing it.

This was an important step in the development of the horizontal integration among communities. Previously, despite the relative proximity of many communities, patterns of vertical integration with Yaruquíes had led them to focus their attention on the town. People's sense of locational identity was vested in the notion of belonging to a particular annex. One was from Amulag, or Cacha, or Querag, and fiestas were celebrated mainly by communities that belonged to one's annex. As one interviewee explained, "Some would say we are from Cajabamba, Yaruquíes, Riobamba, but eventually they agreed that we were from Cacha."[31]

In a long process that began with the workshops and continued through the inauguration of the parish, a sense of being from Cacha became ingrained. This reconstructed history became the basis for political unity and helped to erode the vertical ties established with mestizos in the preorganization period. This new "knowledge" highlighted the existence of a distinct ethnic construction that differed greatly from a stigmatized, generic Indian identity. Cacha identity proved to be a powerful source of collective affirmation and pride. While contemporary Indians were considered ignorant, drunken, and childlike, the Cacha cacique Daquilema had headed the largest Indian rebellion in the nineteenth century. While Indians were considered subhuman and inferior to whites and mestizos, a Cacha princess had initiated the Ecuadorian Inca lineage. The Cachas redefined their identity not merely by reinterpreting the broader meaning of Indianness itself (as occurred in other highland areas) but by constructing a distinct identity as Cachas that highlighted their positive aspects vis-à-vis non-Cachas.

The workshops, as well as the ongoing political education of activists, provided the zone with a sense of history and place, crucial in an area where geography and race were so deeply bound. The creation of Cacha as a political and geographic unit, a place distinguished by a unique and rich (if once forgotten) heritage, a pueblo, provided the tools to construct a political alternative not previously available, to move from doxa to heterodoxy. It was now possible to remain in Cacha, to retain one's cultural identity, and to struggle to improve one's socioeconomic status as a collective. In the words of one woman, "Now we know that we had great consciousness. One day we were big, why not today?" (Arrieta 1984, 60).

CONSOLIDATING RESISTANCE: BUILDING NEW TRADITIONS, MAINTAINING DOMINANT NORMS

Perhaps the most important factor that facilitated the transition to the new order was the creation of the indigenous teniente político's office, which meant the unprecedented indigenous administration of parish justice. The Cacha experience with the administration of justice addresses the second objective of this chapter: the exploration of how rapid and dramatic political change establishes a new framework of meaning, engendering new forms of social action and constraining others. The social construction of resistance itself legitimizes specific sites and agents of resistance while repressing or eliminating others. As Hale (1994) has argued, resistance can appear contradictory, simultaneously challenging certain dominant norms while mantaining others. The creation and institutionalization of the office of the Cacha teniente político provides an interesting example.

The teniente político and the civil registry worked in conjunction with the FECAIPAC to ensure the Cachas' compliance. In fact, a few tenientes have also held positions in the FECAIPAC. The fusing of the state's authority and the organization's is symbolized by the location of the teniente político's office in the same building as the FECAIPAC in Cacha-Machángara, the parish center.[32] The new Indian parish has become legitimized not only through political victory and enforcement of sanctions but also, most important, through institutionalized self-rule. The distinctiveness of this reinvention, however, lies not only in its apparent historical greatness but also in everyday norms. The office of the teniente político provides the best example of the effect of the practice of self-rule. The Indian teniente político represents more than having a representative of the people. He demonstrates how the relocation and reconstitution of public police administration legitimates new forms of collective identity, state power, and authority.

Traditionally, the teniente político in Yaruquíes was a mestizo ally of the caciques who dominated the Cachas in a number of ways. Traditional handling of conflict involved either frequent teniente político abuse of indigenous people or the use of an intermediary that secured somewhat more civil treatment. In addition, the teniente and his assistants as well as the quishquero charged fees, and if no agreement was achieved in a dispute, cases would be sent to trial in Riobamba, at great expense to Indians. The new office of the teniente político, established in 1981, has deliberately differed in four important ways: the office is now elected; the arbitration of indigenous justice by mestizos is avoided at all costs; the exercise of justice is carried out in a collective fashion; and the semblance of noncorruption has become a crucial ethnic marker as distinct from mestizo justice, which is considered corrupt.

The teniente político is an elected Indian from one of the communities. Most discussion and arbitration is held in Quichua, and no fees are charged. The teniente político acts as both arbitrator and punisher. His primary goal is to keep conflicts within the zone and avoid the intervention of canton or provincial authorities or mestizo lawyers, as well as the unnecessary expenses that such an option would entail. Keeping most conflicts in Cacha removes the possibility of police abuse and secures forms of justice that follow community standards.

Another important characteristic of this new office is the way in which it dispenses justice. Use of the Quichua language means the inclusion of a number of people who previously had been excluded from dispute resolution, particularly the elderly and women whose Spanish was limited or nonexistent. While mestizo tenientes políticos would restrict their inquiry to the accused parties of an interpersonal dispute, Indian tenientes follow communal traditions of requesting that all involved family members and friends participate in the conflict resolution session. For example, it is common for in-laws to request that they be present in marital disputes, as they may be considered responsible for the conflict and are ultimately responsible for ensuring that their children follow the teniente's advice. Conflict resolution sessions last until agreement is reached. In some cases, marital dispute sessions have lasted as long as ten hours. In a recent case, a couple that traveled from a town several hours away to resolve their conflict in Cacha were kept in prison until they agreed to a solution. Once they agreed, the teniente asked them to apologize to the dozens of friends and family members who had been present in the office the entire day.

The primacy of keeping mestizos out of the arbitration system reflects the history of opression by mestizos but also acknowledges, reinforces, and legitimizes the break from Yaruquíes and local mestizo mediation as a specific type of resistance. The avoidance of outside interference is also considered necessary to maintain the legitimacy of indigenous autonomy and rule in the parish. At times this can overshadow the goal of justice and democracy, such as in instances in which victims of assault or of automobile accidents are compensated monetarily in lieu of reporting the incident in Riobamba. This meets the organization's goal of autonomy and freedom from outside exploitation, but it also strengthens its position as the sole arbitrator of justice, leaving little recourse available for those who are not aligned with the organization or are not satisfied with the specific resolution. It is important to note that the goal of keeping mestizos out is restricted to local authorities, as both national and foreign members of NGOs such as the FEPP, a Catholic church–sponsored debt agency, FODERUMA, and Swiss Aid are present.

A key aspect of the office of teniente político is the elevation of Cacha justice as purer and less corrupt and therefore more respectful of national and provincial regulations. It is here that the subversive and the conventional coexist, or rather are deeply intertwined. On the one hand, the office has been fundamentally restructured to help Cachas devise their own laws, legitimate their standards of morality and punishment, and eliminate all intrusion from nonindigenous public authorities and intermediaries. They have achieved this, however, not by subverting the state, but by using (and to a certain extent transforming) its own institutions to achieve political autonomy. Moreover, Indian teniente políticos reinforce ethnic pride by claiming a higher standard of morality and compliance than non-Indian tenientes.

In so doing, they are also embracing the dominant notions of the ideal Ecuadorian. Cacha's teniente político is considered a model by provincial authorities, as he complies with official regulations more effectively and efficiently than other tenientes in the province. Most of Cacha's tenientes políticos, for example, have refused payment for services, unlike many mestizo tenientes. Pedro Morocho, who worked pro bono for six years, proudly tells of the day when the governor told other tenientes they should be more like him. In this comparison with mestizos, former teniente Morocho and his successors have self-consciously attempted to embody the more honorable Cacha. Corruption and injustice are purported to belong to the outside. Strictly following the rules demonstrates the Cachas' willingness to posit themselves as ideal, law-abiding Ecuadorian citizens. This pursuit of an administrative moral superiority of the Indian teniente político reflects the moral tone of the parish as a whole. Cachas today are self-consciously law-abiding and constantly preoccupied with following the rules.

Hence, narratives of contemporary Cachas' exceptionalism and superiority to mestizos in the public realm reenforce and sustain the ideal of Cacha superiority vis-à-vis mestizos. In addition, the pursuit of civic virtue and respect for legality allows the Cachas to distinguish themselves from other

Indians. While other Ecuadorian organizations such as the Inca Atahualpa in Tixán, Chimborazo, have reproduced hacienda and communal as well as new forms of corporal punishment, the FECAIPAC has explicitly prohibited its communities from carrying out corporal punishment, describing it as an uncivilized practice.[33] This exceptionalism has also shaped the FECAIPAC's reluctance to affiliate with any provincial or national organizations, unlike the majority of indigenous organizations in the country. This reluctance stems from a desire for autonomy from all explicitly political organizations and from disdain for the mobilization tactics used by activists in other national organizations. Despite the FECAIPAC's official efforts to support provincial uprisings by threatening to fine Cachas who did not participate, many residents and organization officials refused. One organization official expressed his outrage at a recent mobilization organized by other provincial organizations that involved seizing fruits and vegetables from market vendors in a Riobamba market. He said, "I would rather pay the fine than sink so low."[34]

Cacha's isolationism is understandable but problematic for national Indian leaders. It is not difficult to see how resistance to the political and economic control of their neighbors in Yaruquíes has made them deeply suspicious of any linkages to non-Cachas, regardless of racial identity. As one Cacha said, "Why should we get involved with any others? We want to be free, we are free, and we do not belong to any organization."[35]

Contemporary Cacha is a far cry from thirty years ago, when Cachas attacked state nurses who were involved in a vaccination program and who were known for barring outsiders from their community. Here again we can see the effects of the social construction of resistance. The break from the social control of local authorities and mestizos has been accompanied by unquestioned cooperation with provincial and national authorities. Use of the national government as an ally in the struggle for an autonomous parish, reliance on state funds for development projects, and the history of free communities has led to a direct, corporatist relationship with the state that is rarely challenged. The state, in turn, has generously rewarded the Cachas for being good Indians. Cacha's strategy could prove limited if the FECAIPAC decides to pursue political goals that go beyond immediate short-term economic development. Whether this freedom is worth the price of political isolation of the Cachas remains to be seen.

CONCLUSION

Resistance in Cacha involved the securing of political autonomy through spatial excision and political representation. Activists in Cacha had an ethnic project: the spatial, political, and cultural break from Yaruquíes as a precondition for self-rule and empowerment. They accomplished this through the recuperation of a historical narrative, the disruption of vertical integration with Yaruquíes, horizontal integration with three previously separate annexes, and the social experience of institutional political autonomy. Instead of demanding to be incorporated into mestizo society, Cacha secured a space for cultural, political, and economic reproduction. Cacha has relied on state institutions to make the state its own; it is reformulating politics as distinct and distinctively Indian, located at what now appears to be an irreconcilable distance from the white-mestizo practices of Yaruquíes and Riobamba.

In many ways, Cacha and the FECAIPAC's experience is unparalleled in Ecuador in terms of its effectiveness in separating the local mestizo and Indian political spheres, creating the first solely Indian parish. In many other Ecuadorian towns, indigenous intercommunal organizations have had to alternate power with mestizo elites and have greater market and labor interdependence with economically vital towns. Hence, elsewhere local politics and everyday interactions necessarily involve types of racial struggle that the Cachas no longer engage in because a break from the mestizo world is neither feasible nor desirable.

Nevertheless, both empirically and theoretically, the Cacha experience is relevant to the study of other indigenous social movements. Studies of contemporary Andean resistance have focused primarily on former hacienda communities. This is justified by the centrality of the hacienda in the Andean political economy and facilitated by the existence of written documentation on haciendas. Far less is known about free communities. The dispersion of power in free communities presents theoretical and methodological challenges; there is no central node of power and source of information, and the sites of domination and resistance are more varied.

Bourdieu's model of the transition from doxa to heterodoxy provides valuable insight into both domination and resistance. Cachas experienced both coercion and consent; they faced seemingly inescapable objective conditions but also participated in and helped to reproduce some of the necessary subjective conditions through religious rituals and interpersonal relationships. Likewise, the articulation of political alternatives required a transformation of both objective and subjective conditions.

This last point is evident in the transformation of the meaning of space in changing social relations. The Cacha experience turned on its head dominant Ecuadorian racial conceptualizations that view Indians as occupying a separate place, in geographic as well as social terms. In fact, racial domination in practice required vertical integration of free communities. But in a period of rapid economic change and ensuing political vacuum, Cacha was able to recreate itself as a historical and historically important entity, developing its own institutions and building a horizontal integration that enabled a common political front. The construction of a separate geographic realm was a tool in the politics of local resistance.

Finally, theorizing the social construction of resistance enables us to understand the specific constraints of the new order. By focusing on the social construction of resistance itself—that is, the common understandings of how resistance did and should take place—one can explain why contemporary Cacha is characterized by the conflation of territorial and political autonomy, of local power and isolation from mestizo intermediaries, of civic virtue and ethnic identity. Hence strategies of resistance and political identity are deeply intertwined.

A theoretical model that is useful for understanding the Cacha case is what Hale (1994, 25) has called a contradictory consciousness involving a multivalent response to oppression, which he characterizes as combining rejection with partial acceptance, resisting through efforts to appropriate and subvert the cultural symbols of the dominant order. In Cacha, activists subverted the local order while appropriating the national one by reproducing dominant notions of bureaucratic efficiency, citizenship, and virtue. Strategies of resistance played a role in determining which elements of the dominant order were rejected, which were transformed, and which were accepted. This knowledge could prove useful in explicating the relationship between strategy and identity in the formation and development of social movements and the long-term effects of resistance as well as in questioning some of its potential limitations.

Comparing Cacha and Cotacachi

While following very different paths, the UNORCIC in Cotacachi and the FECAIPAC in Cacha have been relatively successful in their quest for indigenous autonomy and empowerment. The UNORCIC has a history of targeting mestizo support, as reflected in its association with the Socialist Party and its affiliation with the FENOC, whereas the FECAIPAC's movement is characterized by a process of ethnic revitalization with little engagement with mestizo locals.

The Cacha experience is a mixed one that shows that while race and ethnicity may at times reinforce each other, they also may be contradictory. The construction of an ethnic identity that is exclusive and exclusionary has discouraged the Cachas' participation in panethnic organization. The Cachas have little solidarity with the Indian movement and have participated in uprisings reluctantly. The same sense of ethnic identity that makes them feel unique has become an obstacle. That they have changed their condition by removing themselves as much as possible from interracial encounters via a process of voluntary segregation may be a further impediment to the positive valuation of Indianness (not Cachaness) and thus to any building of panethnic identification and solidarity.

I selected the UNORCIC as a counterexample to indianista organizations, because it pursued a campesinista discourse and practice, but my field research revealed a more complex experience. Although most of its official rhetoric is campesinista, the UNORCIC is best characterized as pursuing politics in which shared racial and class identification became a resource to generate support for campesinista goals. Hence racial issues were often coded in class terms, and symbolic elements, ceremonies, anniversaries, and everyday practices also reinforced racial affirmation. In this context, race and class are contested terms over which activists try to exercise some control. In the UNORCIC, race and class were often conflated in practice, Indianness was equated with poverty, and class differences between Indians were erased.

After the Indian uprising of 1990 and the eruption of a broader Indian movement on the national scene, however, the relative success of the UNORCIC's double layer politics began to wane as younger activists questioned the campesinista strategy. The influence of the indianista agenda and the panethnic movement throughout the highlands has rendered local Indian politics more complex, forced the few remaining campesinista organizations to revisit their position, and impeded the adoption of a campesinista strategy by new organizations. Moreover, the formation of Pachakutik as an explicitly Indian political movement led to the cutting of all formal ties with party socialists, even though the affiliation with the FENOC continued.

Both case studies illustrate the relationship between the strategy of collective action used and a given social formation, that is, the set of structural, institutional, and cultural constraints that frame a movement. While both organizations were created in response to racial discrimination, their juxtaposition shows how varied Indian politics can be, depending on the socioeconomic and historical setting. Whereas the racialization of space and residential segregation was used by the Cachas to break all links with mestizos, in Cotacachi that option was not possible. The large mestizo population in the canton (49 percent) and the coexistence of many mestizos in Cotacachi city, towns, and rural communities has structured local indigenous politics and led the UNORCIC to pursue the most viable option: building electoral and governing alliances with mestizo socialists. While the Cachas can afford to disregard Yaruquíes, Cotacachi and its surrounding haciendas remain important generators of employment. A rupture from the center, in this context, would be economically and politically suicidal. Hence Cacha's protonationalism in the form of territorial and political autonomy is not an option that is available to Cotacachi or to most cantons with a large indigenous population. The political excision and separation that has made Cacha autonomous would only lead to further impoverishment and disempowerment in Cotacachi.

The differences between these cases lead to two conclusions. First, the use of a specific ethnic identity as a basis for political resistance can simultaneously empower a specific group and interfere with its affiliation with a broader panethnic coalition. The sense of having a unique identity, of belonging to a special and often superior group, may lead members to feel that coalition building diminishes their status. By contrast, the UNORCIC's recent embrace of the CONAIE and active participation in the 1990 and 1994 uprisings suggest that a campesinista platform is not as large an obstacle to panethnic organizing as anticipated.

Second, although these different strategies were relatively successful in achieving their goals, the Cacha model seems more viable and sustainable at the local or parish level. The UNORCIC's model, with its strengths and limitations, is far more likely to be emulated by most other intercommunal, canton-level organizations in which Indians must share power with mestizos. In addition, the CONAIE's participation in Pachakutik in the 1996 national and provincial elections means that in retrospect UNORCIC's electoral strategy is a pioneer example of an experience that is being reproduced across the country at the national level. The tensions in mestizo-indigenous alliances and coalitions, which are reflected not only in relationships between the two sectors but in divisions among activists within organizations; the questioning of the representativeness of political leadership by the grassroots once a social movement becomes a political movement; and the novel coexistence of the politics of protest and electoral participation exemplified in Pedro de la Cruz's takeover of the municipality are factors that pertain not only to the Cotacachi case, but are being reproduced at the national level in the contemporary political setting.

These differences between the two cases, however, should not mask important similarities that shed light on key features of the new Indian politics. In both cases, racial discrimination was the main source of conflict between mestizos and Indians as well as the reason the organizations were created. In both cases, cultural recovery was an important component of the organizations' development. Both organizations sought to generate pride in indigenous identity and history and in local cultural forms as a way of affirming their common bonds and differentiating themselves from mestizos. The simultaneous acts of "recovering" culture and accessing citizenship meant that Indians were seeking to be recognized as equals while maintaining their differences from nonindigenous citizens. For both organizations, it meant, ultimately, that Indians did not have to assimilate or become mestizo to become empowered. Finally, both organizations sought political autonomy that would enable them to gain public authority and decision-making power. While the UNORCIC sought this autonomy through the struggle for electoral nominations in formal political coalitions, the FECAIPAC was engaged in a process of autonomous social and political formation that would render coalition building unnecessary. Despite the different methods and outcomes, political autonomy was a valued goal for both. As the next chapter explains, these three points, antiracism, cultural recovery, and the struggle for political autonomy, are the main features that characterize most local and national indianista organizations and distinguish them from campesinista organizations.

CHAPTER SIX

SEEKING RESPETO

Racial Consciousness and National Indian Politics

The local organizational experiences in Cacha and Cotacachi were informed by activism that was occurring contemporaneously at the regional and national levels. The creation of the new Indian as a political subject by Ecuadorian indigenous activists in the 1970s involved a departure, both ideological and institutional, from traditional forms of oppositional politics. Contemporary highland political discourse and practice originated in a debate held in the mid-1970s between activists who defined themselves as peasants and those who stressed a collective identity as Indians and focused on cultural and racial issues previously neglected by peasant organizations. Whereas most lowland indigenous activism was characterized by a lack of significant influence by the Left, highland activism was defined primarily by what it rejected: the tradition of class politics in which a campesinista political strategy had dominated popular indigenous struggles since the 1920s.

DOUBLE CONSCIOUSNESS

The potential for both a class consciousness and an ethnic consciousness among Ecuadorian highland Indian activists has been the focus of studies by Francisco Rohn (1978) and Roberto Santana (1981, 1984). Despite important differences, both scholars have pursued a phase approach, suggesting that class identity replaced ethnic identity in the late 1970s (Rohn 1978) and that ethnic identity replaced class identity in the 1980s (Santana 1981). Both place class and ethnicity in a dichotomous relationship: Rohn claims that ethnic consciousness among Indian activists in the 1970s was a confused or prepolitical consciousness. Referring to ECUARUNARI's development of an indianista identity in the 1970s, he maintains:

> The decomposition of old structures and appearance of new forms of production, new habits, new values, meant that any effort to attack this reformist process, specifically in the agrarian sector, was useless, like going against a river's current, advancing against the direction of history.... [I]n practice the return to old forms, the attachment to ethnic-cultural ancestry, is meant to adopt regressive positions that are politically reactionary and right-wing. The situation was not defined, the modernization process had just begun, and that is why they do not know where to attack. That is why instead of giving a response that would confront these changes, instead of opposing the new economic, social, cultural and political forms, they [indianista activists] tend to submit themselves to them; their attempts to "respond" are confused and unclear, expressed in some platforms of struggle, as the defense and rescue of their cultural values, those that had remained and that represented the last vestiges of indigenous culture. (1978, 117)

Santana, on the other hand, considers ethnic consciousness a growing form of consciousness that is not only replacing traditional campesinista strategies but is also being suppressed or attacked by campesinista organizations and other sectors of the Left:

> An ethnic option has strong possibilities of imposing itself on Ecuador's political map in the next few years. The other forms of organizations and unions must change accordingly. With the growth of a movement for ethnic rights, the main obstacle is not the Ecuadorian state but the unions and political organizations that are called class organizations, whose current policies and practices are directed at neutralizing the emergent Indian struggle. (1981, 13)

On a theoretical level, one can critique this ethnicity/class divide as a false dichotomy that clouds rather than facilitates the analysis of ethnic politics in Ecuador. On an empirical level, however, this division must be taken seriously, because this dichotomization has also taken place in Indian organizations. The ethnicity-class dichotomy has informed the debates and practices of highland activists and shaped their relationship with lowland Indian organizations, popular organizations, political parties, and the state. From the late 1970s through the early 1990s, as they have been defining their political identity, local, regional, and national activists have held extensive debates about whether they are peasants or Indians. These debates are not merely academic. They have played a crucial role in determining what course activists take at given points, as well as in shaping their relationships with other political actors.

This division among activists can be understood as the manifestation of a process of double consciousness—as peasants and as Indians—that is formed when Indian activists become aware of the contradiction in the strategies of class politics and their experience of racial subordination as a key element of their ethnic formation. Double consciousness, for Du Bois, was the lived contradiction between the ideal of democracy and equality in America and the lived experience of racial inequality:

> From the double life every American Negro must live, as Negro, and as an American, as swept on by the current of the nineteenth while yet struggling in the eddies of the fifteenth century, from this must arise a painful self-consciousness, an almost morbid sense of personality and a moral hesitancy which is fatal to self-confidence. The worlds within and without the Veil of Color are changing, and changing rapidly, but not at the same rate, not in the same way; and this must produce a peculiar wrenching of the soul, a peculiar sense of doubt and bewilderment. Such a double life, with double thoughts, double duties, and double social classes, must give rise to double words and double ideals, and tempt the mind to pretense or revolt, to hypocrisy and radicalism. (1903, 203)

Similarly, the politicization of racial consciousness in the Ecuadorian highlands occurred as Indian activists became involved in class politics and aware of their subordination in an apparently equal but actually hierarchical class structure. In the years following land reform and rural modernization, Indians' frustrated attempts to coexist with mestizos in diverse institutional settings and in everyday life, as well as their attempts to build coalitions with non-Indians along class lines, made their subordination along racial lines painfully evident. Indians realized that despite ethnic and regional differences among them, they were oppressed and treated differently by the white-mestizo population because they were Indian. The altered consciousness that accompanied this realization made organizing along class lines alone insufficient and sidestepping their racial and ethnic identity increasingly difficult. They also realized that their Indianness appeared to deny them a role as protagonists in the discourse and practice of modernity and Ecuadorian national identity. The Indian/peasant tension, therefore, had far-reaching implications not only for the development of indigenous politics or Indian-Left relationships but also for the exercise of indigenous citizenship.

THE CLASS/ETHNICITY DIVIDE

There were three distinct phases of the peasant/Indian debate. The first phase involved the creation of indianista activism during the early and mid-1970s. In the second phase, in the late 1970s, internal conflicts developed between indianistas and both indigenous and nonindigenous campesinistas, as well as among indigenous activists. The new ideological construct of indianismo led to an ideological split between indianistas and campesinistas. Indianistas called for an end to the oppression of Indians by whites and mestizos in different spheres of political and social life. There were two ways in which indigenous activists negotiated this tension. One was the splitting of ECUARUNARI along disagreements about whether to organize around the notion of class or ethnicity. The second path was a "dual strategy," which involved ECUARUNARI's contemporaneous pursuit of coalitions with popular organizations in a cross-peasant or peasant-worker alliance, on the one hand, and a panethnic coalition with lowland Indian organizations, on the other.

The dual strategy, or peasant alliance option, was pursued between 1977 and 1985. ECUARUNARI joined the new politics of popular fronts, in which umbrella union organizations and peasant unions carried out massive demonstrations and strikes, replacing the party politics framework that had become severely debilitated during the military regime. Common goals included opposition to the reversal of land reform, advocacy for land rights and workers' rights, and support of democratization. In the coalition-building process, however, important disagreements among activists and the reproduction of racist practices worked to the political advantage of indianista factions within indigenous organizations and weakened the campesinista activists who had supported the notion of a popular alliance.

The third phase witnessed the failure of the popular alliance and increased contact between highland and lowland organizations. Debates about which form of political identity to adopt were accompanied by new forms of political action in which the Indian/peasant distinction came to be viewed as a political strength rather than an obstacle. This is the phase in which both dimensions of struggle emerged publicly and became a site of negotiation and reconciliation, leading eventually to the prevalence of a materially informed indianista politics. Many former campesinistas became indianistas who came to pursue the viability of the "dual struggle" as peasants and Indians but within the confines of autonomous Indian organizations.[1] The tensions latent in the strict dichotomization of the late 1970s and early 1980s were discussed within the boundaries of a national *coordinadora* (coordinator) created in 1980, the CONACNIE, which eventually evolved into the CONAIE.

During this period, the state played an important role in creating new forms of access for indigenous organizations. The military regime headed by Guillermo Rodriguez Lara in the mid-1970s had affected the perceptions of indigenous activists in newly formed organizations. The state had expanded the meaning of indigenous citizenship by affirming peasants' right to land (through an expansion of land reform), by promoting rural development through land reform law, by creating rural cooperatives, and by developing the Central Bank's FODERUMA to provide rural credit. Further, the new democratic regime initiated in 1979 was neoindigenista: it recognized cultural differences and validated indigenous cultures in its rhetoric and education policy (Ibarra 1992). While neoindigenismo parallels traditional indigenismo in consisting of policy making about the indigenous by nonindigenous people, it departs from it in promoting the more direct participation of Indians in cultural and development policy implementation. Literacy and bilingual literacy programs were implemented on a massive scale, and Indians played an important if controlled role in the planning and implementation of these programs. Also, indigenous activists found new sources of institutional and ideological support from progressive sectors of the Catholic church, human rights groups, academics and NGOs that had been absent in more properly traditional leftist organizations.[2]

By the mid-1980s the indianista option prevailed at the organizational level not because of some natural inevitability but as the consequence of a long and complex process of conflict and negotiation that originated with the creation of ECUARUNARI in 1972 and led to the creation of the CONAIE in the late 1980s. I analyze the decline of campesinismo and the rise of indianismo by focusing on several basic factors that played an important role in this shift: the experience of indigenous activists with the Left and the religious Left, divisions among indigenous activists within ECUARUNARI and between ECUARUNARI and other organizations, and the growing politicization of lowland Indians. The role of the state in shaping indianismo is covered in chapter 7.

ECUARUNARI: PEASANTS AND INDIANS

Since the 1930s, the term *campesino* has been used to refer to all people who cultivated small parcels of land. Although the term itself does not contain any obvious reference to ethnic or racial origin, on the coast it refers to people of mixed Indo-African-European descent, whereas in the highlands it refers primarily to people of indigenous descent.[3] Its use is derived from early Marxist analyses in which the defining element of rural people was their insertion into a precapitalist system of production. Since one's socioeconomic category was presumed to determine individual and collective identity, there was no distinction made between the peasant as a socioeconomic category and the construction of the peasant as a social or political identity.

In the 1970s campesinismo found its expression in syndicalist organizations such as the FEI, the FENOC, and FENOC-affiliated groups.[4] After land reform, the FEI was limited to the legalization of the property rights of former huasipungueros, and the organization had declined significantly in numbers and capabilities. Despite being structured like a union and being an official branch of the CEDOC, the FENOC is a conglomeration of different types of associations, including local unions and cooperatives as well as popular organizations.

At its inception the FENOC focused on land conflicts on haciendas and was particularly successful in the province of Cañar. After land reform, the FENOC was concerned primarily with legal assistance and credit and rural development issues. In the 1970s the FENOC was a large bureaucracy with almost exclusively mestizo leadership on the national front; it paid little attention to Indian issues. Indeed, it was assumed that Indian issues were coterminous with peasant issues. The FENOC operated on the premise that all peasants, regardless of racial and ethnic background, should work together on issues of rural poverty and development and refused to acknowledge any significant difference in forms of oppression.[5] In this early period no effort was made to promote indigenous leadership, as Indians were thought to be just as well represented by mestizo peasant leaders.

In 1973 an alternative to FENOC was created when several religious and indigenous activists met in Chimborazo province. In contrast to the FENOC, this new organization, ECUARUNARI, focused specifically on Indian identity and Indian struggles:

> The objective [of ECUARUNARI] shall be to awaken the conscience of the Ecuadorian Indians, pure or impure, in order to obtain their moral, social, economic and political recuperation, and gain their just rights. All this will be done in a united fashion, that is, the Ecuadorian Indians united in a common effort, with no ideological nor geographic distinctions, with an adequate organization in which Indians assume the responsibilities of directing it.[6]

Spearheaded and supervised by white and mestizo religious leaders during its first two years, ECUARUNARI was considered by religious activists a necessary alternative to the FEI and the FENOC, which were criticized for being too isolated and bureaucratic and having little local presence in the highlands. Created in 1973 by indigenous activists and non-indigenous religious activists, this national organization's rank and file included both indianistas and campesinistas; internal debates increasingly reflected the growing tension between the two.[7] ECUARUNARI began to support local campaigns against racial discrimination and exclusion and lobbied for the election of indigenous local authorities.

After Vatican II (1962–65) and the meeting of the Latin American Episcopal Conference in Medellín (1968), Latin American clergy organized to promote programs in which the church would work more directly with the poor. Like other liberation theology activists in Latin America, those in Ecuador played a crucial role in struggles for social reform between the 1960s and the 1980s. Among the religious and secular organizations that adopted political progressivism and liberation theology were several urban youth groups in the provinces of Chimborazo, Cañar, and Tungurahua and numerous reflection groups, as well as individual priests who organized parishes. In rural areas Indian pastorals modeled on the concept of Christian base communities were organized. This work was particularly important in Tungurahua, Cotopaxi, and Chimborazo, all highland provinces with a large indigenous population (Rohn 1978, 45).

In contrast to FEI activists, who selected specific sites for land or labor claims, determined the relevant issues, and directed the political activities of local Indians, the religious activists followed a methodology based on the teachings of the Brazilian liberation theologist Paolo Freire. This methodology consisted of working in communities by "listening, seeing and acting," using participatory techniques in which the goal was to "awaken" indigenous people, helping them to become aware of their situation and supporting them in their struggle for social change. Liberation theologists developed new readings of biblical passages in which Christ was identified with the poor and landowners and other elites were faulted for non-Christian behavior. Catholic documents usually framed their conceptualizations in terms of poor and rich, exploiters and exploited, not Indians and non-Indians. Yet in practice religious activists referred frequently to indigenous ancestry and cultural identity and exalted those qualities they considered specifically Indian and valuable such as communitarianism, which was posited against the evils of individualism and self-gain.

Freire's methodology also involved a holistic approach. In community and pastoral meetings every aspect of indigenous people's lives was questioned. This included not only specific land conflicts and relationships with landowners but also relationships with town mestizos, including members of the merchant and bureaucratic elite. During these meetings, the secular often overpowered the religious, and issues relating to racial difference and subordination were legitimized as causes for mobilization.

In 1971 some religious activists and priests, members of Iglesia y Sociedad en America Latina (ISAL) (the local branch of Church and Society in Latin America), and nuns of the Laurita order working in El Tejar, a hostel for indigenous migrant workers in Quito, sponsored a series of meetings with indigenous catechists and community leaders in the provinces of Cañar, Loja, Tungurahua, and Chimborazo (Rohn 1978, 48). In Tepeyac, Chimborazo, in 1973, they founded the national organization ECUARUNARI, drawing leadership from indigenous activists of several highland provinces as well as nonindigenous religious and secular activists.[8]

ECUARUNARI had two important characteristics that previous highland organizations lacked. First, it was the only organization that consistently had indigenous activists in top leadership positions.[9] Second, it openly addressed cultural discrimination and racism as important forces that impeded indigenous socioeconomic advancement. Indigenous activists' ability to have independent leadership and address issues of racial discrimination, however, was constantly challenged by factions of the church as well as by the Christian Left. One faction of non-Indian church members active in ECUARUNARI were religious humanists, either independent or affiliated with the Christian Democrats, who eschewed traditional class politics and promoted discussion of indigenous issues as a problem of poverty. Another group of activists organized in the Christian Movement for Socialism, broke from the institutional church and from the Christian Democrats, who they viewed as insufficiently radical. In the National Encounter of Christians for Socialism in Quito, held in 1972, Christian Socialists proposed

> [a] Christianity that is not an ideological-confessional struggle but an ideological-political struggle[,] . . . free from clerical and hierarchical domination, attempting to present a project distinct from Christian Democrats who are present among peasants and to link itself to sectors of the New Left. (Cited in Rohn 1978, 20)

A group of priests, former priests, and others inspired along these lines organized into the leftist Movimiento Nacional de Cristianos por la Liberación (MNCL) and Movimiento Revolucionario de la Izquierda Cristiana (MRIC) parties[10] and became active in ECUARUNARI, pursuing an orthodox campesinista position in the context of a broader popular struggle and dismissing the importance of "cultural" claims as racist and folkloric. The moderate sector of the church, the religious humanists represented by the Laurita nuns and certain priests, were often in conflict with the radical Christians and secular Marxists, and ECUARUNARI was the stage where many of these conflicts were played out. The early years of ECUARUNARI were characterized by strong pressures from members of the Catholic church. Both religious humanists and radical Christians (who were divided among themselves), as well as secular Marxists, pressured indigenous activists to the point where many felt that they were not free to represent themselves as they should and expelled the mestizos from a meeting in 1976. According to a nun who was a founding member of ECUARUNARI, Indian activists' growing impatience with religious activists' influence was due to the radical Christians' opposition to church participation in the organization:

It was not the Indians, it was certain church members who had difficulties with the church. They were former priests who left the church and then linked up with other members of the Left to reject those of us who had collaborated with ECUARUNARI. ... It was a very difficult meeting in Riobamba in 1976 when they [the indigenous] expelled us. They opposed us, using the argument that Indians were dependent on nuns and priests. We explained that it was not a question of dependence but a joint project uniting us all as a people, as children of God. But no, no, no, they did not accept this and they [the radical Christians] began infiltrating, gaining territory and influencing certain groups of Indians, provoking the rupture.[11]

An indigenous activist who attended some of those early meetings suggests, however, that the radical Christians were not simply influencing them but that some activists, on their own initiative, grew tired of what they considered the ideological manipulation of the church:

The nuns would whisper in Indians' ears telling them which position they should take, how they should reply to a certain question or comment. ... All the religious group was highly prepared. We would go to the meeting having some Marxist influence and then we would encounter them [the religious advisers]. So in the meetings the nuns sat behind the leaders, and we also had the intellectuals [Marxists] advising us and when we had group meetings they were all sitting behind us, keeping watch over what we said. ... Finally we got tired of them and asked them if they had to be present. They had already fulfilled their role.[12]

The above comment reflects Indian activists' growing impatience with the tutelage of non-Indian activists of both sectors, regardless of ideological orientation. This early experience in ECUARUNARI led many indigenous activists to reject the option of organizing with mestizos. They believed that indigenous-mestizo cooperation had slowed the development of Indian activists and the adequate articulation of their needs and demands. After a two-year period, Indians literally closed the doors on mestizos. But some mestizos were retained as informal advisers and continued to have an important role in shaping debates. Further, some were able to return to the organization, and a group of disappointed radical Christians in Pichincha province created another campesinista organization, ECUARUNARI-Pichincha

INDIANISMO:
FROM LOCAL ORIGINS TO NATIONAL POLITICS

ECUARUNARI indigenous activists' desire for autonomy within the organization reflected struggles for autonomy throughout the highlands during this period. The emergence of an indianista perspective and the concomitant growth of indianista organizations stemmed from the critical reflection of indigenous activists and the lessons learned from myriad local experiences and new political struggles in the highlands in the late 1960s and 1970s. In the 1970s there was a proliferation of community and intercommunal organizations.[13] Some of the latter developed with the active participation of ECUARUNARI; others developed with the support of the FENOC or the church or without external support.

The increase in numbers reflects a qualitative as well as a quantitative change in the nature of indigenous demands.[14] The post–land reform insertion of the Indian into modern society, the arrival of modernity and capitalism in rural communities, and the mobility of ideas and bodies this entailed created new conditions, power relations, and identities. A consequence was the development of new forms of local struggle in which Indians sought to attack specific racist practices. As Sylva (1991) has argued, some of the organizations were promoted by the state, as both the military regime and the first two democratic regimes' development programs were often predicated on mobilization. The lengthy implementation of land reform led many claimants to organize to negotiate land transactions and protect their landholdings once they were acquired. This alone, however, does not explain all the reasons behind organizing, nor does it explain the origin of many other organizations not involved in land claims.

Anti-Racism and Political Autonomy at the Grassroots

In addition to the struggle for land, local activists and organizations struggled against racism and for political autonomy.[15] Antiracism both galvanized early spontaneous gatherings and became the founding tenet of several organizations. New organizations were created for a number of reasons, including fighting the racial discrimination of authorities in Cotacachi, ending the abuses of mestizo intermediaries in Saraguro, and removing indigenous communities from the authority of a mestizo village, as occurred in Cacha. When asked about her earliest organizing experiences in her native town of Cotacachi, the national activist Blanca Chancoso remembered:

> Our struggle was initiated by land, but with it also came the respect for Indians. Because in those years one could not walk on the streets. They [young mestizos] would remove the hats from men, kick them, play with them. . . . It was our main struggle, respect for the indigenous. We knew it could not be done by decree. . . . I don't even know who was supposed to make them comply with this concept of respect, but it was our principal struggle.[16]

This inequality was difficult to address because it was not formalized legally but sustained through informal mechanisms that structured social relations. The struggle, therefore, was not an explicit civil rights movement that sought individual protection through the law. Instead it was a set of collective mobilizations and protests against de facto everyday abuse, mistreatment by authorities and mestizo elites in the schools, markets, and public offices.

In addition to Cotacachi and Cacha, local mobilizations against racist practices took place throughout most highland provinces. For example, in the southern highland province of Saraguro in 1964, the intercommunal organization Jatun Cabildo was formed because of reported abuses by merchants and intermediaries of Indians. In 1967 a struggle against mestizo lenders who expropriated indigenous lands escalated to the point that the government sent forces to restore order. In 1968 Jatun Cabildo organized a campaign against canteens, labeling them a source of mestizo exploitation (*Nueva* 1983). Imbabura and Chimborazo provinces witnessed a series of indigenous campaigns against chicherías, which were perceived as sites of internal control over communities (Rohn 1962). In 1973 in Cañar province, a group of communities organized the first strike against municipal authorities, in which they paralyzed local transportation for twenty-four hours (CONAIE 1989, 303). In 1975 indigenous activists demanded the resignation of the city council president, claiming that he had abused his authority by using forced indigenous labor. On this occasion activists occupied parts of the Pan-American Highway and the main park.

In Tungurahua province the Movimiento Indígena de Tungurahua (MIT), organized by religious activists in the 1960s, began to question the local fiesta as a form of economic and cultural exploitation. The MIT held political "concientización" courses in communities in which they pointed out public injustices. By 1975 more than one thousand Indians had taken these courses. In this same year the MIT had a conflict with local unions and officials who felt displaced as their mediators. Local activists began to seek mechanisms that would provide broader structural change and political empowerment, allowing them to represent themselves.

One way in which activists believed racial discrimination could be addressed was through the pursuit of some form of political autonomy that would transform power relations. During this period, political autonomy was understood in two ways. The first involved the funding and strengthening of autonomous organizations, which often implied breaking away from dependent relationships with churches and unions. The second was the election or nomination of local leaders who were Indians and who would be able to represent them in formal political institutions.[17]

The first goal, independent organizations, proved less difficult than the election of local officials. Indigenous movements have had more success in securing communal power than in electing tenientes políticos or municipal authorities. In Imbabura province in May 1974, a massive march backed by the FICI and ECUARUNARI asked for their own authorities in political lieutenant offices. Their stated goals were as follows:

> Respect for the indigenous and for the defense of our cultural values, in the struggle against racial discrimination. . . . As an indigenous organization, we must ensure that our leaders belong to our pueblo. (CONAIE 1989, 132–33)

Similar struggles for indigenous parish authorities were undertaken in several highland provinces in the mid- and late 1970s, and in the case of a few organizations such as the UNORCIC, in Imbabura province, local activists were elected to the city council. The efforts to obtain local power have been more or less continuous since the mid-1970s and were increasingly successful in the 1980s and 1990s.

ECUARUNARI's New Political Discourse

In a 1976 letter to the minister of government, ECUARUNARI stated:

> We ask for the recognition of a communal government which should represent the state, and to be involved in planning, administration

and execution.... We want to be represented in canton and provincial councils, in Congress, and we want recognition of the right to administer ourselves in parishes with Indian majorities, through tenientes políticos [and] area chiefs [so] that communes may create their own statutes and judicial norms, [so] that [there is] justice by Indian authorities and not by white tenientes políticos.[18]

This letter indicates the extent to which ECUARUNARI activists were informed by and involved with local struggles. As they attempted to incorporate antiracism and political autonomy into their national agendas, ECUARUNARI activists developed a language that would enable them to address these concerns and explain their position to others. During this period, at least three ideological referents were used to explain the fairness of their demands: the notion of historical rights, the ideal of modernity, and the anticapitalist tradition of the Left. The language of historical rights used the metaphor of sleep to describe the awakening or consciousness-raising process through which Ecuadorian Indians would claim their rightful historical share. A document of one organization states, "Richarimui means to awaken again, the awakening of the Ecuadorian Indian, to be again what he once was and with the same rights and obligations as other Ecuadorians."[19]

Intertwining historical claims and a contemporary language of rights and obligations, activists argued that the expansion of citizenship for Indians was necessary, not solely on the basis of the primacy of individual or human rights, or the injustice of socioeconomic exploitation (a characteristic argument of campesino organizations), but because it restored the dignity and parity Indians had lost on "falling asleep." A just and equitable past (whether historically accurate or not) became the basis for a more just and equitable present.[20] Furthermore, it was the exclusion of this history that was to blame for the contemporary political failures of the nation-state:

> We have been marginalized because we are told that we don't have the capability to analyze the country's problems. Our culture is older. We have preserved our forms. Our marginalization is the reason why national problems haven't been resolved. We have our own cultural and organizational forms.[21]

The second source drawn on was an ideal model of modernity, which, pitted against the subordination of Indians in Ecuador, rendered the country distinctly unmodern. At the same time that it called for a return to history,

ECUARUNARI appealed to the developmentalist concerns of the nationalist military regimes, pointing out the contradiction between the nation's desire for modernity and the existence of premodern forms of social behavior:

> We can't say that we belong to occidental Christian civilization, when people can still chase Indians. Ecuador is retrograde. How can we boast of development projects, be hosts to an OPEC [meeting] and [yet] go 400 years back to when Indians were decapitated?[22]

The historical exclusion and marginalization of Indians was considered the false step that had frozen Ecuador in history. Activists maintained that in its attempt to progress by shedding its Indianness, Ecuador had condemned itself to a backwardness that could be reversed only by becoming whole again through the incorporation of Indian political forms, which contained in them the seed of true national potential. In this unique variant of nationalism, ECUARUNARI activists posited indigenous subordination as the reason Ecuador could not progress, positioning their own emancipation and autonomy as the conduits to future development. In this way indigenous activists, like landowners, tied notions of an idealized Ecuadorian past and a prosperous Ecuadorian future to their becoming citizens and political actors.

The third source of indianista discourse was the reliance of activists on a distinct form of anticapitalism as a basis for demanding change. Indianistas, like campesinistas, were anticapitalists. But instead of focusing only on the economic exploitation attributed to the capitalist system by campesinistas, they viewed capitalism, as embodied in mestizo culture, as the culprit that led to acculturation. Several local organization meetings reflected concerns with acculturation and rejection of indigenous traditions. Stories of children being ashamed of parents and rejecting their origins in front of mestizos were common. Other instances involved conflicts with schools that forced indigenous children to dress in uniform in lieu of traditional clothes. This was often portrayed as the result of an encroaching capitalist culture that forced people to conform. Several local organizations initiated cultural recovery eforts that ranged from art and music competitions to soccer games. One of the main goals of these efforts was to keep indigenous youth linked to their cultures and their communities in a time of their lives when they were most likely to reject their cultural identity. The rescue of the values that capitalism threatened was considered a crucial goal:

[This is] a national encounter of Indians to become conscious of the great social force they represent and to value the race and the communitarian people, contrary to the principles of capitalism.[23]

For indianistas, anticapitalism became intertwined with "making sense" of racial subordination in ways that campesinistas never fully understood or accepted. Capitalism was seen not only or even primarily as the developer of a class system, but as a facilitator of racial exploitation and divestor of culture. Activists started to analyze how their poverty was connected to their status as Indians. In this context the recovering of cultural forms and traditions and the maintenance of Indianness were understood as an anticapitalist struggle.

Hence one of the most important consequences of these early reflections was the weaving together of anticapitalism and antiracism in indianista consciousness. Recuperating respect and dignity and pursuing political autonomy were considered crucial weapons in the broader struggle against a capitalism whose cultural as well as economic ramifications threatened to undermine indigenous livelihood. The antiracist struggle could be (and was) couched in campesinista terms, but it conveyed new meanings. Interrelated race-based and class-based hierarchies were considered responsible for inequalities in the distribution of power, knowledge, and access to opportunity and social status. While socioeconomic struggles continued to be a central concern, it was Indianness, not peasantness, that was increasingly understood as the main problematic that deprived them of citizenship. Some activists even began to resent a campesino identity as something that erased the specificity and complexity of indigenous identity. Ana María Guacho, a longtime ECUARUNARI activist from Chimborazo province, states:

In that period we created an organization called ECUARUNARI in 1972. I was already a militant and I would go because I'm permanently living the economic, social and racial situation that exists in our country with the indigenous. I see how the government in power, the rich, the hacendado, even the church, have always tried to marginalize us and put us all in a same sack, giving us terms that are foreign to us, such as peasants.[24]

Guacho's blending of the economic, the social, and the racial shows that indianistas were questioning peasant identity but not necessarily the material basis of campesinista organizations' claims. Indianista activists were not discarding economic or material concerns by discarding traditional class activism but were in fact reinterpreting them and incorporating them into a new agenda in which they were joined with and at times subsumed under the broadly defined goals of anti-racism, political autonomy, nationalism, and multiculturalism.

With antiracism, political autonomy, and land struggle as a shared agenda, "Indianness" became a common identification and was considered the basis for building a bridge across groups of different provinces in the highlands and (later) among highlanders and lowlanders of different ethnic groups. This was accomplished through the construction of the notion of a single *pueblo indio* (Indian populace) that had historically occupied a subordinate position vis-à-vis white-mestizos.

ECUARUNARI's strategy was to build unity by underscoring Indianness and playing down ethnic or regional differences. As soon as the organization was founded, activists invited members of the Amazonian or lowland Shuar Federation to participate, as the organization's initial goal was to represent all Ecuadorian Indians, not only the highland population. While the Shuars' distance did not allow for regular attendance, they were linked informally to the organization through the 1970s.

Among highland organizations, this link was not a simple process. The construction of a common identification had to overcome the initial reluctance of highland groups who considered themselves ethnically distinct, such as the Saraguros, Cañaris, and Salasacas, as well as the dominance of campesinismo among nonindigenous and indigenous activists.[25] The strong presence of Tungurahua's Salasacas and Cañar activists in the foundation of ECUARUNARI, however, might have facilitated the process. Likewise, the role played by highly educated Saraguros and Otavaleños as the intelligentsia of the movement throughout the 1970s and 1980s opened the lines of communication in both directions.

PEASANT OR INDIAN? THE DICHOTOMIZATION OF IDENTITY AND THE ECUARUNARI DEBATE

In the early years of ECUARUNARI it was not possible to divide indigenous activists neatly into indigenistas and campesinistas, as many of them combined both within a single political perspective. In addition, several shifted their positions through the late 1980s. Nevertheless, by the late 1970s there was an increasing sense among Indian activists that campesinismo and indianismo as general ideological constructs were in conflict. Several ECUARUNARI meetings between February and April 1976 debated whether indigenous activists were pursuing an Indian struggle or a peasant struggle. Much of this debate can be attributed to the tensions between the advisers from the Christian Left and the church and the pressures placed on Indian activists by the Christian Left. But it also stemmed from Indian activists' ambivalence toward indianismo and the fear that it might represent a step backward from the legitimacy gained by campesino political identity. Blanca Chancoso discussed indigenous activists' preoccupations in the late 1970s:

> We were certain that we were indigenous, of the indigenous struggle, of why we were suffering, and we all spoke in that language.... Only that there was a confusion about maintaining the identity, that sometimes we were campesinos. We thought that when we said "campesinos" we were also feeling identified as indigenous as well. We thought that campesinos was what Indians were called. And, well, we also accepted the term *campesino*, being indigenous, because we would say they are referring to us, and we thought the term "campesino" would mean being treated with some respect. And so we would all say "campesinos," and as I say, identifying the campesino with what the Indian was.[26]

Chancoso's words are reminiscent of the early political rhetoric of the UNORCIC organization in Cotacachi, in which "campesino" was the code for "Indian" in public discourse. The association of campesino with respect suggests one consequence of double consciousness—internalization of the negative stigma attached to Indianness. Campesinistas were viewing themselves as others viewed them. What was rarely said openly but is suggested in the passage above is that campesinista activists were hesitant to view themselves as Indians, with all the derogatory meanings it could convey. Campesinista politics and the building of coalitions with nonindigenous peasants and activists had, in the eyes of many activists, lifted them from the status of Indians, empowered them in the public sphere, and offered them a public identity.

These activists' reluctance to highlight difference suggests a fear of being demoted from that status which they felt they had earned. For some activists, the conflation of *campesino* and *indigenous*, while becoming increasingly problematic, appeared racially neutral and erased or mitigated the effects of racial difference. Opponents of campesinismo, on the other hand, felt that the relations of power embedded in constructions of racial difference could not and should not be easily escaped. They thought that to ensure Indian rights they had to highlight the racial difference that rendered them subordinate. For these activists, the term *campesino* was counterproductive because it equated nonindigenous with indigenous and in so doing negated the specificity of their oppression.[27]

The organizational tensions that sprang from these contradictory perspectives continued throughout the mid-1970s. Aside from the conflicts between Indian activists, radical Christians in ECUARUNARI pressed for maintaining campesinismo. After a rift between some Indian activists and radical Christians, the latter responded by creating a branch of ECUARUNARI in Pichincha province, where they concentrated their energies and which they called the real ECUARUNARI. Once ECUARUNARI Pichincha was created as a campesinista organization, members of Tungurahua and Loja provinces refused to attend a Pichincha-planned meeting in 1976 (Rohn 1978, 85–87). The tension between the Pichincha division and the activists not aligned with the Pichincha line escalated when the latter responded to the new military triumvirate's call for a dialogue with popular organizations in 1976. ECUARUNARI activists from Cañar and Imbabura, including Blanca Chancoso, wrote a letter to the government and presented it during a meeting with Minister of Government Richelieu Levoyer. The letter denounced the use of Indians as decoration by CETURIS, the national tourism department, complained about inadequate education, and asked for communal government as opposed to municipal and city council government. Distancing themselves from the blanket condemnation of the military government that had usually characterized ECUARUNARI, they stated, "We must not divide people into civilians and uniformed people but into those with consciousness and those without it" (Rohn 1978, 87).

The Pichincha sector denounced these activists as falsely representing ECUARUNARI (Rohn 1978, 88). ECUARUNARI Pichincha members questioned their right to represent ECUARUNARI and labeled their claims merely administrative and superficial. Further, the Pichincha faction was unable or unwilling to adopt the platform of political autonomy for Indians and was concerned with what it considered one of the most threatening implications of indianismo: the exclusion of nonindigenous actors from indigenous politics. The Pichincha sector accused the activists of focusing exclusively on Indian issues and of therefore being racist agents of American imperialism.[28] This was a problem that the Pichincha sector considered rampant throughout several provinces, where local activists were defining the struggle as an indigenous one. In the same document mentioned above, the Pichincha group identified the focus on the indigenous as ridiculous, claiming that there could be rich Indians (Rohn 1978, 88).

While the Pichincha faction at times had addressed racial difference as a source of conflict, it nevertheless felt that Indians were limited by a racial discourse and that their goal should be the promotion of class consciousness. This would be accomplished, it was thought, once they had established the connection between capitalism and imperialism, ownership of property and the means of production, and thus reached a common identification among peasants of all races. If this had not occurred yet, the Pichincha faction held, it was because of insufficient political education and organizational development that trapped Indians in the immaturity of indianismo.

In the third ECUARUNARI congress held in July 1977, the Pichincha sector dominated and "won" the indio-campesino debate. ECUARUNARI publicly and forcefully declared its position as a classist organization. This victory was due in part to the exodus of many indianista factions. Activists from Tungurahua, Azuay, and Pichincha attended, while Chimborazo and Cañar refused to participate (Rohn 1978, 92). ECUARUNARI defined its class conceptions more clearly: "[We aim to] become closer to the workers' movement as the basis of proletarian struggle, clarifying ideas imposed by the imperialism of exaggerated racism" (Rohn 1978, 98).

The indianista claims adopted were the least controversial, associated exclusively with the recuperation of culture and the right to education. Culture was narrowly understood as the preservation of folklore and educational rights. There was no mention of antiracism or political autonomy. In a political statement, the organization stated the importance of preserving indigenous culture, folklore, language and dress: "We say that we have never wanted to eliminate these customs, despite the claims of agents who have infiltrated the movement."[29] Cultural preservation overshadowed the struggle for socioeconomic justice, and the civil rights dimension of the struggle occupied a secondary position:

In the Third Congress of 1977 we have clearly established that this struggle cannot be indigenista but should be a class struggle, and as such, ECUARUNARI has defined itself as a national movement of peasants whose struggle is indigenista and class based. In other words, we struggle for the defense of our values and culture stepped on for more than four hundred years, but we think that we will only do this in a struggle that proposes the total change from a capitalist society to a socialist society, where together the different peoples and nations will shoulder the struggle for a new society, a socialist society, the society of the working class and not of the indigenous race.[30]

Clearly, official ECUARUNARI rhetoric rejected appeals to the indianista line, subsuming ethnic politics under the broader umbrella of class politics. In a compromise indianistas and campesinistas shared leadership positions. However, ECUARUNARI was quick to denounce any organizational activities by activists who adopted an indianista perspective. A national meeting of indigenous organizations in Sucúa, Morona Santiago province, in 1978 prompted ECUARUNARI, the FENOC, and the FEI to denounce the organizers' "imperialist" ties and the CIA's penetration of the Indian movement.[31] Calling it a false congress, ECUARUNARI and *Nueva* accused the organizers of promoting a separatist racial ideology and of undermining the indigenous struggle by associating it with imperialist organizations that attempted to "distract" indigenous peasants.

The class faction shaped the direction that ECUARUNARI would take in the next few years. But it was not by any means a victory of class vision, as it came at the expense of losing an important number of former supporters. After the campesino "compromise" ECUARUNARI lost its national drive and constituency, as many highland and lowland activists opted out.[32]

BUILDING BRIDGES: THE POPULAR ALLIANCE

We always had both visions. It [the ethnic option] never went away. Maybe our discourse was classist, but we always saw it as an ethnic struggle.[33]

ECUARUNARI until a few years ago called all who mentioned the word *Indian* a racist and insisted on class struggle and class struggle alone. How can they now say the contrary?[34]

The statements above reflect the coexistence of two very different narratives about what actually happened. Given that the campesinista faction of ECUARUNARI had prevailed, was there any basis for Chancoso's claim that they had always engaged in an ethnic struggle?

The origin of indianismo and the couching of antiracist claims in campesinista terms points to the existence of indianista politics before 1977. But Chancoso's description of a continuous ethnic consciousness suggests that this awareness did not disappear after the 1977 victory of campesinismo within ECUARUNARI, a victory in which Chancoso actively participated as an apparently sympathetic campesinista.

An in-depth examination of the post-1977 period suggests that Chancoso may not have been that far off the mark, as campesinista activists in ECUARUNARI returned to an indianista position a few years later. But more important, informal coalitions and alliances between ECUARUNARI and other Indian organizations began to be negotiated shortly after the 1977 congress. To find the existence of an Indian identity, however, one needs to move away from ECUARUNARI's official rhetoric and analyze the organization's relationship with other political actors, such as lowland Indians and state elites. Despite its almost exclusively campesinista rhetoric after 1977, ECUARUNARI was actually conducting a dual strategy: to the Left and the popular sector, the organization was the voice of highland peasants, whereas with lowland organizations and state actors, organization activists were negotiating positions as Indians.

The dichotomization of Indian and peasant politics that led to division in ECUARUNARI was a catalyst for building new relationships among highland activists and other social sectors. Post-1977 ECUARUNARI pursued both campesinista and indianista politics at the same time. While the notion of the "pueblo indio" disappeared from the official rhetoric of ECUARUNARI, it reappeared in the forging of new coalitions with lowland Indians. Following the 1977 ECUARUNARI congress, highland indigenous activism went in two directions. a coalition with class and campesinista organizations and a panethnic coalition, which consisted in reaching out to lowland organizations to create a national Indian alliance.

The crisis of the Left in the 1960s, its ensuing internal cleavages, and the repression of parties by military governments led to a period in which parties were replaced by popular unions. This led to the end of vanguardism and the resurgence of mass spontaneity, involving large strikes and marches organized by workers and peasant unions. ECUARUNARI participated in both popular fronts and party politics. The organization's alliance with workers, campesinos, and the Left entailed three processes: joint campaigns and projects with the FENOC and other campesinista organizations, occasional alliances with the Frente Unitario de los Trabajadores (FUT), the main workers' group that engaged in national strikes and poststrike negotiations with the state, and participation in the FADI.

The post-1977 ECUARUNARI leadership worked with other popular sectors in the struggle for socioeconomic justice during the military triumvirate. As "campesinos," highland activists were committed to the fight against repression and for land reform and other land issues with the FENOC and the FEI, the two national campesinista organizations. They also built coalitions with workers and parties to gain ground on key issues or to win elections.

The relationship with the FENOC was couched in classist terms as this organization's clear campesinista position precluded any discussion of indianismo beyond the preservation of language and folklore. Most combative in 1973 to 1975, the FENOC had rejected the sole focus on Indians as racist and misguided. While the FENOC focused primarily on agrarian reform and credit and commercial opportunities for small landowners, it did not include respect for indigenous language and culture in its platform until the early 1980s. ECUARUNARI's relationship with the FENOC began in a loose coalition with other campesinista organizations, including the FEI, the Asociación de Campesinos Agricultores del Litoral (ACAL), the Federación de Trabajadores Agrícolas del Litoral (FTAL), and the Asociación de Campesinos Agricultores del Ecuador (ACAE), who together established the the Frente Unitario por la Reforma Agraria (FURA) in May 1973. In lobbying for passage of the second land reform law, this coalition held several mass gatherings and national campesino encounters. In the late 1970s this common front was revitalized and called the Frente Unido de Lucha Campesina (FULC). In addition, in the late 1970s and early 1980s ECUARUNARI, in alliance with the FENOC, engaged in several popular projects, including a national campesino-indígena march in 1980 and several May Day marches and strikes.[35] After democratization in 1979, ECUARUNARI continued to work extensively with the FENOC, embarking together on a literacy project. The FENOC hoped to incorporate ECUARUNARI, which was almost exclusively a regional highland organization at this point, under its national umbrella organization, the CEDOC.

The common link among ECUARUNARI, workers, and the Left was established under an anti-imperialist and anticapitalist banner. During the 1970s, nationalism and anti-imperialism were not subversive. In fact, they were state-promoted practices in a decade when the military regime nationalized the petroleum industry and engaged in a dispute with the United States over deep-sea fishing rights. Campesinista anti-imperialism was expressed in struggles against CIA involvement in the CEDOC and other class organizations in the 1960s and against the presence of several international agencies, the Summer Institute of Linguistics and the Evangelical Missionary Organization being the most notable examples.[36] Indigenous activists emphasized what they considered their distinct advantage: presenting themselves as the most authentic representatives of national culture. Also, the common front was considered necessary in the period of the second military regime's "preparation" for democracy, which involved the repression of many popular organizations, the outlawing of land invasions through the National Security Law, and the freezing of land reform.

One of the most critical moments in which Indians, peasants, and workers coalesced was after the killing of approximately five hundred workers involved in a labor conflict in a sugar refinery in Aztra in October 1977. Most of the workers were indigenous peasants who had migrated to the coast. The Aztra dead were peasants, Indians, and organized workers, and the event symbolized the end of the military's popular nationalism and the beginning of a somber transition to democratic rule. The FUT, ECUARUNARI, and the FENOC denounced the killings, demanded an investigation, and participated in commemorative marches in the following years.

The FUT was the second important site for indigenous-Left relations. It was created in 1971 as the political branch of three national workers' unions: CTE, (CEOSL), and the CEDOC. The FUT held a number of important strikes throughout the decade. ECUARUNARI joined the FUT in two national strikes, but the relationship was never an easy one. Although they shared common goals, indigenous activists became increasingly frustrated at their lack of decision-making power in the coalition. The FUT leadership did not allow ECUARUNARI direct access to the FUT as a national-level union of its own but told them they had to join a union (such as the CEDOC, the

FENOC's parent) and use it as their representative or mediator. Fearing a loss of autonomy, ECUARUNARI never joined one of these large centrales and was therefore in the awkward position of being outside the hierarchy of labor organizing. ECUARUNARI was often excluded from negotiations, while the participation of the indigenous rank and file in demonstrations was always encouraged. When ECUARUNARI members wanted to address demands for Indians, they were labeled racists and folkloric by labor leaders. Even traditional peasant issues such as land reform and fair rural prices often were considered secondary to salary and wage issues. This generated discontent among ECUARUNARI activists.

The FADI was the third site for ECUARUNARI activists. A coalition of several leftist parties that sought to unite a dispersed Left and gain electoral support in the new democracy, the FADI was supported officially by the FENOC and has since remained active in the Socialist Party. ECUARUNARI also supported the founding of the FADI until 1984, and many indigenous activists became affiliated with the front in their respective provinces. Several activists, however, resigned out of concern for lack of leadership and candidacy opportunities for indigenous members.

Whether expressed in coalition building with the FENOC, the FUT, or the FADI, the popular alliance had declined by the mid-1980s. Like other social movements under authoritarian regimes, the momentum and unity achieved in the fight against authoritarianism was not sustained after the regime transition. While supportive in theory, even some indigenous activists committed to the idea of class struggle and Indian-peasant alliances were critical of its application. There was general dissatisfaction with lack of indigenous autonomy and leadership and with the inability of the Left to rethink the position of Indians within the coalitions.

Hence ECUARUNARI activists felt that they were relegated to subordinate positions as indigenous people. The question of whether it was better to organize with mestizo peasants and workers or to create a separate space for indigenous organizing drove a wedge between some activists who remained committed to the notion of a popular alliance and others who insisted on the importance of ideological and political autonomy from mestizo activism. This division led to continued tension and fragmentation within the organization. In the meantime, a significant number of disillusioned highland activists both within and outside ECUARUNARI were seeking other alternatives with organizations that were also concerned with cultural specificity, civil rights, and racial subordination and were more detached from traditional campesinista concerns: lowland indigenous organizations.

LOWLAND ORGANIZATIONS AND THE INDIAN ALLIANCE

We are a different people[,] ... a people that is based on one principle, on one ideology, on one culture, on one territory, an entire factor that we argue is the ideological principle of the indigenous.[37]

What we have in common is the same enemy for the highlands, the lowlands and the coast. The enemy is dominant society, which always tries to do what it wants in political and economic situations, while the indigenous peoples are in these conditions.... So this is why there has been a clear orientation to create ourselves as indigenous organizations, or pueblos indígenas, or indigenous nationalities that make up our national organization.[38]

Highland activists worked with Amazonian or lowland organizations to form a panethnic coalition that would struggle for the political demands of all peoples of indigenous descent.[39] Lowland organizations, particularly the Shuar Federation, the OPIP, and the Federación de Organizaciones Indígenas del Napo (FOIN), faced a very different situation from highland organizations. They sought to protect their lands from the increasing encroachment of transnational companies, notably oil, lumber, and palm oil interests that were displacing them from their territories, and from mestizo colonizers who were competing for their land. Lowland organizations also had to protect their water and other environmental resources from the hazardous effects of these enterprises. Like highland organizations, however, lowland activists sought basic rights to education, economic welfare, and health. Also, as lowland activists became increasingly connected with state institutions and nonindigenous social sectors as well as with the national economy, they developed political identifications with other Indians outside their ethnic group, whom they viewed as sharing a common oppression.

Unlike highland organizations, however, most lowlanders had minimal or no experience with campesinista or other class-based organizations. Lowland organizational roots usually originated in the religious organizing of resident missionaries. The Shuar Federation had been affiliated with the once Catholic CEDOC in the 1960s but disaffiliated when it sought more autonomy from the church. Quichua activists from Napo province had worked with the FENOC in the 1970s but eventually left the organization because of ideological differences and dissatisfaction with campesinista politics. In 1973, for example, the Napo province organization changed its name from the Federación de Poblaciones Indígenas del Napo (FEPOCAN; Federation of Peasant Populations of Napo) to FOIN (Federation of Napo Indians), claiming that it did so because "we are not peasants but have our own culture."[40] For many lowland activists, the notion of a distinct culture meant that Indianness was a broader identity that subsumed many aspects of indigenous lives that peasantness did not include. Moreover, the term *peasants*, it seemed, had become such an all-encompassing category that it was devoid of cultural content.

Lowland indianismo was distinct from highland political thought and practice in two respects. First, unlike the broader highland indigenous identity, lowland identifications were much more clearly informed by ethnic affiliations, as Quichuas, Huaoranis, and Shuaras had historically maintained their originary identity and sustained interethnic rivalries. Ethnicity had become politicized, and base organizations only developed within ethnic groups. When they joined in provincial federations of organizations, their ethnic specificity remained an important component of each group's political identity. On changing its name in its second congress, the FOIN stated:

> We identify as Indian because as indigenous people we have our own territory, our own language, our culture, our traditions, different activities in our communities. So in the end we must identify ourselves, because if we say *peasants* it could be a nonindigenous peasant, and an Indian who does not self-identify as such should be considered a peasant. We said if we are indigenous peoples, then let us identify as the Quichua indigenous people of Napo.[41]

The FOIN's statement reveals the importance of racial and cultural specificity as the basis for organizing. Peasants who are not Indians should not be members of the organization. However, racial origin alone was not a sufficient criterion either. The hypothetical of the Indian who does not identify as such reveals the extent to which the FOIN considered the Indian a political category and the claiming of Indianness as a political act.

In addition, lowland organizations aspiring to create a national organization had to go through two distinct processes: first, develop a coalition of lowland activists, and later, work with highland activists toward a national coalition. Instead of facing the indianismo/campesinismo divide that characterized ECUARUNARI, lowland activists had to work out the commonalities of the subordination shared by all lowland Indians, regardless of ethnicity:

> The situation we are confronting has been so difficult in terms of integration into the white-mestizo society and integration into the market economy, obliging us, the leaders, to start realizing and start orienting the organizations, [asking them] what is it worth for us to continue fighting among Indians when our enemies are coming and they fight against us all, Shuaras and Quichuas? [We began] speaking about the petroleum companies, about colonization, about lumber companies, miners. That is when the leader of the organizations start taking initiatives and start unifying forces to defend ourselves. Because the enemy is one.[42]

In addition to interethnic difference, another distinct component of lowland indianismo was the concept of indigenous land as territory and not merely land. *Territory* is an all-encompassing definition of a space as a site of cultural reproduction and political autonomy.

> The discussions were about identifying ourselves primarily as indigenous peoples with territory, not lands. . . . So to speak of territory, a notion distinct from land as understood in the highlands, encompassed an entire social, political, economic, and cultural factor, about developing, inside that territory, a culture, a language, definitely touching on autonomy and self-empowerment.[43]

This concept of territory further embodied the emerging notion of political autonomy developed in the highlands. The notion of territory also includes the sub-suelo, or subsoil, implying that all natural resources found under the land are also part of a community's domain, contrary to the state's definition of all subsoil as state property. It became the basis for a territorial protonationalism that evolved into a more complex nationalist discourse in the 1980s, shaping the way in which highland indigenous activists reconceived of their own land claims.

This notion of territory had great influence on highland activists and was ultimately embraced by national activism in the 1980s and 1990s.

Like the redefinition of capitalism, the notion of territory provided a crucial reinterpretation of material issues. Land was not only an economic resource but a cultural and a political one as well. Land was linked to the cultural reproduction, political autonomy, and self-determination of indigenous people. In the years to follow. land, conceptualized as territory, would be inextricably intertwined with the indianista struggle in every way possible: cultural survival, education, human rights, and multiculturalism.

In 1980 the four provincial lowland organizations joined to form the Confederación de Nacionalidades Indígenas de la Amazonia Ecuatonana (CONFENIAE) in an attempt to present a united and autonomous lowland front and to break away from what were considered the syndicalist influences of highland organizations. While an attempt had been made as early as 1977 to create a united indigenous front combining highland and lowland organizations, it was unsuccessful because of ideological differences between lowland activists and ECUARUNARI members, leading to the estrangement of both organizations until new conversations were initiated in the early 1980s. Cristobal Tapuy, a lowland activist, noted that it was difficult to persuade highland activists to join them. One of the most effective arguments used by lowlanders was the claim that campesinismo was in fact foreign and that indianismo was the nationalist option:

> The idea in the lowlands has been more clear than in the highlands. Because in the highlands they have been led by ideological questions of parties, speaking of parties of the Left, such as the Communist or Socialist Party. They were more carried away by foreign ideas, while we as Amazonians began to define and radicalize our own principles, our own philosophy, and our own ideology as pueblos indígenas ... without taking foreign ideas from outside when we also have our own way of life, our own communitarian socialism. These ideologies are not Ecuadorian. ... So on these terms we began to work with the highlands. And we really liked this work, especially with those leaders who did begin to question. It was a lot of work because the highlanders, since they were focused on this form of ideological organization, started to call us divisive, saying we wanted to break the unity and all that. But the compañeros finally understood.[44]

Surely, lowland indianismo presented an attractive alternative to campesinismo, but the extent to which all highland activists "understood" is debatable. While those who were already questioning campesinista activists and were disgruntled with the peasant alliance were more open to lowland rhetoric, resulting in the creation of the CONACNIE in 1980, several ECUARUNARI activists held on to the campesinista position until the mid-1980s. In fact, Ibarra (1992) suggests that ECUARUNARI started calling itself a peasant-indigenous organization, not out of some dramatic conversion, but because it did not want others to appropriate the indigenous name and cause over which it wanted to keep some control.

Nevertheless, lowland activism and thought, especially its understanding of autonomy and territory, presented a distinct addition to the debate. At first intermittent, after 1980 continuous dialogue among indigenous activists from both regions developed, creating a discourse of and about the Indian outside of campesinista organizations.

THE DOUBLE DIMENSION AND THE PATH TO UNITY

A defeated Indian will never be a proletarian. . . . [T]he conflicts of pueblos indígenas are not only caused by problems of economic and agrarian exploitation, or by the desire for better salaries or better lives. Their roots are cultural, of nationality, territoriality, ethnicity. There is a double oppression of which he must free himself, and one is as degrading as the other. We don't deny any of the two, nor can we reduce the problem to either one of the two.[45]

In 1980 we started clarifying that Indian and peasant did not negate each other but complemented each other, whereas before to be Indian was a shame. We carry a generic name because they submitted us, enslaved us with that, and with the same tools we will rise. There are many ways of naming an organization. We say indigenous nationalities, period.[46]

Both quotations above reveal an important shift in activist rhetoric: simultaneous awareness of double oppression and acceptance of its central role in defining the contemporary Indian struggle. The dual strategy, the coexistence of campesinista and Indianista politics, peaked in the late 1970s. But by the late 1980s campesinismo as an organizational alternative was in serious decline.

Indigenous activism in the highlands experienced a transition from a dual strategy of working with popular groups and lowland organizations to a more open and critical analysis of double consciousness to the adoption of a double-dimension platform that embraced ethnic and class struggles simultaneously. However, the material concerns that had made up the old campesinismo were cast in a new light. The quest for land and the fight against capitalism were not simply appropriated by indianismo but transformed in their meanings and were therefore as different as the new organizational forms and political strategies were from the old ones.

By 1982 the strategy of a coexisting peasant alliance and an Indian front had been exhausted at both the micro- and macropolitical levels. At the macropolitical level, indigenous activists felt they were occupying a subordinate position in a popular front made up of labor unions, the FADI, and campesinista organizations. Nevertheless, at the micropolitical level, campesinismo was still dominant within ECUARUNARI. By 1982 Luis Macas, a CONAIE leader, demanded that other popular groups stop setting aside ethnic claims such as education and development of language and accused them of failing to consider Indian specificity. By the early 1980s there were serious discrepancies between ECUARUNARI and the FUT, because the former's incorporation into FUT was prohibited. ECUARUNARI was never satisfied with this and never affiliated with a labor central.

Efforts to achieve some form of national organizational autonomy as Indians had been carried out as early as 1977 and were principally organized by lowland activists and some highland activists dissatisfied with the campesinista option. The earliest effort to consolidate lowland and highland activism occurred in 1977 at the First Conference of Indigenous Pueblos held in Sucúa, in the lowlands. Despite its initial reluctance, ECUARUNARI insisted on participating, reportedly to ensure that racist elements did not dominate the meeting (Ibarra 1992). The initial goal of uniting to form a cross-regional organization failed because activists could not reconcile their positions to initiate a national dialogue. Although religious, interregional, and ideological divisions created problems, campesinista-indianista conflict halted progress until a second meeting was held in 1980 in Sucúa.

After the creation of CONFENIAE, lowland activists made a second attempt to engage in dialogue with ECUARUNARI in an effort to create a national organization. On October 20–25, 1980, the First Encounter of Indigenous Nationalities of Ecuador was held in Sucúa. This time activists were successful in creating a council (CONACNIE) designed to coordinate future meetings and encourage dialogue that would eventually lead to a national federation of Indians. CONACNIE activists stated that they needed time to unite the double dimension of ethnicity and class as the only way to find holistic solutions. The mission of the CONACNIE, in addition to working toward ideological unity, was to strengthen local organizations, reject the manipulation of political parties, support the political awareness of base groups, and maintain respectful and autonomous relations with class-based organizations that had common struggles. Its stated priority was to advocate for organizing as Indians first.[47]

The ongoing dialogue between lowland and highland activists, as well as debates within the organization itself, finally had an effect on ECUARUNARI. By its fifth congress, held in 1981, ECUARUNARI explicitly acknowledged members' peasant and Indian identity, increasingly emphasizing the same issues that the campesinista congress had scorned two years earlier. In addition to credit and land, ECUARUNARI included the struggle for Indian self-representation, bilingual education, and the defense of cultural values in its platform. Moreover, and for the first time, it defended the concept of the territory of indigenous pueblos. With the exception of bilingual education, however, most of these demands were more accepted in rhetoric than in practice, as the peasant alliance was still considered a priority. Congress documents emphasized the importance of developing a closer relationship with the FEI and the FENOC while simultaneously remaining involved in Amazonian issues and international declarations about indigenous peoples.[48] This congress held the first public discussion within ECUARUNARI of the dual dimension, recognizing the coexistence of class-based and ethnic claims (CONAIE 1989, 223).

This new position was a consequence of both the decline of campesinismo and of several years of interethnic and interregional debate in CONACNIE, which eventually led to its consolidation into the national organization CONAIE in 1986. Hence most of the peasant versus Indian debate occurred between 1980 and 1986, while differences still weighed heavily in different moments in the late 1980s and early 1990s. The double dimension was a compromise between indianismo and campesinismo that facilitated the consolidation of the lowland-highland coalition, making it possible for campesinistas and indianistas to come together under a common banner. In adopting some of the ideological tenets of campesinismo and yet rejecting the racial hierarchies that characterized the campesinista organizations, the CONAIE was able to garner the support of ECUARUNARI campesinistas while maintaining institutional autonomy.

A final important factor in galvanizing indigenous unity and gaining broad popular support was the campaign to expel the Summer Institute of Linguistics (SIL), which was most active in the period 1980 through 1982. An evangelical organization, the SIL had a presence in the highlands but was much more active in the lowland provinces, especially in Napo. Although it functioned formally as a center for anthropological study and translation of the Bible, it was much more concerned with religious conversion and with social control of the lowland Indians. Previously expelled from other countries, it was notorious for "civilizing" Indians, encouraging them to live in sedentary arrangements and relinquish their land rights and preparing them to become a labor force for foreign petroleum and lumber corporations. While this campaign was supported by both labor and campesinista organizations as well as Indian activists, it strengthened panethnic Indian unity instead of boosting an already declining campesinismo. The struggle against the SIL became a site for panethnic organizing, strengthening the indianista option in three key ways. First, it united lowland and highland organizations in an unprecedented common public discourse on the Indian by the Indian, thus generating a new image of the Indian as a political actor. For example, for the first time, lowland Indian activists were featured prominently in national news magazines. Second, it generated the support of human rights activists, academics, NGOs, and other social groups who were becoming increasingly aware of Indian issues. And third, it became popularized as an indigenous struggle that was also a nationalist struggle, effectively managing to combine the notion of cultural recuperation and defense of indigenous rights with the Ecuadorian defense of sovereignty and anti-imperialism.

In a two-year effort activists from most of the highland and lowland provinces as well as national leadership spearheaded a campaign in opposition to the SIL, calling it an imperialist presence primarily engaged with the exploitation and manipulation of indigenous people. Even after President Roldós expelled the institute in April 1981, its slow withdrawal led activists to continue lobbying for the complete departure of all its representatives.[49] In addition to literacy policy, the SIL campaign was one of two main issues that allowed for a common identification between highland

and lowland organizations, touching on central concerns of political autonomy, racism, and imperialism (*Punto de Vista*, December 18, 1981). The second issue, bilingual and bicultural education, is discussed in chapter 7.

The SIL campaign attracted professionals, academics, anthropologists, and human rights groups, who created the Frente de Solidaridad con los Pueblos Indígenas to ensure that the SIL expulsion was implemented. They claimed not only that the state's dependence on the SIL impeded the self-determination and creativity of Indians, but that the untaxed occupation of indigenous territory was a threat to national sovereignty and security, because it occupied an oil-rich area close to the Peruvian border. SIL officials were faulted by the Frente de Solidaridad for being cultural colonialists whose values had nothing to do with Indian culture and therefore tended to work against communal organization. Indians and their communal organizations were considered objects of national defense: "What this [the presence of the SIL] means is that the country has given to the hands of strangers the entire system of socialization of the indigenous peoples of Ecuador."[50]

On the one hand, this position was not far from traditional indigenismo in which the Indian problem is considered the concern of state leaders and intellectuals, not foreign entities. This is why the Frente de Solidaridad could shame public officials by claiming that they were evading their traditional responsibilities. On the other hand, this indigenismo was different in the sense that it gave great symbolic weight to indigenous culture and identity as a bulwark of nationalism, which is in direct contradiction to foreign penetration. Indians in this context epitomized national identity and control over and preservation of indigenous culture, which became an almost patriotic obligation. This discourse was advantageous to the Indians because their problems and issues could potentially become national problems. This was argued not only by indigenous activists such as Blanca Chancoso and Alfredo Viteri but also by the Frente de Solidaridad itself, which claimed that "the indigenous problem in all its dimension demands a broader and more profound reflection on the national economy and society."[51]

In addition to highlighting this issue, the campaign promoted the legitimation of the indianista perspective, providing national activists with a site to discuss other "Indian" issues and Indian struggles, including cultural and land rights on their own terms and not as part of a coalition with the FUT.[52] The direct support of analysts, NGOs, and human rights organizations on this and other issues proved a valuable resource and enabled activists to decrease their dependence on traditional peasant coalitions to have their demands heard.

RETHINKING THE CLASS/ETHNICITY DEBATE: INDIANISMO, DOUBLE CONSCIOUSNESS, AND IDEOLOGICAL UNITY

The reconciliation of campesinistas and indianistas was well under way by the mid-1980s as the emergent, independent voice of indigenous activism, the continued dialogue within ECUARUNARI, and the limitations of the peasant alliance all began to take their toll on ECUARUNARI. In 1984 the organization began to depart from its class-based position. It disaffiliated from the FADI and declined to work jointly with the FENOC and the FUT, instead focusing almost exclusively on strengthening its position within CONACNIE. By the eighth ECUARUNARI congress in 1985, political documents and declarations had eschewed all mention of peasants, replacing it with a discussion of indigenous cultures and nationalities. Moreover, economic exploitation was no longer considered a consequence of capitalist development that affected all the poor but an ongoing part of indigenous history that began with Spanish conquest and colonization. The language of this document made specific reference to racial difference:

> [Indian activism is] a direct challenge to the historic constitution of the Ecuadorian "nation" as a homogeneous country, where the only ones who enjoy equality are whites and mestizos. Paradoxically, indigenous peoples are negated, hidden, and persecuted as a residue of the Ecuadorian nation.[53]

The political unity of the regional organizations was finally achieved when the CONACNIE became the CONAIE (the National Confederation of Indigenous Nationalities of Ecuador) in 1986, after six years of interregional dialogue about the peasant/Indian question.[54] The purpose of the CONAIE was to represent all the national and provincial federations, provid a united front, and coordinate projects on the national level.

Despite the decline of organizational campesinismo, the particular ideological forms that highland indianismo has taken since are a reflection of some of the campesinista/indianista tensions present in early ECUARUNARI history and the subsequent popular alliance politics that generated the politics of a double identity as Indians and peasants. Nevertheless, the concept of the double dimension became a central position within the CONAIE, indicating the importance of this idea in consolidating a common Indian front and reconciling two different perspectives:

> We, the indigenous, are suffering from economic and social exploitation as agricultural workers, and as pueblos and nationalities we are suffering national oppression, in the sense that our historical rights to land, self-determination, politics, and history are not recognized.[55]

Although it may not have appeared evident at first, the acceptance of a double dimension was a challenge to campesinismo. The temporary marriage of campesinismo and indianismo had been obtained initially via anticapitalism and via the Indianization of poverty. In other words, because all Indians were considered poor, the distinctions between Indians and peasants could be blurred rather than reconciled. This initial conflation, similar to the one that ocurred in Cotacachi, would be questioned and undermined, as ethnicity and race were separated in the double dimension discourse. Once these separate identities—and the relationship between them—were analyzed by activists, Indianness was given substantial political weight and was often understood as a root cause for poverty. Therefore, while the concept of the double dimension was effective in forging a political coalition between highland and lowland activists, it was not necessarily effective in bridging the differences between Indians and non-Indians in popular organizations. Ironically, diminishing the apparent "incomensurability" between class and ethnic identity promoted unity among Indians but did not promote further coalition building of Indian and non-Indian activists. On the contrary, the resolved conflict legitimized the more formalized pursuit of indianismo and autonomous organizing.

This line of analysis represents an important expansion to the two major studies of ECUARUNARI (Rohn 1978; Santana 1984). Although they take opposite perspectives, both authors periodize ECUARUNARI: an indianista position between 1972 and 1975; crisis between 1975 and 1977; and then the class-based or campesinista option in 1977. Writing in 1978, Rohn argued that the indianista position was simply a false consciousness stemming from an acute sense of displacement and loss of culture after land reform and rural modernization. In their desperation, Rohn claims, indigenous people clung to their only remaining resource, which was the totality of their traditions, folkways and habits. While this was understandable, according to Rohn, it did not lead to a "deeper consciousness raising" that could only be obtained through forging an alliance with workers in the struggle against capitalism. In fact, the immaturity of indianismo makes its advocates an easy prey for the claws of imperialism. Santana (1984) argued that the 1977 transition to a strictly class-based position was the organization's darkest and weakest moment. Favoring the primacy of ethnic consciousness as a more original and representative position, Santana predicted that in the early 1980s ECUARUNARI's best option would be a return to the ethnic position to free itself from class politics (Santana 1984).

Instead of characterizing all highland indigenous activism as class based and then replaced at some magical moment, I am concerned with the complex way in which highland indianismo was formed. Moreover, early indianismo, while virtually absent from most written documents of the period, did not "disappear" but remained a key influence on indigenous activists. The pre-1977 indio/campesino debates had never really been resolved but rather set aside after the dominance of the class-based coalition. The adoption of a dual strategy that involved coalitions with other Indian organizations as well as with nonindigenous organizations demonstrates that a class-based campesinista identity did not displace the early indianista concerns. If the class victory had been successful, why was ECUARUNARI engaging in conversations and coalitions with other indigenous actors? Contra Ibarra (1992), who claims that it was merely an instrumental choice designed to wrest control over the indigenous platform from lowland activists, it is my view that growing relations between lowland and highland activists were the consequence of a common social and ideological identification, as Indian identity became increasingly politicized.

CONCLUSION

This analysis of the evolution of campesinista and indianista politics between 1972 and 1984 leads to some basic claims. On a theoretical level, the study of the very constitution of indigenous political identity must take into account the relationship between activists and among activists and other political actors. On an empirical level, the specific formation of political consciousness among highland activists provides two key insights. First, it draws a distinction between the lowland and highland positions that have been usually conflated in most analyses of indianista ideology. A consequence of this conflation has been the inaccurate dichotomization of lowland indigenous politics as ethnic and highland politics as class based, impeding any understanding of highland indianista consciousness, cross-regional commonalities, and eventual political alliances among regions.

Second, this analysis of highland indianismo and the related process of double consciousness renders perspectives that describe the replacement of one identity by another (class by ethnicity) as highly problematic on several counts. There was no simple transition from peasant to Indian political identity. ECUARUNARI went from a temporary class-based position to a dual strategy, to the eventual development of a better articulated indianismo that reinterpreted and subsumed some of the original campesinista demands. This can be attributed, I argue, to the existence of double consciousness, which has characterized the highland movement from the early 1970s through the 1990s. Double consciousness helps to explain both the frustration felt by indigenous activists who engaged in interracial coalition politics and their political response to it.

Why were activists frustrated with interracial coalitions? Why, if race and class are intertwined, did activists see them as dichotomous, and why was this dichotomy at the root of factionalism within organizations? The answer lies in the inconsistency between the lived experience of racial discrimination in everyday practices and political life and the promise of equality in leftist discourse. The popular alliance and campesinista politics failed to retain the support of highland Indians, not only because of some abstract ideological disparity, but also because of the racial subordination embedded in the political practices and discourses of non-Indian popular organizations. Race clearly drove a wedge in coalition politics and animated the tensions between campesinismo and indianismo. This led to Indian activists' realization of the contradiction between the discursive and the nondiscursive, between theory and practice, and facilitated the development of antiracist, autonomist politics.

These exclusionary practices led indigenous activists to question the compatibility of the class-based and indianista struggles. Despite the relative feasibility of a popular alliance in a period of national fronts and popular politics and despite ECUARUNARI's willingness to participate in a broad popular coalition, indigenous activists were disillusioned with the subordinate status they occupied in the political hierarchy. While obviously present in the political opposition front, race and racial distinctions were constantly denied in Ecuadorian politics, except when classifying indianistas as racists. The pursuit of autonomist politics, promoted to a certain extent by the state, was thus increasingly considered by activists the only hope for achieving empowerment. The contradiction between leftist rhetoric that idealized the achievement of social and economic equality and the practice of social distinction and inequality was a source for critical interrogation, as well as for the construction of new alternatives that understood racial equality and political autonomy for Indians as necessary conduits for social equality in Ecuadorian society.

However, while double consciousness makes these tensions apparent, it can also be a site for finding solutions. In the politics of double consciousness racial and class strategies can be used alternatively as well as jointly in mobilization, just as they are historically and politically intertwined in the organization of the state and civil society. Despite the apparent race/class dichotomies originated in public discourse and practice, indigenous activists have both recognized and articulated the relationships between class and ethnic demands. Hence the politics of double consciousness implies by definition the coexistence of a relationship between these two forms of consciousness. This relationship may be characterized by tension, contradiction, opposition, and even dichotomization, or it may be more harmonious and less evident but not necessarily less important.

In the case of the Ecuadorian Indian movement, double consciousness explains the development of a materially informed form of indianismo that included socioeconomic demands on its agenda. Indianismo recognized and integrated class demands but redefined and linked them to the new Indian political identity. While campesinismo as a form of organization declined, material concerns traditionally associated with class consciousness were rearticulated: land concerns were intertwined with notions of territory and political autonomy, and capitalism was linked with assimilationism and ethnocide. Double consciousness is characterized by the inevitable and constituting presence of two forms of consciousness that are shaping each other. Political emancipation, therefore, cannot consist of eschewing one form of consciousness for the other but must transform both, a process that the contemporary Ecuadorian movement has engaged in.

The pervasiveness of this double consciousness also helps to explain why, despite the increased popularity of indianismo, campesinista discourse and political practices have not entirely disappeared. Campesinismo was not discarded as soon as Indian politics gained legitimacy.[56] The FENOC remains an important if weakened national organization, and at the local level, there are still several organizations that ascribe to campesinismo, the most notable being Cotacachi's UNORCIC. Nevertheless, as chapter 4 explained, even the latter organization has informal ties with indianista organizations. This is possible because at the national level indianista politics remain grounded in concerns about material conditions, indigenous peasants' social positions, and peasants' role in relations of production.

CHAPTER SEVEN

From Pluriculturalism to Plurinationalism

The Politics of Disruption

> *There is no true Ecuadorian nation. It remains to be constructed. It remains to be defined. When it is defined with all the popular sectors, with all those who make up Ecuador, we will be able to really define nationality.*
>
> ALFREDO VITERI,
> in "Derechos del Pueblo," 1983

The consolidation of several organizations into one umbrella organization, the CONAIE, and the ensuing ideological debate made a national movement possible. Another crucial factor was the state. The Roldós, Hurtado, and Borja administrations expanded the role of the state to include new cultural and educational policies as well as new rural development policies. The state's effort to focus on indigenous issues and establish the mechanisms for a more direct relationship with indigenous organizations has led scholars to describe contemporary Ecuador as a neoindigenista state (e.g., Ibarra 1992).

The state's effort, however, cannot be understood as a mere co-optation. Two approaches can be used to think about the relationship between indigenous movements and the state. On the one hand, one can look at the effect the state, as an independent variable, has on the shaping of social movements. This theoretical model, political opportunity theory, is exemplified by Doug McAdam's (1982) study of the American civil rights movement. He points out that a number of conditions existing in a given political environment could be conducive to mobilization, such as specific state policies, the existence of elite allies, and the creation of social institutions. He argues, for example, that the black church became an important source of support for civil rights activism.

The other approach is to understand mobilization and state formation as interactive, that is, to conceive of social movements and the state as jointly shaping the meanings, process, and outcome of mobilization. Omi and Winant (1986) use the concept of racial formation to explain the dynamic tension between the state, pro–civil rights activism, and anti–civil rights activism in shaping the American civil rights movement, its effects and implications. Likewise, Radcliffe (1993) discusses how social movements often use the terms and ideas of state leaders to dispute and reconstruct meanings and identities and set new terms of negotiation between activists and the state. Finally, Foweraker (1995) argues for an approach that does not separate issues of identity from the practical politics of resources, mobilization, and state responses to mobilization.

All these authors posit the political arena as the site of identity production and transformation. Relying on this approach, I focus on the relationship between the state and activists, arguing that it is precisely in the interaction between the two, not solely from above or from below, that collective identity is produced. I argue that the Ecuadorian case provides a poignant example of the interrelationship of identity, political environment, and the politics of mobilization. The platform of plurinationalism that was developed and adopted by the movement was greatly informed by the experiences of state officials and movement activists in the pursuit of cultural policy and in movement politics.

By understanding state–social movement relations as interactive we can understand why new advantages provided to a group will not always result in organized and sustained resistance. Opportunity alone has not always led to mobilization. For example, a group of targeted organizations may take advantage of a given opportunity simply to work within the parameters of state policy. This was the case in Ecuador in the 1980s. It is also the case in Colombia, where a constitutional assembly that guaranteed indigenous groups several new rights has not resulted in an explosion of activism. The passage from participation in formal or institutional politics to extrainstitutional politics, that is, a sustained uprising politics, such as Ecuador's, begs one question: Why, precisely at the moment when the state had arguably presented more opportunities for indigenous empowerment than ever before, did Ecuadorian activists critique the limitations of this policy, highlight its gaps and contradictions, and by 1990 stage the largest Indian uprising in contemporary history?

I argue that indigenous mobilization was triggered by the gap between the state's and indigenous activists' notions of pluriculturalism. The latter's shift from formal politics (negotiation and accommodation with state elites in the planning of literacy and bilingual education) to the politics of disruption initiated in the national uprising of 1990 can be explained as the consequence of the exhaustion of the cultural policy model pursued by the state, consisting mainly of the National Literacy Program (1979–84) and the Intercultural Bilingual Education Program (1988–present), legal-cultural initiatives, and the creation of indigenous government units, to the exclusion of land, commercialization, and significant rural development and redistribution concerns.

The gap between models of pluriculturalism occurred for several reasons. First, whereas indigenous activists had a notion of culture that integrated material and cultural demands, the state's notion of culture was limited primarily to education and artistic endeavors. This cultural policy was ultimately deemed insufficient by activists because they believed it separated cultural demands from material and political ones. The ability of the state to do this for a prolonged period was limited, as this same separation had been addressed and problematized by activists in internal debates. Having experienced a historical rift between indianismo and campesinismo and having spent a six-year period attempting to resolve these differences, activists were suspicious of the state's attempts to maintain the separation between "Indian" issues and socioeconomic concerns.

Hence one of the movement's main goals, as expressed in the discourse and practice of the uprising politics of 1990 and 1992, was to lay bare the limitations of this dematerialized neoindigenismo that considered indigenous concerns as primarily educational. Activists who had dealt with the separation between the cultural and the material had, to some extent, recognized the falseness of such a dichotomy and were actively exploring ways to reconcile the two in their pursuit of pluriculturalism. While initially they were eager to participate in the design and implementation of this cultural policy, ultimately they were unwilling to accept what they perceived as a dematerialized notion of culture and cultural policy offered by the state. As a critique of this separation presented by the state, they developed a broad ideological approach that provided a material basis for their struggle. Rejecting the denomination of ethnic groups, they declared themselves nationalities and Ecuador a multinational country, opting for a more materially informed conceptualization of Indian identity and difference.

THE PLURICULTURAL STATE

The democratic regime inaugurated in 1979 opened up opportunities for indigenous empowerment. Economic subordination and social discrimination of Indians continued, but the new regime provided them with unprecedented political opportunities and institutional mechanisms through which they could channel their demands. The transition to democratic rule began with the election of a new president, Jaime Roldós, who represented a Center-Left coalition that assumed power in 1979. Roldós's government was known for its symbolic appeals to Indians, as well as for its active pursuit of cultural policies that would improve their status. Before the transition, the military triumvirate had granted the illiterate the right to vote, which expanded the voting base substantially, and had encouraged the Roldós regime to appeal to this new electorate. Roldós was the first president to include a small speech in Quichua in his inaugural address, a gesture of great symbolic significance to Indians and non-Indians. His regime was also the first to openly speak of a multicultural state and to carry out a full-fledged literacy campaign implemented in most of the highlands. Roldós's and subsequent administrations were characterized by their focus on cultural and educational policy, particularly literacy policy, on which they spent great amounts of energy and resources, precisely at a time when agrarian reform and other rural policies began a slow decline.

This new state approach in Ecuador and other parts of Latin America has been called neoindigenismo. Although it represents a new variant of indigenismo, it is also the outcome of a radical critique of traditional indigenismo in Latin America, specifically, its integrationist approach. In contrast to policies in the 1970s that used a racially neutral language to refer to all peasants and marginalized people, the cultural policies developed in the early and late 1980s openly reflect public debates about the Indian.

Whereas traditional indigenismo attempts to integrate Indians into a homogeneous model of the nation-state, neoindigenismo denounces the assimilationism and paternalism of the former and seeks an alternative. Neoindigenismo, which can be traced to the international meetings in Barbados in 1972, was developed by anthropologists as well as activists. The first Barbados Encounter was organized in reaction to ethnocide occurring in Colombia and Brazil. Scholars such as Guillermo Bonfil Batalla and Stefano Varese from Mexico and Darcy Ribeiro from Brazil helped to draft a declaration that critiqued the integrationism of traditional indigenismo.

This new indigenismo had two main premises. First, it argued that Indians should be considered subjects, not objects, and that difference should therefore be respected and not attacked. Moreover, as subjects, they should freely associate and participate in the planning of their own development. Second, it recognized the role of the nation-state in cultural ethnocide. It called for the reconceptualization of national societies with indigenous populations as plurilingual, pluriethnic, pluricultural, and plurinational. This conceptualization called for a new role for the state, as the main agent responsible for protecting the rights of Indians. According to the declaration, the state was responsible for guaranteeing to all the indigenous population, by virtue of their ethnic distinction, the right to be and to remain themselves; recognizing that indigenous groups possess rights prior to those of other national constituencies; sanctioning indigenous groups' right to organize and to govern in accordance with their own traditions; and extending to indigenous society the same economic, social, educational, and health assistance that the rest of the national population received.[1]

Important implications of this critique were (1) that the direction of ethnic politics should no longer be dictated by indigenista officials and writers but informed by the needs and demands of Indian activists; and (2) that there would be a renewed role for the state as protector of Indians from the acculturation and assimilation that capitalism promoted.

The early efforts at the Barbados meeting were developed in subsequent meetings and documents.[2] Moreover, international organizations such as the International Labor Organization and, much later, the United Nations organized international encounters in which a common agenda designed to preserve native American rights in all the Americas could be agreed on. These early meetings and declarations sensitized many Latin American anthropologists as well as some bureaucrats, while others remained uninformed, uninterested or critical.[3] Nevertheless, in the Ecuadorian case, the

1980s reveal a gradual awareness, and acceptance by some, of the principal tenets declared at Barbados and elsewhere.

Since the Roldós regime, the Ecuadorian state has been almost continuously concerned with the expansion of indigenous citizenship through Indians' involvement in rural planning and education.[4] Indigenous culture would be maintained through the preservation of language and the exaltation of tradition and customs incorporated into bilingual education and other state-sponsored cultural programs. Government declarations and documents have recognized indigenous organizations as privileged interlocutors with respect to the problems of their population and adopted many of the principles of the Declaration of Barbados, including the right to self-determination and the concept of ethnodevelopment as an alternative to capitalist development and ethnocide (Ibarra 1992; Appendix).

While the military regimes had referred to the Indian populations as marginals who must be integrated into the state, the new democratic governments spoke of a nation that was characterized by "pluriculturalism," respect for and support of indigenous peoples and cultures as a key component of national development. This vision did not explicitly address racism, but it did acknowledge the right of the Indians to articulate their own concerns, organize independently of class- and peasant-based groups, and represent themselves in direct communications with public officials (Ibarra 1992, 186). It meant that for the first time Indians would become participants in policy debates that affected their communities. While some direct access to institutions occurred during the military regime of the 1970s, it is only in the 1980s that we can speak of any type of state-sponsored dialogue between indigenous activists and state officials at the national level.

The Ecuadorian state pursued this notion of pluriculturalism throughout the development and implementation of cultural and educational policy. It is important to note that while this new pluricultural policy was being pursued, economic and land policies that did not publicly address Indians, but greatly affected them in detrimental ways, were being pursued. Land reform cases diminished noticeably when the budget of IERAC was slashed. In addition, colonization in the lowlands was increasing at dramatic speed, leading to the dispossession of several lowland groups. The coexistence of these policies with the new cultural policies would result in tensions that would deeply shape the movement.

STATE PLURICULTURAL POLICY: ITS PROMISE AND ITS LIMITS

Pluricultural policy in Ecuador between 1979 and 1990 can be divided into three types. The first initiative, which I call the legal-cultural rights initiative, involves the signing of international treaties to uphold indigenous rights and lobby for cultural preservation, as well as for policies and programs designed to support Indian languages and cultures. Supported by new rhetoric and practices that were spreading throughout the Americas, these policies combined a preoccupation with the legal entity and rights of Indians with the preservation of cultural rights.

The second type is governance policy, referring specifically to attempts to create governmental divisions dedicated to the study of Indians and the implementation of indigenous policy. These include all efforts to create ministries, secretariats, or subsecretariats of the Indian. These are the most obvious examples of different regimes' attempts to create a corporatist framework, in which all the organizations' demands and claims, and all indigenous policy would be coordinated by the state.[5] Corporatism, derived from an Iberian tradition and consolidated in Latin America in the second half of the twentieth century, is based on the notion of regulation of private associations (Stepan 1978; Wiarda 1981). Regulation of popular groups is achieved by enabling unions and other popular organizations to exist while restricting their autonomy (Lehmann 1990, 34). While corporatism can lead to some group empowerment, it also entails co-optation by the state.

The third and most important type of policy covers literacy and bilingual education projects, which were under the direction of the Ministry of Education and involved unprecedented attempts to change literacy and education rates at massive levels. These projects primarily targeted Indians but also affected other rural and poor urban populations. Of all three policies, the latter was the most interactive and therefore the site where state and activists' notions of multiculturalism would be aired.

Government Agencies

Like other Latin American countries, Ecuador has created special governmental entities to manage indigenous issues and to coordinate the various branches of the state in charge of policies targeting the Indian population: the Ministries of Social Welfare, Agriculture, Culture and Education,

Labor, and Health. The first such entity, the Oficina de Asuntos Indígenas (OAI) (Office of Indigenous Affairs) within the Ministry of Social Welfare, was created in 1983 by the Hurtado administration. The OAI was created two years after the government organized a working group on public policy and the Indian, which began with the 1981 Technical Meeting on Indigenous Affairs of the Amazonian treaty countries, held in Puyo, Ecuador (Sánchez-Parga 1988, 88). The objective of OAI was to

> [r]escue, conserve and develop the values of aborigenous cultures, respect the autonomy of their cultures, and promote their development . . . and to support the joint actions of aboriginal groups and peasant associations.[6]

The OAI was involved primarily in education and training, publication of books and pamphlets, production of documentaries, and support of popular education (Sánchez-Purga 1988, 90). In 1984 the Febres-Cordero regime created the Dirección Nacional de Pueblos Indígenas (DNPI) as part of a broader plan to scale back resources and keep tighter governmental control over programs for the indigenous population. For example, by October 1984, the Febres-Cordero regime had decided to renew the government's contract with the Centro de Investigación para la Educación Indígena (CIEI), despite repeated protests from indigenous organizations concerning their exclusion from the process by CIEI officials. In January 1986 the president moved the Servicio de Desarrollo Rural Integral (SEDRI), the agency in charge of rural development projects, and FODERUMA to the Ministry of Social Welfare, creating a subsecretariat of rural development. Under the Hurtado regime, SEDRI had been under the control of the presidency and received considerable attention and funds. Further, while land reform had declined, the attention paid to SEDRI and FODERUMA programs gave activists the impression that the government remained somewhat interested in rural development issues. By removing SEDRI from the president's control, the Febres-Cordero administration was deemphasizing its importance and dismantling rural social policy.

Also, by transferring SEDRI to the Ministry of Social Welfare instead of the Ministry of Agriculture, the administration was disavowing the connections between rural development and agrarian policy designed to generate growth and productivity. Policy targeted to Indians was segregated in the DNPI. Instead of being coordinated together with agricultural policy writ large, it was now confined to the realm of social policy. The transfer was accompanied by a cutback in spending in SEDRI programs as well as many other cultural and education programs (Ibarra 1992; Sanchez-Parga 1988). Giving up hope of accomplishing anything through the executive branch during the Febres-Cordero presidency, activists shifted their attention to Congress, working with the Socialist Party on a law for Indian nationalities designed to uphold indigenous rights.

Despite the obvious differences between the Hurtado and the Febres-Cordero administrations, they shared one thing in common: reliance on a separate body that would oversee all policies related to indigenous people. Most Indian organizations feared that such governmental bodies would co-opt or replace independent organizational leadership. Activists were vigilant even as they asked for services and funds from these agencies. Further, the state's support of parallel indigenous organizations that were happy to declare their support for the government led activists to think that such efforts were designed to protect state interests and not popular indigenous interests.

The creation of these separate agencies, however, should be understood in the context of Ecuadorian political tradition and therefore as more than a simple effort to control organizations. It also reflects civil society's understandings of political and social organization, derived in great part from a tradition of corporatism and sectoral representation in the early part of the twentieth century. Citizens are subjects of the state as members of a group, not as individuals. They organize and demand as groups or, more specifically, as sectors. Hence before the military regimes, the Ecuadorian constitution guaranteed sectoral representation in Congress to workers and Indians (always by non-Indians, however). This tended to favor vertical relationships between public officials and sectors, instead of cross-group cooperation.[7] Therefore, instead of focusing mainly on civil and individual liberties as such, the focus of the Ecuadorian Indian movement has been the guarantee of group rights as Indians (as a political actor distinct from peasants).[8] Activists have focused primarily on the cultural and legal entity of the sector as a whole, demanding respect for Indians as a group through the promotion of social, economic, and educational policy and through the incorporation of Indians into local and national power structures.[9]

Likewise, the state's approach involved addressing all the group's joint demands through one single entity, in an effort to establish a vertical relationship with the executive branch and thus incorporate the organizations under its umbrella. Indigenous organizations, however, feared that the state would use traditional clientilistic mechanisms to wrest control from them. In this period, most activists kept a healthy distance from these agencies. Most directors of the agencies were not indigenous people who were linked with the organizations, and the few activists who were involved usually became distanced from their organizations in the process.[10] Fear of co-optation and mutual distrust between state agents and organization activists leery of losing their autonomy led to competition of sorts between state officials, the leaders and parallel organizations they incorporated, and the majority of the organizations. Activists preferred an autonomous political space from which they could negotiate with the state instead of becoming a part of it. State officials, nonetheless, continued to establish special agencies. In subsequent administrations, the idea of a special government body continued under different names in different administrations. In the last year of Osvaldo Hurtado's administration the Oficina nacional de Asuntos Indígenas (ONAI) was created. In 1984–88, Febres-Cordero replaced the ONAI with the DNPI. Finally, in 1988 Borja created the Presidential Commission for Indigenous Affairs, inviting national activists to participate in meetings with Commission members.

The Legal and Cultural Rights Initiatives

The legal and cultural policy has been concerned with creating a framework that clearly expresses the state's intention to recognize the rights of indigenous people and their cultures. The three main types of legal-cultural policy are symbolic declarations and speeches promoting pluriculturalism, the specific allocation of funds for "cultural preservation," and state participation in national and international meetings on protection of Indian rights.

Among the government's symbolic efforts was former president Jaime Roldós's inaugural speech in August 1979, during which he spoke for a few minutes in Quichua, inviting all Indians to participate in the new polity and describing Ecuador as a pluricultural nation. More important than the actual message was the fact that a president had used Quichua, a language spoken by most highland communities and by lowland Quichua groups in the provinces of Napo and Pastaza and never previously used publicly by non-Indian elites.[11] Another important moment occurred in Cacha, when

Roldós landed in a helicopter and inaugurated the new Indian parish. In his speech, he spoke of Cacha as a standing symbol for cultural preservation and Ecuadorian roots. The national government's support of this effort in light of significant local opposition by white-mestizos was confirmation for indigenous activists throughout the country of the state's dedication to ensuring the legal and political rights of indigenous organizations. Roldos's symbolic effort was repeated by his successor, Osvaldo Hurtado. At his inauguration he wore a presidential band written in the language of the Shuar, a lowland nationality.

The Roldós administration marked a significant departure in cultural policy by emphasizing the pluricultural nature of Ecuador.[12] Roldós allocated substantial funds, either directly, by supporting national and local festivals, dances, and musical performances, or indirectly, through institutions that channeled funds to different cultural events, such as the Casa de la Cultura (House of Culture), the Catholic University of Quito, the Central Bank, and the National Institute of Anthropology.

During the Roldós and Hurtado regimes (1979–84) there was a marked increase in the number of indigenous cultural events, which were promoted or supported by the state (Sánchez-Purga 1988, 76–96). This policy was well received by indigenous activists who were engaged in their own process of cultural recovery as a political strategy (see chap. 6). In a virtual cultural renaissance, Indian music and dance was performed in practically every province. While countless events were provincial or intercommunal, many were national in scope. In addition to festivals and dances, events might have included handicraft workshops and exhibits and special programs dedicated to the recognition and preservation of indigenous cultures (see table 4). Also, the Ministry of Education and Culture commissioned studies on indigenous cultures. For example, in June 1984, the Subsecretariat of Culture, in conjunction with the Anthropology and Linguistic School of Pichincha, initiated research on the vernacular cultures of the country, focusing mainly on lowland and coastal groups. According to the subsecretariat, "[T]he objective of this investigation is to make known the historical and social importance of the existence and evolution of different ethnic pluralities [in Ecuador]."[13]

The cultural renaissance and the rediscovery of popular culture was initiated by the state in conjunction with several sectors of civil society, including academics, NGOs, Indian and non-Indian artists, indigenous organizations,

TABLE 4.
New Festivals and Artistic Events

1981	Festival of San Antonio, Pichincha
1982	Handicraft Festival of Cañar Province
1983	*Ritual of the Solstice of the Sun, Cochasquí, Pichincha
1984	Ceramics Festival, Victoria, Pujilí, Cotopaxi
	National Festival of Authentic Music and Dance
	Festival of Popular Bands, Peguche
1985	Indian Handicraft Festival of Ecuador (held in Otavalo)
	National Encounter of Indian Artisans
	Festival of Indian Nationalities of Ecuador
	International Seminar of Health of the Quichua People
1986	National Festival of Indian Music
	Artisan Exhibit Commemorating the Inti Raimi, or Feast of the Sun
	National Festival of Indian Culture
1987	Festival of Indian Dance and Music of Ingapirca
1988	Encounter of Indian Music

NOTE: This list includes most of the larger festivals initiated in the period between 1981 and 1989 in the highland provinces. It does not include smaller events at the cantonal level, including festivals, dances, plays, and poetry readings. The asterisk indicates no government participation in the funding. Except when specifically described as a provincial event, all these events are interprovincial.

SOURCE: *Kipu* 1983–89.

and students. The latter were among the most active in promoting local dances and music. For example, in Otavalo province in 1985 the Causanacunchic, a cultural workshop, organized a large exhibit and formed liaisons with fifteen cultural groups in the region. These groups were made up mostly of high school and college students interested in reclaiming or recovering their own cultural forms.[14]

The third aspect of legal-cultural policy was the promotion of the legal rights of Indians at the national and international levels. Since the Barbados declaration, the legal guarantee of Indian autonomy and rights was viewed as the necessary condition for the development of indigenous cultures. Given Latin American states' history of infringing on these rights in different ways, neoindigenismo called for a self-conscious state role in securing these rights. However, historically there has been little agreement on what those rights should entail. Main points of contention are land rights (particularly the right to the subsoil), which conflict with property laws in most of the region, and *ley consuetudinaria*, or customary law, which would allow indigenous communities to regulate themselves according to legal precepts and norms different from those practiced by society at large.[15]

The Ecuadorian state held meetings and seminars during the 1980s to discuss the legal rights and socioeconomic status of Indians. One of the most important was a 1984 seminar organized by the Ministry of Social Welfare's OAI called "State Policy and Indigenous Population," designed to evaluate state policy regarding Indian populations and to create new conditions that would lead to their economic and social improvement. Attendees included representatives of public and private institutions as well as members of indigenous organizations. It was the first national-level meeting planned by the state to discuss indigenous issues.[16]

Public officials, academics, and indigenous activists agreed on strengthening indigenous organizations as a common goal.[17] Scholars and activists pointed out that Indians' own cultural forms, systems of labor, and technologies had not been recognized. There were also discussions on how Indians historically had been discriminated against and marginalized from national decision making. Press coverage of the event was broad, and the proceedings were published. The event played a key role in legitimizing the concerns and demands of new Indian organizations. In addition, state institutions responsible for agricultural policy, such as the IERAC and FODERUMA, conducted several workshops to promote indigenous organization and leadership.[18]

Literacy and Bilingual Literacy: The Early Years

Educational policies initiated in the Roldós government and continued by subsequent governments were the main focus of the pluricultural state, and the main point of contention among indigenous activists who developed an alternative notion of pluticulturalism. Literacy policy provided Indians with the first serious opportunity to participate in the public sphere as Indians and to develop cross-racial coalitions that facilitated the subsequent creation of the CONAIE. Hence the state played a crucial role in the development of the new Indian political identity. The politics of literacy policy shaped the indigenous politics of the subsequent decade, simultaneously encouraging indigenous participation through institutional channels and providing a site in which new ideologies of opposition would develop.

The Roldós regime began a massive literacy campaign that had great impact on the countryside, raising the indigenous literacy level from 30 percent in 1974 to 55 percent in 1982 (Sánchez-Parga 1992). Literacy policy, while implemented broadly throughout the country, consciously focused on bilingual indigenous education as the path to a more profound nationalism and to national development. The pillar of national development was the new notion of an authentically representative Ecuador, envisioned as a unitary nation that could not operate until all its components, particularly the indigenous communities, were developed. The government's National Office of Literacy, located in the Ministry of Education, released a series of documents discussing these goals. Literacy was also seen as having important sociological and political functions. Because it consciously promoted popular participation in the process, it was considered the path to true human liberation that would develop critical individuals who could participate in society and provide alternatives. In this view, literacy was a form of emancipation, because it was considered an essential precondition for significant social change:

> This new type of education, capable of liberating the illiterate man from his state of dependence and alienation, will be based on one basic principle: all and each of us human beings are born free, equal and capable of contributing to the common good.[19]

Literacy was also believed to expand citizenship by allowing its target population to practice its options and participate in political and civil society in ways it had not before. Another government document discusses the concept of participatory literacy as one in which participants take consciousness of their ability to act critically and reflexively on the phenomenon of change and on the transformation of their social, political, and economic environment:

> Those who become literate can lay out alternatives and freely opt for the role they will perform politically.... The social function of literacy is to achieve national integration and popular mobilization in search of the great aspirations for social justice and of the overcoming of the great sociocultural contradictions that exist among the diverse classes or social strata.[20]

This last statement views literacy not only in its more traditional function as social equalizer but also as carrying within it the potential for the eventual socioeconomic improvement of its target population. This discourse had a strong impact on indigenous activists who were becoming involved in the literacy campaign. However, while they also aspired to exercise the deeper and more meaningful citizenship offered in this discourse of literacy, activists would come to believe that this aspiration could only be accomplished under two conditions: if indigenous activists exerted more control over program design and implementation and if literacy policy was complemented with other socioeconomic policies that would offer more resources and opportunities to indigenous communities.

For indigenous activists, literacy was also understood as a space to socialize political knowledge and exert some political control and unity. Indians "saw this as an important factor for the strengthening of ethnic identities, the unification of communities, the discussion of development strategies, in sum for ideological clarification in terms of indigenous autonomy (Santana 1984, 108). Much like Rigoberta Menchú's realization that learning a language could be empowering in itself, enabling ethnic groups to unite and organize, Ecuadorian activists understood the implications that learning language could lead to empowerment by facilitating consciousness-raising and organization (Burgos 1984). A locally produced literacy document in Tungurahua stated that the literacy project was about empowerment as well as education: "Through education one can obtain more power and consciousness, escape one's marginal conditions, and have the same possibilities as the whites."[21]

Program implementation was preceded by a number of unprecedented meetings between state officials and local and national highland organization activists who wanted a decision-making role. Activists had two concerns: ensuring some control over policy and pushing for a broader agenda that included material demands. The first point was established in the initial meetings. These meetings were considered necessary, Santana (1986, 105–6) argues, because the policy itself "did not guarantee the benefits the Indians wanted. . . . [T]hey had to secure that" (Santana 1986, 105–6). In a series of work meetings between the government and Indians between 1979 and 1981, activists took great care to ensure that they were not simply managed from above. They insisted on playing a key role in all national decision making concerning bilingual literacy as well as on local control over the selection of promoters and implementation of policy (Santana 1986).

The second concern was made clear in a subsequent national encounter. In 1979 the government organized the National Encounter of Aboriginal Cultures, Peasant Organizations, and Neighborhood Associations in Colta, Chimborazo, with the purpose of creating the Instituto de Culturas Aborigenes y Acción Comunitaria (INCAYAC), responsible for governing the administration of literacy. Public officials were surprised when indigenous activists asked to expand the agenda. Activists stated that any cultural policy designed to benefit peasants could not be conceived at the margins of reality and had to incorporate land and rural development issues into discussions of literacy (*Nueva*, December 1980, 72). Literacy would be meaningless, they argued, if it was not accompanied by policies that ensured socioeconomic improvement. Activists also wanted the institute to be autonomous and directed by indigenous organizations (in lieu of coadministration with government officials), claiming that this arrangement would enable them to pressure for solutions to land, education, health, and housing problems. None of these recommendations were accepted, and the activists refused to cooperate with a government that did not want to grant them more autonomy. The INCAYAC project was soon suspended, and several smaller meetings that followed were limited to negotiating the terms of literacy implementation that would satisfy state officials and activists.

The activists' efforts to incorporate socioeconomic demands into the government's cultural agenda was an important political consequence of the politics of double consciousness in which the classic concerns of campesinismo and the newer concerns for cultural demands could not be separated. It was evident that the new Indian organizations had not dropped the old demands of campesinista organizations, but they had rearticulated and integrated them into the indianista agenda. The material concerns, expressed in the demand for socioeconomic rights, made it difficult for the government to confine its Indian policy to literacy and education.

Another occasion on which indigenous activists' agenda encountered the state's occurred on April 14–18, 1980, at the government-sponsored Nueva Vida (New Life) Seminar, at which dozens of indigenous activists from throughout Ecuador met to codify the Quichua alphabet. Nueva Vida was important on several levels. Despite its obvious limitations as a government-controlled event, it demonstrated the state's willingness to include indigenous people in the literacy agenda. More important, it presented a unique opportunity for indigenous activists to develop ties with activists from other provinces. Before Nueva Vida, many activists had not been exposed to their cohorts in other parts of the country or participated in a national-level dialogue with high-level officials. Activists attending the seminar demanded full representation on the National Council of Literacy, community election of local promoters, and indigenous selection of promoters. They also demanded the right to Quichua names for their children in the civil registry and the elimination of the state-mandated use of Spanish-language names. For use in Quichua readers, they chose the Spanish-language alphabet as opposed to the English-language alphabet proposed by the Catholic University of Quito's Institute for Indigenous Education.[22] In addition, they asked for resolution of land problems and expulsion of the Summer Institute of Linguistics.

After extensive discussion, public officials and activists reached agreement: activists were granted some power over local administration of policy. The local selection of literacy promoters by indigenous organizations and some indigenous participation in the national and provincial literacy programs, the use of Quichua in the civil registry, and the expulsion of the SIL were approved by the government; the autonomy of the literacy council and indigenous control over national program design and implementation were not. Of these concessions, the first ones were important victories that allowed indigenous educators and activists to play a central role in the local administration of bilingual literacy. However, the socioeconomic demands that would have given literacy policy a material dimension were removed from the table.

Nueva Vida thus marks the beginning of an unwritten and tenuous pact between the state and activists that excluded demands for economic empowerment while allowing for some local ownership of literacy policies. For Indian activists, there was tension between participating in governmental incorporation and continued engagement in resistance, as this pact clearly contained its own contradictions. In an effort to generate popular support for its literacy program, the state had forcefully laid out the politically liberating and economically empowering potential of literacy, especially in terms of its ability to raise social consciousness and enable individuals to develop social alternatives and in so doing expanding their own citizenship. In the negotiation process, however, the state sought to divest cultural policy of political content, dematerializing neoindigenismo and claiming that education and language policy alone were part of a specific "cultural" public sphere in which broader political and economic demands did not have a place (Ibarra 1992). Although literacy policy was designed to stimulate critical thinking, as far as the state was concerned, there was only one correct way of thinking about literacy policy.

However, while the state was still ignoring most of their socioeconomic demands, the unprecedented opportunity to participate in national educational policy could not be dismissed. The unofficial pact between the state and indigenous activists sidestepped not only campesinista politics but also much of the political agenda that campesinismo had considered central and that remained a major concern of indigenous activists. It cannot be explained, however, as the mere co-optation of an indigenous sector that was ridden with false consciousness and "blinded" by the neoindigenista practice of a monolithic state, as Ibarra (1992) suggests. Instead, it reveals (1) the complexity of state practices that led to an opening of institutional channels in some policy areas and the closing in others and (2) the ability of indigenous activists to use state discourse and policies to gain some access to the state and self-empowerment, despite the obvious constraints. Both the state and movement activists, in a dialectical fashion, were involved in the creation, negotiation, and re-creation of concepts and policies. Both, I would argue, had something to gain from this arrangement.

Despite the limitations, activists' experiences with the literacy project and related cultural policy benefited indigenous organizing on two counts. First, they facilitated the politicization of the indigenous grassroots throughout the highlands and lowlands. At the local level, for example, intercommunal organizations strengthened their relationship with communities as they became responsible for implementing the education policy. The state's effort to foreclose mediation by labor and the Left gave scores of grassroots activists the opportunity to engage directly in political negotiations with the state. Moreover, literacy projects enabled local leaders to develop their political bases, recruiting new cadres, expanding their sense of citizenship, politicizing themselves and others in the process.[23]

Second, literacy policy was a new arena in which agendas pertaining to political autonomy and antiracism could be discussed and put into practice. Political autonomy referred to autonomy from local authorities as well as from the Left. It encompassed the practice of communal justice and indigenous communities' selection of their own public officials, a goal that with few exceptions had not been achieved. Activists considered the local selection of literacy promoters and their increasing control over program administration necessary for their independence from all political parties, state bureaucrats, and nonindigenous teachers. Nueva Vida activists stipulated that literacy promoters had to be Indians. This displaced many mestizos who had initially been appointed and eventually led to conflict with the teachers' union, Union Nacional de Educadores (UNE), made up mostly of mestizos. While the main argument for Quichua teachers in the highlands was that they would be better able to develop course material that validated indigenous culture, a subsidiary argument was that mestizo teachers could not and were not willing to take indigenous students seriously or to be responsible for the bilingual and bicultural nature of the education they were seeking.

A literacy program under some local indigenous control also provided an unprecedented opportunity to address racial discrimination, affirm a panethnic racial identity, and create an imagined community. Despite the differences in language and curriculum across ethnicities, the literacy projects promoted national Indian unity. They forced activists to address what an "Indian" education should be, what general components it should have to be effective, and what common identifications and generalizations one could draw across ethnicities in the design of a general curriculum that was conscious of economic realities. In this process pre-Columbian origins and history, the common history of colonization and oppression, the five-hundred-year commemoration, and the teaching of alternative Indian history and models of thought were all common themes discussed nationally and locally and incorporated in curricula.

Finally, the acquisition of the "secret knowledge of writing" as the historian Galo Ramón (1993) refers to it, was considered indispensable for indigenous empowerment, because it allowed access to institutions that had excluded them. Literacy, and the knowledge and skills that would follow from it, would enable indigenous communities to do their own accounting and resolve their own civil and legal problems, instead of relying on often distrusted mestizo mediators. This in turn would diminish the probability of abuses such as inaccurate weighing and accounting by mestizos in the market and unequal treatment in the judicial system and public offices. It would also undermine the racial construction of the Indians as ignorant illiterates.

Hence although the tacit pact meant temporary neglect of material claims and little access to political institutions and processes that went beyond local policy implementation, local control over literacy policy led to important grassroots gains for the indigenous movement. It provided a space for the education and political maturation of local and national indigenous activists (many of whom started out as literacy educators), and for the politicization of hundreds of indigenous communities that would later participate in massive mobilizations. As I explain below, it also provided an arena for indigenous educators and activists to push for more access to national power.

Bilingual and Bicultural Education: The Second Phase

The National Literacy Program initiated by Roldós and continued by Hurtado declined considerably during the Febres-Cordero regime. Rodrigo Borja's campaign and presidency marked an important transition, as he expressed a renewed commitment to indigenous affairs. Indigenous support for Borja's candidacy followed an intense campaign by the Izquierda Democrática to win the indigenous vote. Chiriboga and Rivera (1989) show overwhelming support for the ID in the rural highlands, in areas with a large indigenous population. While the Febres-Cordero regime had brought a hiatus to the program, the Borja administration (1988–92) began a new literacy campaign and continued bilingual education.

In 1988 the state gave national indigenous organizations substantial control of bilingual and bicultural education. Borja directed the campaign specifically at Indians and called it the Monseñor Leonidas Proaño Literacy Campaign, after the liberation theologist and bishop from Chimborazo province. Also in 1988, after significant CONAIE pressure, the Ministry of Education signed an agreement with the CONAIE that established the Dirección Nacional de Educación Intercultural Bilingue (DINEIB), to be administered by the CONAIE. Housed in the Ministry of Education and Culture, DINEIB has a primarily indigenous staff and serves the dual purpose of managing literacy and bilingual education projects.

This event marked the acme of the state's pluricultural agenda, as well as indigenous empowerment. The state's open promotion of pluriculturalism through education was unprecedented in giving Indian organizations the lead in implementing education, what had so far eluded rural development projects, despite the anti-integrationist, pro–alternative development rhetoric often used by state officials. Indigenous activists' input into curricula at the national and local levels as well as their attainment of leadership positions in the national and provincial bilingual education coordinating offices were perhaps the most important gains of the educational policy enacted since redemocratization. Even as Indians continued to be excluded from decision-making bodies at large and from leadership positions in agricultural policy, educational policy was the site where mestizo hegemony had been broken. The vehement protests of the UNE, which cried racism when mestizo educators were replaced by indigenous ones, as well as countless disputes between mestizo and Indian educators over control evidence a significant disruption of social norms and expectations.

But transferring the directorship to the CONAIE also laid bare the limit of indigenous power. To an extent, the politics of cultural policy had been exhausted as a site of empowerment and political growth for activists. It had legitimized a pluricultural agenda and met some basic indigenous demands but failed to go far enough. The other issues in their agenda, which had been dismissed by the state almost a decade earlier, had not been forgotten. The gap between the implementation of cultural policy and the absence of significant social policy and economic redistribution became the basis for a critique that would take the movement to a new stage.

LAUNCHING A CRITIQUE: WHOSE PLURICULTURALISM?

By the late 1980s, state pluriculturalism had become institutionalized. Although the new policies had facilitated the creation of an indigenous class from which new leaders emerged and had increased the educational level of many rural Ecuadorians, they were not accompanied by an improvement in the socioeconomic status of the majority of Indians. In fact, as Rosero (1990) has shown, indigenous people's standard of living decreased substantially during the 1980s. By the mid-1980s the CONAIE and ECUARUNARI had begun to express dissatisfaction with the general direction of state pluricultural policy. Three sets of criticism were evident.

First, cultural policy was considered suspect because it could lead to the the manipulation and folklorization of indigenous culture. Activists often discussed their concerns about state-guided historical and cultural preservation that might lead to the objectification of indigenous culture and Indians themselves. Moreover, the preservation of culture and the handicraft programs designed to market it led some activists to claim they were being used for profit in the guise of pursuing pluriculturalism. As early as 1983

CONACNIE had charged that the CIEI, which had been the primary recipient of public funds to address cultural issues, was actually engaged in the systematic control and penetration of indigenous organizations. In a May 6, 1983, letter to President Hurtado the organization wrote:

> We cannot conceive that this government continues to consider indigenous people as an object of investigation and experimentation as it has been doing with bilingual education. Programs fail because the government does not listen to our proposals. The CIEI is outside the reality of Indian communities.[24]

Hence, for most national activists, all cultural policy was a site of political struggle, and vigilance was of utmost importance. In addition to written critiques, some activists staged alternative cultural events designed to present Indians' own representation of themselves, maintaining some autonomy from state-funded programs. Such was the case of the Causanacunchic, a cultural workshop organized by students in Otavalo who wanted to ensure that indigenous cultural production was not appropriated by others. In one declaration they stated that they were there to defend their aboriginal culture, "which has not been valued or respected. . . . [I]t has been taken advantage of by whites [to be used] as folklore for tourists."[25] In the same province, Otavalo activists refused for a few years to participate in the Yamor festival because they believed it had been appropriated by the mestizo population of the city.

Second, indigenous organizations complained about the lack of indigenous control over policy. The fear was that the very programs designed to assist Indians would also serve to control them, either by depriving indigenous leaders of autonomous decision-making power, by dividing indigenous organizations through favoring one over the other, or by using educational and cultural policy to gain indigenous support for the political party in power.[26]

Despite obtaining control over the administration of bilingual education, indigenous activists realized that they still lacked access to broader political power that would enable them to have more meaningful input in pluricultural policy generally. The new pockets of political gain could not erase or significantly diminish the political effects of a polity in which Indians were grossly underrepresented outside of education policy. In 1985, for example, there was one Indian from the highlands in Congress.[27] There were no Indians in the higher levels of ministry bureaucracies or at the executive level in national or provincial politics. Further, there had never been an Indian mayor even in cantons with a large Indian population. Indian municipal council members were rare, but there were usually no more than two per council, elected sporadically in cantons in Imbabura and Loja provinces.[28] Most local tenientes políticos were not Indian, even in parishes with an overwhelming Indian majority. The lack of political representation and power at all levels of government made it difficult, even for the best-intentioned national bureaucrats, to guarantee Indian activists any amount of political control at the local or national level.

The final complaint about state pluriculturalism was the exclusion of material demands from the agenda of cultural policy. It highlighted the limitations of a policy approach that sought to protect cultures without improving their lives, assuming that education in itself was sufficient for long-term rural development. Often the three types of complaints would be condensed in one declaration or statement, such as this one made by ECUARUNARI in 1984:

> The current government and the bourgeoisie in its totality do not consider our rights and needs globally. The bourgeoisie says that the culture and language of the Indian must be rescued, but they deny our right to land. They speak of national integration but they integrate us into capitalism as proletariats and semiproletariats. They use our right to literacy and education as a mechanism of control and division of peasant organizations.[29]

Part of the problem was the existence of two very different perspectives on what culture was and what constituted cultural politics. For state officials, pluriculturalism was sufficiently embodied in educational and cultural policy and upheld in theory by adhering to international law. For indigenous activists, there was a three-part component to pluriculturalism: cultural rights, economic rights (including land), and political empowerment. They feared that while the first component was being addressed to a certain extent, the latter two were not addressed sufficiently or at all. Further, they feared that the mechanisms used to implement the first were undermining the others.

Two organizations, ECUARUNARI and the CONAIE, were most influential in these critiques. First, ECUARUNARI was hesitant to join a national coalition because it feared traditional class issues would be abandoned. The six years between the creation of the CONACNIE and the creation of the CONAIE had been dedicated to resolving the tensions between organizations of different regions and ideological tendencies. The central issue, as evidenced in the campesinista/indianista debate, was whether indigenous activists should organize as peasants or as Indians. ECUARUNARI members had felt that abandoning their class identity as peasants meant abandoning basic demands for land and rural development, whereas highland and lowland indianistas felt that the neglect of their cultural specificity had led to their subordination in the ranks of the Left. The many years of disagreement and debate led to acceptance of a dual identity in which both class and ethnicity could be claimed. In addition, it led to the development of a new language in which to incorporate material and cultural concerns into one agenda. Culture was redefined to include not only artistic production and language but also a way of life, an economic rationale, a system of law, and the right to territory.

By the 1986 CONACNIE congress, land, education, and tradition were all considered cultural manifestations. The new understanding of land as both cultural and material was internalized by national activists and was a central point in the declarations preceding and following the 1990 uprising. Many national and provincial organization documents argue that land is the indispensable and necessary condition for the life, health, education, and development of Indian communities and for the reproduction of indigenous cultures:

> The difference between us and the peasants is that our struggle is cultural as well, in the sense that we have a proposal that views land as community, and then land as nationality.[30]

> We believe that there will be no solution to the Indian problem unless there is a solution to the land problem. The recuperation of our land is essential. (Macas 1991, 10)

For these activists, a cultural struggle meant conceptualizing the demand for land as cultural, not as neglecting or superseding the demand for land. In this conception, the term *pluriculturalism* represented, as stated in the Barbados declaration, a critique of land dispossession and a belief that respect for indigenous cultures was respect for and defense of land rights and for the economic empowerment of indigenous peoples. The bridges that were built between lowland and highland indianistas and highland campesinistas during the 1980s were possible because of common agreement, by the late 1980s, that there was no strict dichotomy between material and cultural demands. In this new perspective, there was a cultural dimension to all material needs and demands, and cultural issues and policy could not be separated from the material needs of the population. The notion of a pluricultural nation, which for the state meant artistic festivals and bilingual education, conveyed a much broader set of goals for activists.

The difference between this conception of pluriculturalism and the conception of state officials became evident in congressional debates about approval of the International Labor Organization's Convention 169, concerning the protection of indigenous nationalities. As Borja's minister of labor, Cesar Verduga took Ecuador's position to the ILO in 1989. Following a modified version of the language first posited in Barbados, Ecuador proposed that all states recognize in their legislation their pluriethnicity and seek to legalize the recognition of Indian pueblos with their own forms of social organization and self-development. In addition, Ecuador stated that the document should include the guarantee and respect of Indians' integrity and social and cultural identity, their customs, traditions, and institutions.[31]

From the start, this proposal met with opposition within the administration. According to Verduga, it was opposed by several members of the Ministry of Labor who could not understand why Ecuador would become involved in this proposal, and much less cling to such a radical thesis.[32] Although Congress was in agreement with most of the treaty's points concerning recognition of ethnocultural diversity, education, preservation of identity, and territory (as long as the subsoil was not included), it did not approve the accord because it considered the defense of indigenous law and customs unconstitutional.[33] Indigenous activists continued to push for the ratification of Convention 169, and it was finally approved in 1997.

The effort had two important effects. First, it showed indigenous organizations that the executive branch was significantly more open to their claims than the legislative branch. While Indian organizations had relied more on Congress during the Febres-Cordero regime, in the Borja presidency they relied more on the presidency.[34] Staging of the first national uprising a year after congressional repeal of Convention 169, according to several activists interviewed, was a calculated risk, based on their two-year experience with an executive branch they predicted, quite accurately, would be relatively tolerant and more prone to negotiation than repression.

Second, the ILO experience revealed Congress's interpretation of what was meant by pluriculturalism and, more important, what was not: territory, as long as it did not include the subsoil; and legal rights, as long as these did not include Indian customary law. Moreover, even without the subsoil, territory and land remained an unmet demand, as little significant land distribution had occurred since the late 1970s.[35] In this light, a state that was claiming to protect and promote pluriculturalism but set aside land reform demands and actively promoted colonization and the incursion of transnationals in the rainforest was not perceived by activists as pluricultural or democratic. Hence, despite the significant gains in cultural policy, by the mid-1980s many regional organizations as well as the CONAIE were claiming that culture—as defined by the state—consisted of an excessively reduced agenda.

These initial critiques and the consolidation of a common front marked the beginning of a transition to extrainstitutional politics. It was clear from the CONAIE's 1986 decision to call for indigenous abstention from elections that the official realm of politics had disappointed most activists, particularly many of those who had been directly involved with the design and implementation of educational policy and other state efforts.

FROM CRITIQUE TO DISRUPTION: THE POLITICS OF NATIONALISM AND DEMOCRACY IN THE 1990 UPRISING

> The Ecuadorian state, following the principle of the French revolution, one state, one nation, conceives of Ecuador as a homogeneous country in which all are equal, [and] no differences exist. It is clear that the only ones who enjoy that equality [are] the dominant white-mestizo classes. They appropriated the millenarian historical and cultural legacy of the indigenous civilizations. Paradoxically, the pueblos indígenas are negated, hidden, and persecuted.[36]

The transition from institutional to extrainstitutional, or uprising, politics occurred when national and provincial activists had more power than they ever had before and yet were more certain that the majority of their demands would not be met through regular channels. Moreover, the Borja administration's neoindigenista rhetoric and the yielding of bilingual education control to the CONAIE led activists to think that this government would be more willing to negotiate than to engage in massive repression.

In June 1990 the massive national uprising symbolized the exhaustion of pluricultural politics as usual. The sixteen-point platform presented by the CONAIE included education and cultural rights but also demanded land and improvements in rural development and the cost of living. The scope of these demands and the central place of material demands indicated a general unwillingness of leadership at all levels to be relegated to the cultural realm, as it had been conceived by the state. While traditionally cultural issues such as respect for culture, the right to practice medicine, and the right to speak and learn in native languages were included, it was clear to the CONAIE and eventually to government officials that land was the central and long-neglected concern.

The demand for land clearly clashed with the state's policy. The first negotiations, which involved the CONAIE, ECUARUNARI, and the CONFENIAE, were difficult: Indian leaders had a long list of land conflicts that had not been resolved in years. Initially the government wanted these issues to be addressed by the Ministry of Agriculture alone, but leaders refused, claiming the ministry was dominated by landowning interests. In December the CONAIE withdrew from the negotiations, claiming that the government did not want to address land issues. After accusations that internal divisions had created a rift, the CONAIE announced that it was indeed united and with church intervention went back to the negotiation table. Finally, it was agreed that fifty-six land conflicts would be resolved; most of the other demands were set aside for future discussion. Negotiations after this point involved local and national leaders and dealt with the minutiae of resolving each land case.

The ability to get some major long-standing land conflicts addressed if not resolved was a significant gain and made the uprising more than symbolic. Early negotiations rested on the common understanding that land and local political empowerment would be the main points of discussion. While many activists since have complained about how other points of the platform were not addressed, the negotiation of land cases marked the direction of policy for many years to come and ended the belief that mere "cultural" policy would be sufficient.

The focus on material demands was accompanied by a quest for more political empowerment and self-determination. In July 1990 the already vulnerable relationship between the CONAIE and the state was complicated further when the CONAIE presented a declaration written by the OPIP titled "Agreement concerning the Territorial Rights of the Indian Peoples of Pastaza." This document called for recognition of land rights, self-rule, political autonomy, respect for customs, and Indian participation in decisions concerning oil exploration on Indian lands. It also opposed military intervention in indigenous people's affairs, asking for the revision of military statutes. With regard to self-determination, the document stated:

> Self-determination and autonomy of the Indian pueblos is also a principle consecrated in international law and should be applied by the state, especially if it declares itself a plurinational and multiethnic country.... This implies the self-government of the peoples.[37]

This proposal combined demands for socioeconomic improvement and political autonomy in an agenda that prioritized self-determination, autonomy, and territorial rights. Although the government had been willing to discuss economic demands, political demands, particularly self-determination, seemed out of the question. When President Borja met with national Indian activists, he categorically rejected the proposal, accusing Indians of threatening national sovereignty by attempting to create a parallel state. He proceeded to lecture the Indians on constitutional law. "You are simply an Indian community inserted in national territory. You have to respect me, because I am the president of Ecuador," Borja stated.[38] He informed them that they could have land rights but not sovereignty.

He reviewed the main points of the document, stating that self-government meant the creation of a parallel state and secession of Pastaza province; that upholding traditional law meant the suppression of Ecuadorian law and of the administrative state; and that the rejection of military involvement in indigenous affairs suggested Indians' desire for absolute withdrawal of the military from the area. In August 1990 Minister of Government Gonzalo Ortiz Crespo stated:

> The indigenous may not use the textual words "a parallel state," but all their proposals imply the creation of such a state. This means autonomy, self-government, and self-determination in the soil and subsoil,

the retreat of the armed forces, and the suppression of Ecuadorian law in this territory. All this added together is the creation of a parallel state. We cannot discuss these proposals because in doing so we would be violating the Ecuadorian constitution and working against national sovereignty.[39]

Unable to speak during the meeting, CONAIE activists responded via the press. They defended their document, claiming that it had been misread and misinterpreted. Self-determination, they claimed, merely implied the recognition of the law of customs, which already existed in fact; that Indian participation in decisions regarding oil extraction and profit did not mean depriving the state of its rights to a rational and controlled exploitation; and that it was not denying the military's right to be there. On each count, however, they were on the defensive, denying even the most basic aspects of what had indeed been some of their major tenets. Clearly, activists had not believed that the declaration would be heeded, but they had hoped to pressure the state to engage in negotiation.

The president's statements about the proposal had a broader societal effect. Other popular movements as well as sectors of the Left also warned against the threat this movement presented to national sovereignty. There was no political support for the OPIP proposal outside of the CONAIE, and in most governmental and political circles it was overwhelmingly rejected. Several politicians and congressmen stated their rejection of this position publicly. Many intellectuals and analysts began to claim that the Indians had gone too far. For members of the Chamber of Agriculture and of the military forces, this incident confirmed that their warnings had been on target.

The short-term effect was disruption of the negotiation process, which would not resume until the following year. There was one important long-term effect, however, that curtailed the CONAIE's likelihood of pursuing a nationalist agenda: the state's refusal to discuss Indian empowerment at the national level, whether through representation in national institutions or changes in the law. Borja's "we will give you land, not sovereignty" reflected which "Indians" the state was willing to accept (those with specific economic demands) and which it would not (those seeking political autonomy). This put indigenous activists in an untenable position, because economic and political demands were often intertwined and were both key parts of their agenda. True to his word, When the OPIP's and the CONAIE's lowland march was held in 1992 between Puyo and Quito, the government guaranteed the Indians 1,115,000 hectares but rejected the demand that Ecuador be considered a pluricultural country. Several months later, when it was proposed as a constitutional amendment to Congress, it was also rejected.

This rejection indicates that by 1992, the state was not only aware of this competing notion of pluriculturalism but was actively engaged in containing it. While the state had embraced a pluricultural model in the 1980s, it did not bear much resemblance to the model presented to it by indigenous activists in the 1990s. Indigenous activists had appropriated state discourse in order to transform it. The indigenous movement's struggle for its own version of pluriculturalism had provided a new framework of meaning, rendering the discursive and political fields more complex and making previously "safe" terms into points of contention.

In this new framework, Ecuador was seen by activists not only as a pluricultural state but also as a *plurinational* one. If the state's reaction to indigenous resistance was to shy away from pluriculturalism, activists' response was to press for the more radical notion of plurinationalism, expressed in the 1992 lowland march to Puyo and subsequent demonstrations and declarations. Indigenous activists rejected the categorization as ethnic groups or cultures and defined themselves instead as nationalities. Through this definition, activists sought to give political and economic substance to what had been considered primarily ideological or superstructural by the state. Plurinationalism seemed to capture as well as wed the material and political dimensions that the state had ignored in order to offer a critique of the nation. Plurinationalism did not originate as a secessionist movement but as a strategic response to state negligence of political and material concerns that were central to activists. This was a representation of Ecuador that was diametrically opposed to the construction of Ecuador as a mestizo, homogeneous, and unitary nation-state. The reaction of state officials and civil society to this new concept (mainly to what they imagined the concept to be rather than to actual formulations of it developed and openly manifested by activists) reveal the limitations of state conceptions of pluriculturalism as well as the distances between indigenous and nonindigenous popular sectors' relationship to the polity.

The discrepancy between the state's and indigenous organizations' understanding of pluriculturalism was not a mere semantic one, but needs to be understood in its political context. While difference in customs, dress, traditions, and political and social organization were signifiers of pluriculturalism, it was the struggle for economic demands and political empowerment that embodied it. Indians' decision to demand plurinationalism and not pluriculturalism was the direct result of a decade of cultural policy in which the distance between the state's use of culture and the activists' understanding of culture was not breached. While many activists had not completely worked out the details of their plurinational platform, what was clear was that it consisted of something distinct from the pluricultural policy pursued by the state and that it could not be subsumed under the rubric of cultural rights and preservation of history, folklore, and education. It had to include the substance and the effects, not only the signs, of ethnic and racial difference. Because the idea of plurinationalism problematized the dominant construction of nation, these early conceptualizations of nationalism contained a critique of the notion of a homogeneous nation and an attempt to reveal the underlying power relations of the Ecuadorian nation-state. As early as 1985, an ECUARUNARI declaration stated:

> The Ecuadorian nation is not a stable community. It is kept by force. It was not historically formed with the consent and will of all the national sectors and the originary pueblos. It appropriates our history to justify its existence, [and] the historical elements that should constitute it are destroyed.... [I]n conclusion, the Ecuadorian nation does not exist. It exists through the law of the dominator, by force. Therefore, neither the state nor the Ecuadorian political experience represents all the pueblos and social classes but only the exploiter and the oppressor.[40]

There is a link between the critique of homogeneous nationalism and the lack of democracy. Ecuador, as a "homogeneous nation," could never be democratic because it had to impose itself by force. The statement that "neither the state nor the Ecuadorian experience represents all the people" establishes a relationship between democracy and plurinationalism and also provides a broader political justification for the Indian movement: it serves the interests of all citizens. The legal incorporation of plurinationalism became, in this view, a precondition of justice for all.

CONCLUSION

The Indian movements' concept of plurinationalism was negotiated and contested in the process of resistance. There was a dialectical relationship between the politics of nationalism developed by movement activists and the culturalist policy promoted by the state. The pluricultural platform adopted by the state simultaneously incorporated indigenous organizations and elicited a more critical response that demanded that pluriculturalism include economic rights and political autonomy.

The partial recognition of material demands that went far beyond cultural and educational policies implemented to date is the most important policy effect of the national Indian movement. This was not the result of further concessions by state officials in the course of everyday politics but of pressure from the extraordinary politics of activists in the national 1990 and 1994 uprisings and the 1992 lowland march. Mobilization and disruption pushed the indigenous agenda forward and sensitized civil society as well as international actors to the long-standing demands of lowland and highland activists.

However, as these material demands were being addressed, it became clear to activists that the recognition of indigenous citizenship and further access to political power would take much longer. The state's rejection of plurinationalism did not constitute a simple rhetorical move. It had practical effects, enabling state officials to ignore crucial questions of political empowerment at the national level. In the state's view, no discussions of empowerment with Indians were possible, because they had proven themselves incapable of respecting the nation-state.[41] Hence the exchange between indigenous activists and the state after the OPIP proposal shaped and constrained future state policy and movement activism, despite both actors' adherence to a pluricultural Ecuador.

How can we explain the mixed effects of indigenous mobilization? In her study of Peruvian peasant women, Radcliffe (1993) discusses the relationship between peasant women's political protest and the state. She argues that while certain "femininities" are considered acceptable, others are repressed. In the case of Peru, the state had promoted the image of the Indian fighter Micaela Bastides alongside the image of Tupac Amaru during a land reform campaign in the 1970s. It later repressed that image, opting instead to promote the image of women as mothers. Policy was only targeted to women insofar as it addressed their role as mothers. Women who wanted to be seen as workers and were struggling for land and loan rights used the Micaela Bastides image in their struggle to oppose the "woman as mother" image.

Likewise, in the Ecuadorian case, much of the leadership's concepts and ideologies were inspired by state discourse on pluriculturalism, popular culture, and Indian rights. President Borja himself had made many previous declarations in which he described Ecuador as a plurinational country, and Minister Verduga had proposed Indian territorial rights at the International Labor Organization meeting. The OPIP document's interpretation of that language two years later, however, was vehemently rejected, and the image of the Indian, or "Indianity," that was being articulated (as autonomous and self-governing) was rejected. The accepted Indianity revealed the limitations of state pluriculturalism. It was an Indianity in which the state was open to certain material demands, as Indians were equated with poor peasants who merited land concessions but not political power. As Borja stated in 1990 in a speech in Azuay province on the opening of an electricity project that would benefit Indian communities:

> There are a few Indian agitators who do not have a job, who do not use tools to work the land, who do not get up early as you do, who don't sweat or care for the cows, but who support themselves by exploiting the Indians in the field.... [T]he peasants and Indians must not be fooled by these agitators who do not feel their problems, and my government is willing to lend a hand, in solidarity, to solve in a peaceful manner the problems of education, housing, sewage and electricity.[42]

Mobilized Indians, politicized Indians, were viewed as agitators, or *indios alzados*, unworthy of state support and constructed as beings who were distinct from the deserving, working Indians who were vulnerable to their enticements. The effect is to deny most indigenous citizens political identity or political agency. By rendering hardworking indigenous peoples vulnerable to false agitators, the state underscored its own role as protector of indigenous peoples and guardian of their affairs and resources. Hence Indians were a group targeted as recipients of aid, but the extent to which they could practice their citizenship was questioned and even curtailed. They were still not seen as equal participants in legal, economic, and political decision making. In this context, the nationalist Indianity constructed by activists was judged a threat to Ecuadorian nationalism and sovereignty.

This discourse on nationalities and plurinationalism gained strength and legitimacy as a critique of the state's corporatism and neoindigenista approach and as a more viable alternative for social and political organization. The development of a nationalist platform was met with effective state resistance expressed in coercion and co-optation but most important, with constructions of the movement as antinational. Although the state promoted some forms of Indianness, it rejected others that were considered too radical. Although activists continued to use nationalist rhetoric, they were forced to downplay the plurinationalism platform and rely on other strategies. The tensions and differences between pluriculturalism, as defined and exercised by the state, and plurinationalism, as conceptualized by indigenous activists, shaped Indian collective identity and forms of resistance throughout the 1990s.

CHAPTER EIGHT

INDIANS IN THE PUBLIC SPHERE

*Comparative Reflections on
the Negotiation of Difference*

The creation of a new Indian political identity was produced by changes in the economic, political, and racial structures of post–land reform Ecuador, as well as by changes in the political consciousness of indigenous activists engaged in resistance. This interaction of both factors, the macropolitical and the micropolitical, prompted massive local and national mobilization. The new political economy, the new state, and new forms of racial consciousness also served to create a new framework of political meaning, in which campesinista concepts and approaches were questioned and abandoned, while the substance of some basic material demands was rearticulated in a new indianista platform.

On studying the politicization of Indian identity and the transition from campesinismo to indianismo, I am left with this question: How does this matter? In other words, how have these new political identities, organizational forms, and ideological constructs transformed the politics of struggle and the ways in which the scholarly community studies them? I would argue that this development has important implications for the study of indigenous politics, Latin American politics, and social theory.

The relevance of this book for the study of indigenous politics is fourfold, as it sheds light on four main features of many contemporary indigenous movements throughout the world: (1) a broad agenda with ideological flexibility, (2) the negotiation of political coalitions with non-Indians, (3) the plight of double consciousness, and (4) continuous reliance on the politics of disruption.

One of the most notable differences between indianismo and campesinismo is the fact that the former is a broad ideological construct that has a specific frame of reference and a general agenda, but does not purport to be either ideologically rigorous or follow a specific revolutionary path, as many leftist organizations do. While antiracism and the struggle for political empowerment, socioeconomic survival, and cultural recovery are objectives shared by most in the movement, and there are some basic strategic guidelines that activists follow, there are no detailed blueprints describing how this must be accomplished in Ecuador or in the region.

This characteristic has often made the indigenous movement the target of campesinista and other leftist groups that complain it is not ideologically or politically consistent. However, it is also the characteristic that has afforded the movement the most flexibility and strategic versatility, as well as promoted the allegiance of a variety of social movements, political actors, religious organizations, NGOS, and local movements. It is precisely because indianismo is so porous that it can be many things to many different people and can mobilize local movements as disparate as the ones in Cacha and Cotacachi. This flexibility has allowed indianismo to inspire and inform a national movement whose scope far outweighs any previous campesinista efforts to obtain national indigenous unity. Like other minority movements, this umbrella-like quality of indianismo is derived in great part from the fact that it relies primarily on racial consciousness and racial solidarity as the glue that holds activists and their constituencies together.

However, the breadth and flexibility of this movement also has drawbacks, as no movement can be all things to all people. The ambitious panethnic and almost panideological national movement has been vulnerable to rupture and must be constantly reinforced and sustained. There are deeply embedded differences in the movement, and regional, ideological, class, and religious divides have been sources of tension and dispute. In addition to potential fragmentation, the success of indianismo can also render the organizations that promoted mobilization unnecessary. We saw this in the the case of Cotacachi: the organization lost its role as organizer of elections once an Indian who was not from the organization became mayor. In addition, the CONAIE's rhetoric and symbolism have been appropriated by other organizations. This tendency of other groups to claim Indianness and question the CONAIE's representativeness can be attributed to an extraneous or symbolic effect of indianismo. While the positive valuation of Indianness and the subsequent national political mobilization are due in great part to the consistent work of the CONAIE's national activists and regional and provincial affiliates, the symbolic success of this project has permeated local organizations throughout the country. As the cases of Cacha and more particularly of Cotacachi have shown, local activists can be informed and inspired by indianista ideologies and ascribe to a political identification as Indians without being affiliated with the organization.

This symbolic effect has political consequences. First, despite its privileged position as the main representative of Indians in negotiations with the state, the CONAIE's monopoly on the "Indian voice" is often questioned by parallel organizations, evangelical groups, and campesinista organizations. Second, the growth of organizations that claim an Indian identification while not sharing an ideological affinity with the CONAIE has in some cases been promoted by the state; in other cases, these organizations have been targeted for state-funded development projects, Cacha being a notable example. Further, the popular resonance of Indian identity may lead not only to a fragmentation of indigenous movements but also to an individuation of Indianness, that is, to an adoption of a positive valuation of Indianness without any accompanying collective mobilization. This, perhaps, is an unavoidable consequence for social movements that have achieved some level of ideological and political success. Nevertheless, students of indigenous politics must also examine how this popularization and individuation of indigenous identity may affect indigenous political identity and mobilization in the future.

Another feature that is reproduced in other indigenous movements is the reliance on coalitions with non-Indians. This may not seem logical, as this book explains how national indigenous activists sought ideological and organizational autonomy from the Left. This autonomy, however, has been followed by the fairly recent establishment of coalitions with other social movements in electoral and protest politics. Yet these new coalitions are quite different from the ones that took place before the consolidation of indianismo. First, they are not constitutive alliances. In other words, social movements and leftist organizations are not involved in the creation of indigenous organizations or in mediation for Indians. Second, the power dynamic among movements is far more equal than it was thirty years ago, and nonindigenous activists would not dream of excluding Indians from their protest plans but rather actively seek them out. Third, Indians no longer have to struggle to have their issues included in a broader agenda, nor do they have to wait their turn. In sum, these coalitions are different because indigenous activists arrived at them from a position of relative strength, having already achieved organizational and ideological autonomy. They are loose networks rather than tight affiliations, and indigenous activists no longer fear being excluded from the process. For example, while the Pachakutik–Nuevo País agenda is designed to represent the needs of all poor Ecuadorians and popular sectors, most of its elected officials are Indians, its electorate is predominantly Indian, and its electoral support depends to a great extent on its ability to struggle for the demands of indigenous organizations. Hence the Ecuadorian experience teaches us that the establishment of separate, autonomous organizations can help disempowered groups to gain political strength vis-à-vis other groups.

Nevertheless, as the Cotacachi experience has shown, these contemporary coalitions are far from perfect. The creation of new interracial coalitions has renewed old questions about autonomy and self-representation, albeit in different ways. This includes questions of equal balance of mestizo and indigenous concerns in the political agenda, of equal power in the party leadership and in negotiations with the state, of nonbetrayal by nonindigenous social movements, and of equal sharing of the risks and benefits of mobilization. While Ecuadorian Indians acknowledge the political need to engage in these coalitions, the history of interracial relations, the reluctance of many political elites to take Indians seriously as political actors, and the persistence of a homogeneous model of the nation-state, despite the important inroads of pluriculturalism, have made them suspicious of interracial coalitions as well as of the actions of indigenous political leaders in Pachakutik–Nuevo País.

The conflicts that can arise in an interracial political party such as Pachakutik–Nuevo País are reminiscent of the debates that most racial minorities have held about whether to participate in interracial parties, create an exclusively race-based party, or participate in elections at all. Each of these options can present opportunities as well as limitations. The CONAIE went from abstention from elections to participating in an interracial party as the best option for obtaining some key electoral gains at the local and congressional levels. Although an exclusively Indian party would eliminate some of the interracial tensions within parties, it would probably hinder rather than help the establishment of interracial bridges for common causes. One interesting area for further inquiry is comparative research on the effectiveness of different methods of political participation used by indigenous actors in Latin America and other regions.

The use of double consciousness as a theoretical tool can also prove useful for analyses of indigenous peasant mobilizations that took place earlier in the century. Instead of categorizing peasants as lacking a workers' consciousness, or peasant struggles as isolated and prepolitical, focusing on the gaps or incongruencies between leftist ideology and practice and indigenous ideologies might yield alternative histories of resistance. In addition, applying the notion of double consciousness to studies of other Indian movements in the region can shed light on theoretical debates about the primacy of ethnicity or class and potentially steer analyses away from the false dichotomization of the two. Instead of insisting on the primacy of class politics that is no longer constructed as such by the activists themselves, analysts could focus on how previous class concerns have been reconceptualized. Likewise, instead of focusing exclusively on the differences between indianista and campesinista politics, ethnicity-centered analyses could benefit from theorizing the linkages and relationships between the two.

This approach implies taking indigenous subjectivity seriously as a crucial link between agency and structure. Studies of Indian and peasant movements would benefit from making a distinction between objective definitions of class, race, and ethnicity and the subjective processes through which these are constructed and become central sources of identity. This would rescue analysts from the seemingly inevitable and static categorization of all indigenous demands and struggles as "ethnic" and all mestizo demands as "class based," suggesting instead that there are multiple axes of identity that can become politicized by different actors in specific historical contexts. (For example, although I focus primarily on race and class, I illustrate some of the ways in which dominant constructions of nation have both shaped indigenous political consciousness and been contested by indianista activists). Even after the emergence of contemporary uprisings in Latin America, Indian movements have been naturalized in a different way, as they are often considered the continuation of a millenarian struggle that was temporarily sidetracked by the imposition of class politics. It is precisely these forms of theoretical essentialism that future studies of Indian movements in the region must avoid in favor of analyses that focus on the construction of identity and related forms of consciousness. While the strategic essentialism that characterizes indigenous organizations themselves both within borders and transnationally (exemplified in the 500 Years of Resistance campaign) is understandable insofar as it serves activists' specific political objectives, social analysis of these movements should remain committed to historical and political research. In sum, the subjectivity inherent in the process of social formation and the constructivism of class, ethnicity, nation, gender, and race cannot be skipped over or assumed but must become the focus in analyses of peasant and Indian mobilizations.

The final implication of Ecuadorian indianismo for indigenous politics is the creation of a model of politics that relies on sustained capacity for disruption. In fact, the Ecuadorian indigenous movement has developed such a strong and sustained capacity of disruption that it has pioneered a fourth path for regime change in Latin America: the popular coup. In 1996 and 2000 massive indigenous mobilization played a crucial role in the removal of two presidents, Abdalá Bucaram and Jamil Mahuad, respectively. Whereas the 1996 mobilization was part of a broad popular coalition, the 2000 mobilization was predominantly the result of an alliance between the CONAIE and the military. Previous removals of presidents in Latin America have been the result of elections, a military coup, or an elite coup with military support. The implication of this fourth path, and how it may continue to affect electoral politics and the electoral system, is an important question for future research.

However, while the 2000 coup revealed the formidable force of the movement, as well as its ability to establish alliances with junior military personnel, it also revealed the limitations of indigenous power, as the upper ranks of the military and the vice-president-elect were able to seize the temporary control earned by Indians and junior military. As regards broader reaction, the political commentaries that followed in subsequent weeks could be summarized as a combination of relief that the president had been forced out and putting Indians in their place. In essence, Ecuador had a half-coup. No one questioned the need to remove Mahuad or clamored for his return, despite his undemocratic exit. Moreover, his exit was accomplished with no bloodshed and little effect from mestizo members of the major parties, who benefited greatly from indigenous activism. However, Indians were accused of being undemocratic and irrational for thinking they could hold and keep power over a contemporary liberal democracy.

Repeatedly, Indians were characterized as lacking the knowledge of political and economic policy that could help Ecuador to face its crisis. Accompanying this familiar characterization of Indians as premodern were not very subtle assertions about their audacity in attempting to govern the country. An editorial in the major newspaper *El Comercio* stated, "No creerán los indios que nos van a gobernar" (The Indians cannot believe that they are going to govern us).

This incident brings me to two reflections on the politics of disruption. First, although there has been a significant level of popular support for policies that address pressing indigenous issues (in response to a decade of intense activism), there is reluctance to accept Indians as equal political actors who can participate in decisions that affect all Ecuadorians. Moreover, the prominence of indigenous politicians from Pachakutik–Nuevo País, such as the attorney Nina Pacari or Cotacachi mayor Auqui Tituaña (who has been lauded in the press for mediating between the CONAIE and the government after a massive mobilization in 2001), has led many Ecuadorians to distinguish between people like them—considered exceptional, different Indians, who are safely engaged in formal politics—and "the others"—the CONAIE activists who are often viewed as less able to occupy positions of leadership. This underscores not only the existence of a racial hierarchy against which activists must struggle but also the effects of decades of ventriloquism, speaking for Indians and not with them, while rendering them politically invisible. The Ecuadorian polity and the public identity of Ecuadorian political leaders have relied for years on the absence of Indians from the public sphere. After more than ten years of mobilization, some Indians, elected and active in the political movement, have been validated as worthy representatives of the indigenous population, while the main leaders of the social movement are often vilified and their representativeness questioned.

Consequently, for all the state's inclusion of multiculturalism and despite key gains in electoral power, Indians are aware that their main power lies not in their elected officials (even when engaged in congressional coalitions with the Left and the center) but in *their capacity to disrupt* and in their ability to sustain this capacity over time. The need to rely on the power of disruption evidences the incomplete "inclusion" of Indians in the polity. As *El Comercio* illustrates, while many support "Indian rights" and the mobilizations when they agree with the cause or share a common enemy, this support has not translated into acceptance of increased indigenous power over mestizo citizens.

The second reflection stems from the question, who benefits from the politics of disruption? Is it only indigenous activists or even primarily indigenous activists? Although the politics of disruption have played a key role in limiting and at times halting neoliberal reforms that would raise the cost of living and cut social spending, they have also benefited the Right. In the Ecuadorian example, the right-wing PSC was eerily quiet and tacitly supportive of the indigenous coup against Mahuad (whom they opposed) but was outspoken soon afterward in denouncing indigenous activists' efforts to retain power after the coup while supporting the new vice president, Gustavo Noboa, who was more likely to support the Right's agenda. What has ensued is not only politics as usual but a more right-leaning and repressive government than the one the Indians had helped to remove. Hence, without much effort, the PSC got what it wanted, thanks in great part to indigenous efforts for political change.

This last point also highlights another issue that indigenous activists themselves have raised. That the indigenous movement has assumed the costs of two massive mobilizations that have benefited political elites is in some ways reminiscent of the mita. While Indians actually do the labor involved in a president's removal, it is the white-mestizos who frequently benefit the most. This division of labor leads to questions for activists as well as researchers about specific relationships that cannot be assumed as given: Is there always a positive relationship between the politics of disruption and policy outcomes? Can indigenous activists actually pursue their agenda once mobilization has taken place? Are the politics of disruption always an effective conduit for social and political change? Given the current political system, is there an alternative? Future research on the pros and cons of the politics of disruption could prove useful to students of indigenous movements.

This study also has implications for the study of Latin American politics. Specifically, I have aimed to analyze how racial consciousness served to stimulate panethnic unity and alter the political landscape at the local and national levels. This book, therefore, joins other recent works on contemporary racial constructions and racial relations to underscore the role played by race in structuring contemporary Latin American politics (Wright 1990; Wade 1993; Hanchard 1994). As scholarship begins to whittle away at the notion of racial exceptionalism and the myth of racial democracies, increasing attention will need to be paid to how populations of color are placing themselves on the political map. The emergence and growth of indigenous and Afro–Latin American movements in the region means that increasingly the racial questions that were considered outside the sphere of politics are being politicized and that efforts to counteract racism are both becoming institutionalized and transforming political institutions. An example of analyses that focus on the relationship between racial movements and political institutions is Van Cott (2000), who engages in a comparative study of Latin American constitutions that have been changed in response to indigenous mobilization. Another area for future comparative research is the role that indigenous movements are playing in altering cultural and legal institutions, political parties, and the political process itself.

In addition to affecting Latin American political systems, the influence of indigenous movements on other social actors and movements is a relatively unexplored topic that begs for future research. In Chiapas, Mexico, for example, the Zapatistas have inspired and mobilized urban movements, leftist politicans, and rural indigenous movements throughout the country. In the case of Ecuador, the indigenous movement has energized old social movements and helped to stimulate new ones. Also, the movement's focus on multiculturalism, autonomy, and self-determination has influenced the rhetoric and actions of local movements throughout the country. Some interesting areas for future research are the role that indigenous politics is playing in shaping and transforming social movement politics, popular expectations of the political system, alternative conceptions of nation and democracy, and state-society relations in the region.

Finally, this case study contributes to our understanding of a more global transition from class politics to a politics of identity in which the cultural and the material are deeply intertwined. The Ecuadorian Indian movement teaches us that the global decline of class politics need not be equated with the end of ideology, the end of the politics of opposition, or with a declining articulation of socioeconomic demands (as new social movement theorists have speculated). Instead of disappearing, the politics of the material is undergoing a metamorphosis, as former class demands are rearticulated and reconstructed in new ideological frames and become the basis for new and renewed political struggles. Hence indigenous movements across the region are not only challenging their polities and expanding citizenship and democracy but also changing preexisting academic categories. If the Ecuadorian case has shown anything, it is not that class politics has disappeared or become defunct, as some have contended, or that the new Indian identity that has supposedly replaced it is its opposite, representing a dematerialized, solely culturally based identity. Rather, it has shown that new conditions created by political and economic modernity generate new identities and political processes that challenge our existing academic categories. Indigenous movements have demonstrated great political creativity in articulating a new type of discourse and politics for the twenty-first century. The challenge for their students lies in producing analyses and categories that adequately reflect and understand a new political discourse and a new political world.

APPENDIX

Sixteen Demands Proposed by the CONAIE in the 1990 Uprising

1) Public declaration that Ecuador is a plurinational country (to be ratified in the constitution).
2) Grant of lands and titles to lands to the nationalities.
3) Solutions to water and irrigation needs.
4) Absolution from indigenous debts to FODERUMA and the National Development Bank.
5) Freezing of consumer prices.
6) Conclusion of priority projects in Indian communities.
7) Nonpayment of rural land taxes.
8) Expulsion of the Summer Language Institute.
9) Free commercial and handicraft activity.
10) CONAIE protection of archaeological sites.
11) Officialization of Indian medicine.
12) Cancellation of the governmental decree that created parallel land reform granting bodies.
13) Immediate granting of funds by the government to the nationalities.
14) Granting of funds for bilingual education.
15) Respect for the rights of the child.
16) Fixing of fair prices for products.

Notes

CHAPTER 1

1. *Indigenous* is a term commonly used to refer to peoples of Native American descent who, despite their differences in ethnic origin, are defined by their shared experience of socioeconomic and political subordination. *Indigenous organizations* refers to local and regional cooperatives, unions, and communes, as well as national federations, confederations, and fronts that have represented or claimed to represent indigenous peasants' interests. In this book I often use *indigenous* and *Indian* interchangeably. *Indian*, as a self-referential term, is most frequently used by national activists who are referring specifically to the new Indian identity and purposely reversing the meaning of what was once a derogatory term to one of positive national affirmation. Most local activists, however, use the term *indigenous*.

2. In South America, the censuses in only four countries ask for self-identification of ethnicity: Brazil, Surinam, Guyana, and French Guyana. In Ecuador, language data were collected only in 1950 and 1990. Knapp used the 1950 language data to create an ecological census that determines predominantly Quichua-speaking zones. Knapp uses the same data to project onto 1987. Zamosc uses Knapp's 1950 parameters, because the decline in monolinguism means that language is no longer a useful indicator.

3. In fact, the awareness of themselves as Quichuas is quite recent, since *indigenous* has been the primary form of self-identification.

4. *Mestizos* refers to people of mixed descent who do not identify themselves as Indians. *Blancos*, or whites, refers to people who claim no mixed descent. Because these are cultural as well as phenotypical categories, self-definitions of blancos and mestizos will vary across the region. I use the term *white-mestizos* to refer to the nonindigenous population. The term is also used as shorthand by several activists and academics. However, it inaccurately excludes the Afro-Ecuadorian population.

5. These protests began in Sincay and Quingeo in 1920, spread through Azuay, Imbabura, Pichincha, and Tungurahua in 1923, followed by Cayambe and Tiguas in 1926, Cotopaxi in 1927, Columbe and Colta in 1929, Licto in 1935, and Pull in 1938.

6. Some of the unions created in this fashion in the period of 1927–30 were the Juan Montalvo Union in Cayambe, El Inca, Pan y Tierra, and Tierra Libre.

7. All of the above-mentioned mobilizations were brutally repressed. The government's fear of the ramifications of indigenous organization is evidenced by its persecution and imprisonment of indigenous leaders who were about to meet in the first national Indigenous Congress in 1931. In that same year, the government passed the Law of Communes, which restricted the forms that Indigenous mobilizations could take, rendered strikes illegal, and undermined Indian unions.

8. Recent academic analyses have claimed that despite the obvious violence and dispossession that characterized the hacienda system, it was also the site of a social pact that guaranteed indigenous survival as well as mediation between Indians and the state. This pact between the dominators and the dominated allowed Indians to reproduce their culture in the hacienda and legitimized the hacienda as a social unit. For extensive discussion of the hegemonic pact between landowners and huasipungueros, see Guerrero 1991 and Ramón 1986.

9. In contrast to several scholarly and political works that have addressed this mediation and paternalism, Becker (1997) contends that the relationship between mestizos and Indians in Cayambe in the 1930s and 1940s was an equitable one. I would argue, however, that the reality lies somewhere between equitable and manipulative. While not questioning the good intentions of the socialists and communists who worked directly with Indians and mediated for them, the power differential between Indians and mestizos lies beyond the realm of interpersonal relations, encompassing vast differences in literacy, levels of knowledge about the state, and access to public officials.

10. The administration of León Febres-Cordero (1984–88), a right-wing conservative from the Partido Social Cristiano (PSC) froze or reversed these policies.

11. Interview with Nina Pacari of CONAIE, Riobamba, September 1, 1993.

12. An analysis of the events held during the uprising is beyond the scope of this book. For more detailed analyses of the uprising itself, see Macas, 1991; ILDIS, 1991; Moreno and Figueroa 1992; Rosero 1990. For a detailed description of events as they occurred, see *Kipu* 14, a compilation of newspaper reports about the uprising.

13. "Una Condena al Racismo," *Punto de Vista*, June 11, 1990, 7. Transcript of a Chimborazo Indian's speech.

14. "El Tribunal Indígena de Cotopaxi," *Punto de Vista*, July 2, 1990, 10.

15. The year after the uprising, there were debates over whether to prioritize the national struggle first or to focus on local struggles as a conduit to a more extensive and profound transformation. The latter option, given the politicization of many activists at the local level, was considered not only viable but necessary and was emphasized most in moments when national negotiations were at a standstill.

While some evaluations of the national uprising claim that results were not as significant as hoped for, the gradual changes in local power relations should also be seen as an effect.

16. "Indians of Ecuador Coalescing in Quest for Political Power," *Washington Post*, July 23, 1996.

21. Ibid.

CHAPTER 2

1. For a history of indigenous mobilizations, see Albornoz 1971.

2. For examples of these portrayals of early indigenous mobilizations, see Velasco 1979 and Ibarra 1992.

3. Notable exceptions are Santana (1984) as well as Muratorio (1982), who addresses the unlikely role of Protestantism in this transition. Most works addressing the movement acknowledge this transition as a matter of fact but do not attempt to explain it.

CHAPTER 3

1. The huasipungo was a system of landownership in which a large landowner allowed a group of peasants to use small plots of his or her land in exchange for labor. Peasants engaged in this specific relationship are called *huasipungueros*, whereas *yanaperos* and *arrimados* are usually relatives of huasipungueros or inhabitants of adjoining free communities who exchanged labor for access to water and pasture. For more extensive discussions of the huasipungo system and its termination, see Barsky 1984; Velasco 1979.

2. Policies designed to supplement land reform include the Fondo para el Desarrollo Rural marginal (FODERUMA), a credit and infrastructure program for farmers administered by the National Bank for Development and Desarrollo Rural Integral (DRI), which consisted of a series of specific commercial and agricultural development programs implemented in selected zones, among other smaller pilot projects. These projects were initiated in the late 1970s and have been implemented through the 1980s and 1990s, with varying rates of funding, contingent on the politics of the administration in office.

3. Landowners were threatened most by the decline in the amount of land they could own, a fear that became more substantial in the early 1970s, when pressure from neighboring free communities threatened further limitations on plot size. It was this threat against private and absolute property, not the termination of peonage relations, that large landowners found most unsettling. Although initial landowner reaction against reform was based on claims that labor supply would decline, this was not actually the case. The low quality and small size of the plots peasants received meant that most former huasipungueros could not even subsist off the land; the intense competition for higher-paying work in adjoining towns and distant cities and communal and familial attachments to their place of origin led

many "free" indigenous peasants to work on their former haciendas as free laborers for little more than what they had made as huasipungueros.

4. Barsky (1984) argues that Ecuador's agrarian reform law was a consequence of the initiative of modernizing landowners, claiming that while it was presented as a social policy enacted on popular demand, it actually reflected the will of the ruling class. Other scholars, among them Guerrero (1983), Chiriboga (1988a), and Sylva (1986) have questioned this thesis, arguing that only northern highland landowners stood to benefit from reform, while central highland landowners vehemently opposed it, this fact being demonstrated not only by significant evidence of landowner campaigns against the 1964 and 1973 reforms but also by the acknowledgment that both laws could only have been passed by military regimes. In addition, the mounting pressure of peasant struggles for improved wages and working conditions played a much greater role in the enactment of reform than Barsky admits. Finally, even if Barsky's thesis about the policy process were accurate, implementation was assured only on haciendas where indigenous peasants carried out long struggles on both the national and local fronts. In her seminal study of Chimborazo province, Sylva (1987) shows the direct relationship between peasant struggles and actual land transfers. Regardless of the existing law, it was only through extended and well-organized confrontation that indigenous people were able to claim lands in an environment in which local landowners circumvented the law through selective repression and tight control of labor.

5. In actual land transfers, landowners often disregarded the location of the huasipungueros' original plots. Instead, they assigned huasipungueros the poorest lands located at the highest altitudes, keeping the more fertile valley zones for themselves.

6. After years of struggle, several national organizations were able to obtain state nationalization of water resources, as a first step in the eventual concession of water resources to legal communities.

7. The FEI, the FENOC, and ECUARUNARI were the three main national organizations in the 1970s. While the FEI and the FENOC are what I would call more popular organizations, focused on peasant issues, ECUARUNARI was developing its own position using a combination of peasant and Indianista lines. I discuss the genealogy and positions of each of these organizations in chapter 4.

8. *Anejos* or *caseríos* were groupings of indigenous households whose spatial layout was designed according to the landowner's need to control labor. *Comunidad*, or community, refers to a group of families living in one specific location. Community sizes vary, ranging approximately from 100 to 600 people. They differ widely in the form of property ownership, ranging from shared ownership of most land to sets of individually owned plots. The most common arrangement is a combination of individually owned plots and one communal plot designed to benefit all. Other community characteristics include a *cabildo*, or council, with elected members who govern the community, and *mingas*, or regular arrangements of collective works in which members assist each other in labor-intensive agricultural and infrastructural tasks.

9. The political uses of this concept were present in agrarian modernization debates over a new agrarian law in 1994 in which landowners, despite their efforts, were unable to abolish prohibition of sales of communal lands to individual purchasers.

10. The historian Galo Ramón Valarezo has written extensively about the symbolic meaning of the community and the political importance of its recuperation. Further, he (1993) suggests that the growth of communities as political entities as well as geographic space is a political and territorial project in the making.

11. For a more extensive discussion of indigenous migration, see Carrasco and Lentz 1985.

12. Bucaram's party, the Central de Fuerzas Populares (CFP), was a populist party based on the coast that derived its electoral support from the urban mestizo working class. In 1972 Ecuador began to export oil recently discovered in the lowlands region. Since then, the income generated from oil exports has consistently been the largest contributor to Ecuador's GNP.

13. The only political party that ever officially supported the Rodriguez Lara regime was the Communist Party.

14. Pre–land reform indigenismo can be followed by studying old copies of socialist magazines such as *Mañana* and *El Pueblo* during the early 1960s. While denunciations of the horrors of debt peonage and the need to liberate peasants from hacienda bondage were considered radical in the early part of the century and mostly attributed to the Communist Party, by the 1960s and 1970s it had become a mainstream component of popular culture.

15. República del Ecuador, 1974. Filosofía y Plan de Acción del Gobierno Revolucionario, 1974, 25. This and all subsequent quotations were translated by the author.

16. República del Ecuador. Presidential Address: "F.F.A.A. Segundo Aniversario," February 1974. Presidential Address.

17. Filosofía y Plan de Acción, 79.

18. Ibid., 26.

19. Ibid., 6

20. Ibid., 3–4.

21. The Rodriguez Lara regime implemented the second agrarian reform law in 1973, funded the IERAC generously, and supervised the largest transfer of lands in a four-year period. Many land transfers after his regime were actually adjudicated during his presidency. In addition, the regime implemented the first pilot rural development projects. The state also encouraged the creation of indigenous organizations, which it hoped would legitimate the nationalist revolution. While this was clearly a corporatist frame of thought in which popular organizations would lack real independence and policy control would be controlled from above, it helped to create political opportunities for Indian organizations at the local and national levels. One example is ECUARUNARI, the first regional organization, whose original meetings were funded by the president. While this was allegedly a favor Rodriguez Lara did for his niece, Sister Genoveva Rodriguez, one of ECUARUNARI's founders,

it also reflects—at least in the early years—the government's generally encouraging posture toward ECUARUNARI. Interview with Genoveva Rodriguez, August 1993.

22. Although it occurred a few years after the Rodriguez Lara regime, a specific example is the UNORCIC's experience with the state agency FODERUMA in the late 1970s (see chap 4). FODERUMA planners designed and implemented a public water project in the communities surrounding Cotacachi but failed to finish it. UNORCIC activists, involved only in name, played almost no role in the plans but lost political support in the canton after the interruption.

23. This was designed to include the claims of indigenous peasants from free communities adjoining haciendas who felt they had historic claims to the land because of decades of work for hacendados but had not benefited from land concessions to huasipungueros.

24. *Mensajero*, July 1973. This text was later found to be an early draft of the law that had already been discarded by the drafting committee. The mysterious appearance of this text in the media led critics to speculate that a group of hacendados were responsible for its release.

25. *Acción*, No.1, *Boletín Informativo Agrario* (August and September 1979).

26. "El Grito en el Cielo," *Nueva* 94 (January–February 1983), 30.

27. Ibid., 31.

28. Conference at the Catholic University of Quito, June 1992. In this conference the international research group IDEA presented a study of the positive relationship between land reform and decline in economic productivity. CONAIE representatives present as well as other analysts pointed out that IDEA's report excluded some important factors such as the great differences in soil quality between indigenous land and producer lands, and lack of technology, credit, and infrastructure for indigenous communities.

29. "Quinchuquí: El alto precio de la lucha," *Nueva* 59 (November 1979), 51.

30. Ibid.

31 "Campesinos de Quinchuquí: Morir luchando antes que morir en casa," *Nueva* 53 (November 1978); "Quinchuquí: El alto precio de la lucha." "Quinchuquí: Ya basta!" *Nueva* 67 (July 1980); "Quinchuquí: Hasta cuando patrón IERAC? *Nueva* 76 (April 1981).

32. The teniente político is the main police authority in the parishes or rural local governments.

33. Ecuador is divided into twenty-two provinces, each of which has several cantons, or main settlements, as well as several parishes (*parroquias*).

34. While Burgos's *Relaciones interétnicas en Riobamba: Dominio y dependencia en una región indígena* (1977) remains the sole treatise on interracial relations in one province, most of the patterns are documented extensively in thousands of local and national organization documents, congressional archives, newspaper and magazine articles, and teniente político archives throughout the highlands. These forms of mistreatment also have been corroborated in several interviews by the author.

35. Interview with Delfín Tenesaca, Santa Cruz, Riobamba, August 10, 1993.
36. Interview with Gladys, August 16, 1993, Riobamba.
37. Interview with Manuel Paca, August 13, 1994, Tixán.
38. Interview with Segundo Andrango, July 7, 1993, Topo Chico.
39. Interview with Blanca Chancoso, October 1, 1993.
40. In the 1990s mestizos maintained tight control over traditionally mestizo turf. Besides migrant labor opportunities in the large cities, most opportunities for real socioeconomic or professional advancement for Indians were created by state-funded literacy and bilingual education projects, which hired hundreds of Indians as teachers, or by a growing Indian petit-bourgeoisie of artisans who hire Indians to work in their factories. Many successful Indians are self-employed as market vendors or artisans.
41. Interview with Gladys, August 16, 1993, Riobamba.
42. Interview with Manuel, a migrant worker from Chimborazo province living in Quito. Cited in Carrasco and Lentz 1985, 98–99.
43. Interview with Segundo Andrango, July 7, 1993, Cotacachi.
44. Interview with Pedro de la Cruz, August 6, 1993, Cotacachi.
45. In several interviews with indigenous activists from various highland provinces, I found that narratives of incidents in which Indians were expected to serve mestizos in some way were not only common, but were consistently used to exemplify the extent of the racial humiliation they had suffered and express moral outrage. What remains striking about these accounts is the inclusion of parents' and grandparents' experiences as one's own, counting them as part of the present (something not entirely unusual in communities with oral traditions and more circular notions of time) as well as the specific humiliation attributed to patterns which re-create hacendados' specific racist acts. In this re-creation of hacienda servitude lies the specific nature of the racialization of Indians, which is not shared by the mestizo poor in the highlands or other parts of the country.
46. Interview with Pedro de la Cruz, August 6, 1993, Cotacachi.

CHAPTER 4

1. República del Ecuador, INEC, *V Censo*, 1992, 180–81.
2. Unfortunately, there are no data available on the sizable number of Indians living in the urban zones, particularly in Cotacachi.
3. Zamosc 1995, 76; *V Censo*, 1992, 181.
4. Leather manufacture and sales have become important activities only in the past twenty years. There are no economic analyses of the reasons this sector is exclusively mestizo, or of the ways in which Indians have been systematically excluded from production, commercialization, and retail opportunities. In addition to leather manufacturing, and with the exception of the production of indigenous handicrafts and handwoven goods, most retail stores, restaurants, and shops are owned by mestizos. In addition to handicraft production and agricultural labor, selling produce

and operating food stalls in the local market are the main economic activities for indigenous people. The only other alternatives are migrant labor and working for commercial haciendas in the zone.

5. The neighboring city of Otavalo, however, a half-hour drive, is notorious for a far greater income disparity between indigenous people because of a substantial Indian middle class that has marketed its handicrafts in the international market.

6. As Barsky (1984) explains, most Imbabura haciendas were able to preempt land reform policy by making their haciendas "efficient," by converting them to cattle grazing and developing a dairy industry. In the zone of Cotacachi the most important case of land reform occurred on the Tunibamba hacienda, where indigenous peasants were able to acquire land after more than a decade of political struggle. The Tunibamba decision, however, is fairly recent, the final adjudication occurring in 1992. It was considered one of the outstanding land reform cases during negotiation between the CONAIE and the government after the 1990 national uprising.

7. UNORCIC, *Report on Economic and Geographic Characteristics*, UNORCIC archives, n.d. The percentages are based on raw data obtained from this document. Most UNORCIC statistics have been elaborated in conjunction with the Coordinadora Andina de Acción Popular (CAAP), a Quito-based NGO that has channeled international foundation funds to the UNORCIC. The isolation of UNORCIC communities does not reflect the rural status throughout Cotacachi canton, as it excludes the communities of the Intag zone, made up mostly of mestizo parishes.

8. Interview with Blanca Chancoso, October 8, 1993, Quito.

9. Interview with Segundo Andrango, July 7, 1993, Topo Chico.

10. Ibid.

11. Despite the key role of urban Indians in creating the UNORCIC, the number of urban Indians who refuse to be involved with the UNORCIC remains high. Those urban Indians who wish to distinguish themselves from rural Indians reject the UNORCIC as a representative of rural interests. Others complain that urban Indians are entirely neglected by the organization. This suggests that the common identification created by these activists was one based on rural interests: UNORCIC activists did not address urban interests, nor did they achieve a more general politicization of urban Indians under their banner.

12. Several oral histories suggest that a number of fights stemmed from intercommunal conflict between indigenous people, as well as interracial conflict between rural Indians and urban mestizos.

13. The jefe político oversees the reports and activities of the tenientes políticos of a canton, in addition to regulating city dwellers.

14. 110 Teniente Político Report to the Governor of Imbabura, 1975, Archives of the Jefatura Política of Cotacachi.

15. Archivos del Jefe Político, Cantón Cotacachi 1960–80.

16. Ibid.

17. The lack of will to arrest mestizos for assaults or crimes against Indians was a generalized problem. The use of forced labor, the charging of taxes, and sexual

and physical assaults mentioned earlier were activities that rarely resulted in the arrest and imprisonment of mestizos.

18. Interview with Segundo Andrango, July 7, 1993, Topo Chico.

19. Ibid.

20. In most accounts of police brutality there are different versions of the nature of Perugachi's intervention. Some accounts state that he merely told the police officer he had no right to beat the man; others state that he pinched the officer, after which the officer hit him.

21. Interview with Alberto Andrango, July 8, 1993, Topo Chico. In 1977, 28 sucres equated U.S. $1.00, and 240 sucres equated U.S. $8.50, while median income was approximately $40.00 a month.

22. With a certain degree of political and demographic strength secured in this initial incident, the UNORCIC, like other second-degree organizations, institutionalized a set of rules and procedures to facilitate its rule over all intercommunal relations. It created a cross-community government in which general assemblies of community leaders would be held once a month to report the activities of the organization and listen to the needs of the communities. It established its position as the sole representative of the communities in the zone through government programs such as FODERUMA's loan programs and water projects and demands that international organizations as well as religious groups seek its approval before beginning development work in specific communities. It oversaw council elections in every community to ensure that the teniente políticos did not "persuade" voters to select a candidate of their choice but also to maintain the organization's presence in each community and keep informed of the communities' political developments.

23. UNORCIC, Executive Committee's Report to the Fourth Congress, 1992, UNORCIC archives.

24. Letter to Provincial Director of Education of Imbabura, June 25, 1986, UNORCIC archives.

25. Until the constitutional referendum in late 1994, Ecuadorian law demanded that all candidates for office be affiliated with a party, barring independent candidacies. For indigenous people who wanted to run for office, this meant required association with one of the seventeen parties. Indigenous candidates throughout the highlands and lowlands have tended to associate with parties of the Left, but also with populist parties and the center.

26. The local division between the UNORCIC and the FICI has remained a long-standing rift since the creation of the UNORCIC, a rift that has enabled the FENOC to keep UNORCIC as a member despite the national organization's decline and eventual disaffiliation of several member organizations.

27. Electoral Statistics, Tribunal Supremo Electoral, 1979–92.

28. There is an important distinction between representation, or simply having an Indian in office, and incorporation, in which Indians initiate and develop policy. In the case of Cotacachi, the possibility of incorporation depended on the particular activists who were in office and the possibility of establishing governing coalitions

with nonindigenous council members on specific issues. In addition, it is important to distinguish an electoral coalition, or the alliance of urban mestizo socialists and rural Indians who brought UNORCIC activists into power, and a governing coalition, in which the two parties cooperate in developing a common policy agenda and devising strategies to enact it. In the case of Cotacachi, when Andrango was alone in the council, he used his vote to bargain for his demands, but with the exception of brief periods in which Intag and UNORCIC activists governed together, there has been no consistent or long-term governing coalition.

29. While other indigenous candidates have been proposed for local elections in highland provinces, it has been sporadic and without the support of the organization, much less planned as an organizational strategy.

30. The underlying assumption here is that if the FADI felt it was possible to win the elections it would have put some "bankable mestizos on the ballot," as has historically occurred in areas where despite the existence of a large indigenous population and the presence of several Indian activists interested in becoming candidates, the FADI and other parties of the Left opted to exclude them from the races.

31. Organization document (ca. 1979); interview with Alberto Lima, August 5, 1993, Cotacachi; interview with Segundo Andrango, July 7,1993, Topo Chico.

32. República del Ecuador, Tribunal Provincial Electoral de Imbabura, Resultados Electorales del Cantón Cotacachi.

33. It was impossible to obtain a breakdown by parish of the vote via official electoral documents, as parish breakdowns are not listed in the electoral records of the Tribunal Supremo Electoral until the 1992 elections.

34. "Como indígenas tenemos nuestros planteamientos políticos," Ecuador Debate 12 (1986). Interview with Alberto Andrango.

35. The UNORCIC's break with the FADI coincides with the party's own dissolution. When one branch of the FADI decided to support the Izquierda Democrática two groups broke out, each creating its own party: Liberación Nacional (National Liberation Party) and the PSE. UNORCIC activists reluctant to accept the new alliance with the ID decided to associate with PSE.

36. Andrango, Speech, July 9, 1986, UNORCIC archives.

37. Interview with Pedro de la Cruz, August 6, 1993, Cotacachi. Emphasis added.

38. Municipality of Cotacachi Archives, Minutes of City Council Meetings, 1988–92.

39. Interview with anonymous UNORCIC informant "Carlos," August, 1993, Cotacachi.

40. Aro's sidestepping the organization as the mediator for these communities is consistent with the traditional behavior of state bureaucrats and local public officials. While some national agencies such as the National Development Bank and several international foundations have shared the "understanding" that any activity in the communities must meet with the approval of and be coordinated with the UNORCIC, politicians and candidates of other parties as well as other state development programs have disregarded the organization and developed direct communications and

negotiations with targeted communities. This is a matter of conflict shared by most highland intercommunal organizations vis-à-vis development-oriented organizations and state institutions. Intercommunal organizations are zealous guardians of development in their communities, and they are often reluctant to approve projects in which they have not been involved. The intervention of intercommunal organizations meets two important goals. First, it complies with a model of grassroots development in which communities and their leaders, as well as intercommunal activists, play a role in the decision-making and administration of programs. Second, it strengthens the organization's position vis-à-vis its member communities as a distributor of resources.

41. Interview with Pedro de la Cruz, July 5, 1993, Cotacachi.
42. The UNORCIC holds a congress every four years, in which it elects its leadership. Activists and members of all the affiliated communities participate and discuss the political direction and goals of the organization.
43. Video, 1992 UNORCIC Congress.
44. Interview with Segundo Andrango, July 7, 1993, Topo Chico.
45. Interview with anonymous informant "Pablo," August 1993, Cotacachi.
46. This includes repeated statements from FENOC president Mesias Tatamues about the political limitations and racist nature of an Indian struggle and reflects the position of other activists and politicians working closely with the FENOC. For example, in one FENOC workshop in 1993, to discuss the notion of multiculturalism, a PSE politician was on hand to underscore the FENOC's distinction from the CONAIE position and to point to the racism involved in indigenous people's perception of themselves as nationalities and their perception of the state as multinational.
47. Interview with anonymous informant "Juan," August 1993, Cotacachi.
48. Interview with Pedro de la Cruz, August 6, 1993, Cotacachi.
49. The large size of the indigenous parishes could lead one to believe that the mestizo vote was not necessary to get Tituaña elected. Indigenous parishes, after all, made up 7,038 of the 9,067 valid votes, or 77.62 percent. Moreover, indigenous parish rates of participation were similar to those in mestizo parishes, and Sagrario and San Francisco had the highest rates, averaging 80 percent of the voting-age population. But the slim margin of Tituaña's victory (2,186, or 24.11 percent of the votes, compared to 2,113, or 23.0 percent of the overall vote, for the PRE candidate) shows that those marginal mestizo votes for Tituaña did in fact make a difference.

CHAPTER 5

1. *Fiesta* is a generic term that refers to most indigenous celebrations. Fiestas are usually held to celebrate a religious holiday or mark the harvest season. They usually last several days and involve a number of symbolic rituals of evolving social meaning and political significance. In Cacha the most important fiestas were Cacha Fiesta in November, *la fiesta de Pascua* on Easter weekend, *la fiesta de Alajahuán*, or Corpus Christi, in March, and *la fiesta de carnaval* in February.

2. One example of coercion is the kidnapping of the bride. The reigning alcaldes would kidnap a woman who pleased a Cacha so that he could marry her, later "encouraging" the groom to whom the favor had been granted to become a prioste in the following fiestas.

3. Interview with Manuel Janeta, November 7, 1993, Cacha-Machángara.

4. The *chicheros* were mainly mestizos who owned *chicherías* (chicha bars) in the town as well as on the roads between communities and Yaruquíes. Burgos (1977) states that in the early 1970s it was still possible for a young, poor mestizo couple to open a chichería and make a very good living. The biggest problem indigenous people encountered were chicheros taking advantage of their illiteracy or of their highly inebriated state to grossly overcharge them.

5. Interview with José Morocho, November 1, 1993, Cacha-Machángara.

6. The idea that they "owned" the fiestas gave the Cachas a sense of control over their cultural reproduction; it also enabled Yaruqueño racial constructions of indigenous people as avid fiesta makers and drunkards who misspend their money irrationally on lavish preparations.

7. The alcalde system was the only form of community government until the late 1970s. The cabildos as self-elected governments were nonexistent or nonfunctional until the mid-1970s.

8. According to the Ecuadorian census, in 1982 only 37.62 percent of Cachas over ten years of age were literate, compared to a 78.2 percent literacy rate in the province of Chimborazo. By 1990 the literate population had increased to 55.78 percent.

9. Commonly known in the area as *quishqueros*, intermediaries are more generally known as *tinterillos*. The tinterillo is not just a translator, but often considered something more akin to a lawyer, someone who will intervene in favor of indigenous people and use his knowledge to help them conduct their affairs adequately. Because tinterillos needed to understand both worlds, it was not uncommon for them to be recent descendants of indigenous people who had become educated and used their knowledge of language and local culture.

10. Interview with José Morocho, November 1, 1993, Cacha Machángara.

11. Interview with Pedro Morocho, November 1993, Cacha-Machángara.

12. Longo is a pejorative term used for a young male highland Indian.

13. Interview with Pedro Morocho, November 1993, Cacha-Machángara.

14. Interview with Agustina Asqui, November 7, 1993, Cacha-Obraje.

15. According to several indigenous and mestizo informants, vendors and chulqueros were usually those most interested in keeping the indigenous uneducated and as isolated as possible. They would spread rumors that the military was going to seize children who went to school. In addition, according to Arrieta (1984), an attack by Cachas against vaccinators in an inoculation campaign was instigated by mestizo vendors, quishqueros, and other compadres.

16. Interview with Hector Lovato, November 1993, Riobamba.

17. While all Ecuadorian communities have been eligible to apply for legal status since the 1937 ley de comunas, many communities were not even aware of the potential advantages of this status until the 1970s. It could also be argued that until the 1970s, the advantages to be gained by becoming a legalized community were few, as it was only in that decade that the state pursued rural development aggressively.

18. Arrieta 1984; interview with Agustina Asqui and José Janeta, November 7, 1993, Cacha Obraje; interview with Pedro Morocho, November 3, 1993, Cacha Machángara; interview with Pedro Vicente Maldonado, November 10, 1993, Cacha Machángara; interview with Manuel Janeta, November 3, 1993, Cacha Machángara.

19. Arrieta 1984; interview with Agustina Asqui and José Janeta, November 7, 1993, Cacha-Obraje; interview with Manuel Vallejo, November 1993, Yaruquíes.

20. On consultation with several sources, it appears that these claims were never verified despite a formal investigation.

21. *Verdugo* means "executioner." It is a derogatory term used to refer to Indians in the Chimborazo province. It signifies the representation of Indians as violent and prone to attack mestizo pueblos. Documentation in the 1960s reveals that it was already used then, and its origins may be much earlier.

22. Interview with Agustina Asqui, November 7, 1993, Cacha-Obraje.

23. Interview with Pedro Morocho, November 1993, Cacha-Machángara.

24. Interview with Manuel Abagalla, November 9, 1993, Riobamba.

25. The teniente político position, however, did not become a state-paid position until six years later. Pedro Morocho, the first teniente político, did not receive compensation during this entire period.

26. Interview with Manuel Janeta, November 3, 1993, Cacha Machángara.

27. Interview with Agustina Asqui and José Janeta, November 7, 1993, Cacha-Obraje.

28. According to some historical accounts, the Duchicela family of Cacha was a noble dynasty that intermarried with Inca nobility, founding the Ecuadorian Inca dynasty. In addition, Cacha was the site of the largest uprising in the nineteenth century that was led by a local cacique, Fernando Daquilema.

29. *Kipu* 9 and 10.

30. There is a clear separation, however, between this mythical dimension and the administration of the organization. According to one source, when the Duchicela princess began to intervene in organizational affairs, she was informed by federation members that she had no right to do so and was interfering with the work of the activists who had earned their position through struggle and popular support.

31. Interview with Pedro Morocho, November 1993, Cacha-Machángara.

32. This observation was made initially by Carrasco (1993).

33. For a discussion of the Inca Atahualpa organization, see Cervone 1995.

34. Interview with anonymous Indian informant "Miguel," November 1993, Cacha-Machángara.

35. Interview with Manuel Abagalla, November 9, 1993, Riobamba.

CHAPTER 6

1. The contemporary legitimacy of the indianista position is such that despite evidence to the contrary, many former campesinistas deny ever having held a campesinista position.

2. It is important to point out, however, that the crisis of the Left caused by internal divisiveness led some of its activists to defect and participate in NGOs, state institutions, and academia in collaboration with indigenous activists. It is not unusual, therefore, for certain former leftists to have a long-term relationship with the indigenous movement in new and different capacities. The role of the church in the movement, however, merits a separate analysis and is beyond the scope of this book. While recognizing the importance of the church, I want to distance my work from explanations that give full credit to the church for instigating Indian activism. This is not only an argument that is frequently used by opponents of the movement to deny the indigenous activists any agency, but as a quasi-academic argument it fails to explain the relatively autonomous course of Indian politics in the late 1980s and 1990s in areas, such as Imbabura province, where the church played no role in Indian activism.

3. Carchi and Azuay provinces are two exceptions in that peasants are predominantly mestizo.

4. The FENOC originated in 1960 as the rural branch of the CEDOC, designed to address rural labor issues and as an alternative to communist unions. The FENOC has undergone several divisions since its founding in 1968. As sectors of the Catholic church became more progressive, the more moderate branch of church progressives affiliated with the Christian Democrats turned away from the old leadership in 1973.In 1976 a second division within the organization was created as a more radical branch turned away from the Christian Democrats to create the FENOC-CUT (more radical) and the FENOC-CLAT.

5. Since the mid-1980s the FENOC has made a serious attempt to incorporate more indigenous people in the national leadership and has changed its name to FENOC-I (the "I" stands for "Indigenous") at indigenous members' insistence, but its basic position remains the same.

6. *Boletín Mensual de ECUARUNARI*, 1, no. 1 (1974).

7. For alternative perspectives of the history of ECUARUNARI, see Rohn 1978 and Santana 1984.

8. Many of the indigenous members were not representatives of organizations but active in the church or in their community's affairs. This is the case because in many provinces provincial or intercommunal organizations were not created until the late 1970s or early 1980s. Nevertheless, the ideas and concerns of these activists both reflect local struggles and inform new organizations. Although ECUARUNARI had national aspirations and had some members from the coast and lowlands, it was predominantly made up of highland activists.

9. The FEI was founded by Dolores Cacuango and Jesus Gualavasí, both of whom are Indians, but after Gualavasí's death, the organization did not always have indigenous people in the top positions

10. The MCLN predates the MRIC. Many nonindigenous activists left the MCLN to participate in the MRIC. Both parties were small and short-lived and were dependent on indigenous support for their survival.

11. Interview with Genoveva Rodriguez, August 16, 1993, Riobamba.

12. Interview with Segundo Andrango, July 7, 1993, Cotacachi.

13. By "community," I mean the creation of working electoral bodies in existing communities (many in which the council had only existed in name or where the community government if not the territory had been undermined) as well as the organization of new territorial associations that chose to acquire the legal status of communities. Communal councils are considered first-degree organizations. Intercommunal organizations that represent a plurality of communities located in one specific canton or zone are called second-degree organizations. Third-degree organizations means provincial units, and fourth-degree organizations means regional-level organizations.

14. For a more detailed analysis of organizational growth during this period, see Sanchez-Parga 1992 and Sylva 1991.

15. ECUARUNARI was most active in local land conflicts between 1972 and 1975. Communities struggling for land, with ECUARUNARI support, found fierce opposition from local landed elites, leading to the deaths of the ECUARUNARI activists Lazaro Condo in 1973 and Cristobal Pajuña in 1974, both in Chimborazo province. After their deaths, mobilizations diminished, as local activists feared the consequences of future actions, particularly once the military triumvirate came to power (Rohn 1978). The most important aspect of ECUARUNARI's role in these conflicts was its ability to turn national attention to these deaths and move the national government to resolve the cases. In addition, particularly in the case of Condo, the focus of ECUARUNARI's claims was not only land but the inhumanity of everyday discrimination against the Indians that these deaths symbolized.

16. Interview with Blanca Chancoso, October 8 1983, Quito.

17. The most important official was the teniente político, who handled dispute resolution and channeled most local conflicts through the legal system. Tenientes políticos have usually been mestizos who favor local elites' interests over indigenous claims and have used their power to make the indigenous comply with forced labor as well as other forms of social control. Because tenientes políticos usually are nominated by the governor, many local protests in the 1970s and 1980s asked for their election in parishes with a high percentage of indigenous people, which will most likely result in an indigenous teniente.

18. Letter from ECUARUNARI to Minister of Government Richelieu Levoyer, February 29, 1976. Cited in Rohn 1978, 133–35.

19. Ibid.

20. The notion of individual rights, specifically, human rights, did not become popular until the early 1980s, when a number of national and international human rights organizations developed in the process of democratization and incorporated indigenous rights in their agendas.

21. ECUARUNARI letter cited in Rohn 1978, 133–35.

22. *ECUARUNARI Bulletin,* June 11, 1974. Cited in Rohn 1978, 128.

23. Minutes of ECUARUNARI meeting, December 1, 1972. Cited in Rohn 1978, 107.

24. Interview with Ana María Guacho, August 20, 1993, Riobamba.

25. The differences among Saraguros, Salasacas, and more "generic" highland groups whose originary identification has disappeared are discussed in chapter 2. While more studies of these interethnic distinctions and their political implications are necessary, my position is distinct from those that group all highland indigenous (Quichua) based on a common language. I hold that although language is an important basis for common identification as well as a political symbol, it is not the only basis for ethnic formation or for political unity and that other shared processes are just as if not more important.

26. Interview with Blanca Chancoso, October 8 1993, Quito.

27. Interviews with Luis Macas, August 4, 1993, Quito; Miguel Llucu, July 1, 1993, Quito; Juan Lligalo, September 15, 1993, Quito; and Blanca Chancoso, October 8, 1993, Quito.

28. The use of the term *race* in political discourse was considered unacceptable by the left and by academics. Analysts consulted by indigenous activists proposed *ethnicity* as a more "scientific" and acceptable term.

29. *El Campesino,* 18 (September 1977). Cited in Rohn 1978, 98.

30. Open letter by ECUARUNARI Pichincha to all the indigenous in the country, document in Rohn 1978, 144–47. While the term *indigenista* was used by those opposed to indianista claims, it was not a term of self-identification for many indigenous activists.

31. The leftist magazine *Nueva,* in its four-part series in 1978, openly accused Lema and defended the FENOC's and ECUARUNARI's claims.

32. Interviews with Cristobal Tapuy, September 20, 1993, Quito; Luis Macas, May 11, 1993, Quito; Genoveva Rodriguez, August 16, 1993, Riobamba; and Rogelio Housse, October 1993, Quito.

33. Interview with Blanca Chancoso, October 8, 1983, Quito.

34. Interview with anonymous informant "Rodrigo," June 1992, Quito.

35. That these annual marches are called campesino-índigena marches is a reflection of activists' attempts to incorporate this new political identity and give it some public status.

36. While the Summer Language Institute's purported purpose was to translate the Bible into indigenous languages, in reality it has carried out a campaign of religious conversion and social control of indigenous populations in the lowlands and in pockets of the highland provinces.

37. FOIN, "La Lucha de los Napo Runas," 1987.

38. Interview with Cristobal Tapuy, September 20, 1993, Quito.

39. The major lowland ethnic groups are the Shuaras, Quichuas, Huaoranis, Cofanes, and Siona-Secoyas, the first two groups having a much longer history of organizing. After the Shuar Federation, most lowland organizations were created

in the late 1970s, including the FOIN, which includes the lowland Quichuas of Napo, the OPIP, which includes the Quichuas of Pastaza, and the Jatun Común Aguarico.

40. FOIN, "La Lucha de los Napo Runas," 1987.
41. FOIN, *Sacha Runas*, n.d.
42. Interview with Cristobal Tapuy, September 20, 1993, Quito.
43. Ibid.
44. Ibid.
45. UNAE, Problema indígena y colonización, 1983, 7.
46. Interview with Luis Macas, August 4, 1993.
47. "Resolutions of the First Encounter of Indian Nationalities," cited in CONAIE, 262.
48. ECUARUNARI, "Declaration of the Fifth Congress," 1979.
49. According to some oral sources, the institute left in name, but several former members as well as resources were channeled into World Vision, an evangelical organization that remains active today.
50. Frente de Solidaridad con los Pueblos Indígenas, "Por que el ILV debe salir del país," June 30, 1981.
51. Ibid.
52. While "peasant" does not entirely disappear, the media, informed by the activists' language, began using the terms "indigenous" and "Indians" to refer to these movements in 1981.
53. ECUARUNARI, Report of the VII Congress, 1983.
54. This dialogue was a lengthy and difficult process, at times involving heated disputes and occasional physical confrontations when agreement was not found. As late as 1985 there were still many key points that were being debated. One August 1985 workshop had different committees addressing questions such as does the concept of social class reflect Ecuadorian reality, especially Indigenous reality? and are there differences between the exploitation of mestizos and the exploitation of the indigenous?
55. CONAIE, Comision Politica del Primer Congreso de las Nacionalidades Indígenas del Ecuador, 1986, 2.
56. In fact, the Summer Language Institute experience appealed to the anti-imperialist feelings of leftist supporters and Center-Left public officials.

CHAPTER 7

1. IWGIA, "Declaration of Barbados," 1971.
2. See the full declaration in the Appendix.
3. For a critical perspective on this neoindigenismo, see Díaz-Polanco 1997, 73–75.
4. This chapter focuses primarily on education and cultural policy, not on rural development. However, the most important programs developed by the state to

achieve alternative participatory development were Foderuma and SEDRI. Both of these programs sought to include Indians in some decision-making capacity and to offer an alternative to leftist struggle. In most cases, indigenous organization leaders played some role in administering projects but did not have great decision-making power.

5. I have intentionally excluded rural development policy, which encompasses all government initiatives to provide infrastructure and credit and improve economic production in the countryside. This is discussed more thoroughly in chapter 4. I have excluded it here because it does not specifically address pluriculturalism or target Indians as such. These policies, however, disproportionately affected highland Indians in great numbers. The rural highlands received 66.7 percent of the funds FODERUMA allocated for projects between between 1979 and 1984 and 49.4 percent of the credit. While an evaluation of these rural development policies is outside the scope of this book, according to most experts, they did not lead to redistribution of income or land sufficient to meet the economic demands of most Indian communities.

6. Article 1 of Decree 617, creating the OAI. Cited in Sanchez-Parga 1988, 88.

7. Interestingly, this very principle can be applied to the organization of local power in highland communities, as exemplified in the vertical relationships established between town caciques and elites and members of Indian communities in Cacha (see chap.7).

8. This is also due in part to the fact that the Ecuadorian constitution, like all Latin American constitutions, theoretically, treats all individuals as equals. However, it is this universalism in rights in theory but not respected in everyday practice that has been the brunt of attacks by indigenous and Afro–Latin American activism throughout the region. While U.S. and South African activism could point to specific laws that had to be abolished, after the abolition of slavery and debt peonage activists in Latin America were confronted with the legal "invisibility" of the inequalities of power that ensured their subordination. Hence the political strategies used in Latin America have been the opposite of those used in South Africa and the United States: they have focused on the distinctiveness and specificity of the conditions of subordinate groups and attempted to then use that specificity to demand policy changes. This is commonly referred to in Ecuador as the politics of "Igualdad en la diferencia," or equality amid difference.

9. This is one reason token appointments of Indians as directors of these agencies has failed to satisfy the demands of organizations that do not see any Indian representative who is unlinked to organizations as legitimate.

10. This trend has changed, however, since the late 1990s since the Bucaram, Alarcón and Mahuad regimes have incorporated indigenous leadership into their respective agencies.

11. Interestingly, Roldós had been coached by Luis Macas, who at that time was getting a doctorate in linguistics at the Catholic University of Quito and would later twice become president of the CONAIE.

12. According to Sanchez-Parga (1988, 31–40), the military regimes of the 1970s had claimed to promote national culture in name but never elaborated a conceptualization of culture apart from the broader developmentalist goal or recognized pluriculturalism.

13. "Investigarán las culturas vernáculas," *El Comercio*, June 1, 1984.

14. "Indígenas de Otavalo organizan movimiento cultural," *El Comercio*, November 19, 1985.

15. These two issues gained more salience in the 1990s, as the CONAIE included them in its main platform.

16. One has been held in the lowlands (see Sánchez-Parga 1988).

17. "Seminario Sobre Política Estatal y Población Indígena," *El Mercurio*, February 21, 1984.

18. The state was not alone in this activity. The Socialist Party, research institutes, and national Indian and peasant organizations created conscientization and leadership workshops.

19. Oficina Nacional de Alfabetización, "La alfabetización participatoria como proceso político," 1981.

20. Ibid.

21. "Bilingual Education in Tungurahua," n.d. (ca. 1982).

22. Until Nueva Vida there had been no consistent use of standard written Quichua, as it primarily had been an oral language. The debate revolved around the use of the "k" to represent the "k" sound in Quichua, as opposed to the "q" used in Spanish. While CIEI officials argued that the "k" would remove the stigma of Spanish colonialism, a group of activists at Nueva Vida claimed that the "k" represented American imperialism and that indigenous students already familiar with written Spanish would find the Spanish alphabet more accessible. In the end the activists' perspective won, and contemporary Quichua education projects are written with the Spanish alphabet.

23. Many contemporary leaders of intercommunal and provincial organizations first became politically involved when they were literacy teachers and promoters in the early 1980s. In a process not dissimilar from the methods used by progressive Catholics, literacy teachers selected by communities or intercommunal organizations considered consciousness-raising one of their main functions and would habitually engage students in critical analyses of their socioeconomic conditions and political alternatives. Many literacy manuals and books prepared in this period have a great deal of political content, including lessons on local organizing, social injustice, and cultural preservation.

24. CONACNIE, "Carta dirigida al Presidente Osvaldo Hurtado," May 6, 1983.

25. "Indígenas de Otavalo organizan movimiento cultural," *El Comercio*, November 19, 1985.

26. Bilingual education teachers from a number of provinces who were interviewed often complained, for example, that their selection was contingent on joining a party. These complaints apply to all three parties that have been in power since

1981: the Democratic Party (PD), the Social Christian Party (PSC), and the Democratic Left (ID).

27. Manuel Naula, from Cotopaxi, was harshly criticized for speaking Quichua in the congressional chamber. Politicians and journalists took different sides on this debate, most supporting Naula's right to speak Quichua.

28. Only Cotacachi canton, in Imbabura, had at least one council member (almost continuously) since 1979. The specific case of Cotacachi is discussed more fully in chapter 8.

29. ECUARUNARI, "Nuestra posición," 1984, 16. Presented at the Seventh Congress on October 1983.

30. Blanca Chancoso, interviewed in "El despertar indígena se da en la Lucha por la tierra," *Nueva* (June 1983).

31. "Ecuador defiende estado multi-étnico," *Hoy*, June 11, 1989.

32. Interview with Cesar Verduga by Marta Roldós, August 1993, Quito.

33. Ibid.

34. During the Febres-Cordero regime, for example, Indian activists cooperated with the Socialist Party in an attempt to get the Law of Indian Nationalities passed. This law would have declared Ecuador a pluricultural country and guaranteed the legal and cultural rights of Indians. It was submitted to Congress in 1988 but did not pass.

35. For a statistical study and an in-depth analysis of the land redistribution situation, see Rosero 1990. Rosero shows also that while there were many legal and transfers during the Febres-Cordero and Borja regimes, most of these were simply the giving of land titles to people who had lived on the land for many decades, not actual land redistributions.

36. ECUARUNARI, Eighth Congress, November 1985.

37. "Una administración a lo interno," *Hoy*, August 31, 1990.

38. Cited in "Despierta el gigante," *Vistazo*, July 15, 1990.

39. "Vías no están Militarizadas," *Hoy*, August 29, 1990.

40. ECUARUNARI, Declaración del Octavo Congreso, November 1985.

41. In this light a second uprising in 1994 was necessary because although Indians were political actors, they had not been involved in formal political national decision making at the national level. This realization led to a second phase of debate within the movement that led Indians and other social activists to form a new party and participate in elections in 1996.

42. "Borja entregó Sistema Eléctrico," *Hoy*, September 10, 1990.

Glossary of Spanish and Quichua Terms

Alcalde	Mayor. In the specific case of Andean Ecuador, it is also used to refer to the members of indigenous communities who were selected by caciques to organize the fiestas and maintain order in their communities.
Alpargatas	Sandals used by indigenous peoples in the Ecuadorian highlands.
Anejo	Annex. The name given in Cacha to different sections of the zone before Cacha became a parish. Each anejo usually consisted of several communities.
El arranche	Literally, "the snatching." Refers to an act in which a white or mestizo/a takes a product from an indigenous vendor first and then pays the price he or she sees fit, which is usually below the vendor's asking price.
Autodesarrollo	Self-development. Refers to full indigenous participation in the design and implementation of social and economic development projects.
Autodeterminación	Self-determination.
Cabildo	Council of elected members that governs an indigenous community.
Cacique	Chieftain. In twentieth-century Cacha, caciques were mestizo leaders, usually of indigenous descent, who held both symbolic and real power over indigenous residents of communities.
Campesinismo	Peasant politics, in which indigenous peasants' activism is the central form of political identification.
Cantina	Small bar.
Caseríos	Groupings of households.

Central	Central or center. Usually used by leftist organizations to mean a union or group of several affiliated organizations throughout the country.
Chapa	Slang term for police officer.
Chicha	Alcoholic drink made of fermented corn that is consumed in the highland and lowland zones. Variations of chicha are consumed in all the Andean countries.
Chichería	Small bar where chicha is sold.
Chichero	Chicha vendor.
Chulquero	Moneylender.
Compadrazgo	Relationship between two adults in which one is the godparent of the other's child. On this act, a man becomes a *compadre*, and a woman becomes a *comadre*.
Compañero	Comrade or partner. Popularized by the Latin American Left, it is frequently used by most indigenous organizations to refer to their own membership as well as to outsiders who are supporters of their cause. The political connotation is that a compañero is "one of us."
Comunidad	Group of families living in a specific location.
Concertaje	System of debt peonage that held conciertos criminally liable for debts to landowners.
Concientización	Consciousness-raising.
Concierto	Indigenous rural worker who exchanges his labor for the use of a small plot of land and remains indebted to the landowner for many years or for life.
Coordinadora	Coordinator. Specifically, the CONAIE used this term between 1980 and 1986 for self-reference. A coordinadora is meant to group several autonomous organizations and establish a dialogue between them.
De manos	Hands-on relationship, based on personal experience.
Diezmo	Tax charged to Indians; remnant of the indigenous colonial tribute, which was not officially abolished in Ecuador until 1857. However, Indians continued to be taxed in informal ways.
Fiesta	In the Ecuadorian highlands, refers to a large celebration in which indigenous communities come together to celebrate a religious occasion or a cyclical event, such as the harvest, or a combination of both.
Fuerzas vivas	Literally, "live forces." Refers to organized groups of mestizo and white town dwellers.
Gamonal	Hacendado, or large landowner.
Gamonalismo	System in which a few wealthy landowners own most rural land and exercise social, political, and economic control over local peasants.

Guarapo	Popular drink.
Hacendado	Large landowner.
Hacienda	Large landholding.
Huasipungo	Before the 1964 agrarian reform, the name given to the small plot used by an Indian in exchange for providing labor to the hacienda's owner. The indigenous worker, however, did not own the huasipungo.
Huasipunguero	Indigenous worker who uses a huasipungo in exchange for his labor.
Indianismo	Panethnic form of political consciousness and mobilization that is based on a common identification as Indians.
Indígena	Indian or indigenous person. This term was used by most indigenous activists to refer to themselves.
Indigenismo	Discourse and practices of intellectuals, academics, politicians, and other social practitioners concerned with the problem of addressing indigenous needs and incorporating Indians into society.
Indio	Indian. Originally the term used by Spaniards to refer to the inhabitants of the Americas, it has also acquired pejorative connotations. However, Ecuadorian and other indigenous activists throughout the world have used the term for self-affirmation and as a symbol of resistance.
Indios alzados	Name given to Indians who are considered agitators.
Jefe político	Political chief; administers the law and addresses civil and criminal disputes in a specific canton. The jefe supervises the tenientes políticos (see below).
Levantamiento	Uprising.
Ley consuetudinaria	Law of customs based on practices in indigenous communities.
Ley de comunas	1937 law that recognizes communities as legal entities.
Longo	Pejorative term for a person who is Indian or of indigenous descent.
Maltrato	Mistreatment; abuse. Term commonly used by highland Indians to refer to everyday forms of racial discrimination.
Mestizo	Both a physical and a cultural category, meaning a person of mixed descent, not Indian. In Ecuador, the terms *blanco* (white) and *mestizo* are often collapsed to refer to non-Indians and nonblacks.
Minga	Group or community work effort, based on voluntary reciprocity.
Minifundio	Small plot of land.
Minifundización	The proliferation of small plots after the 1964 land reform.
Mita	Forced labor.

Mitayo	Name given to Indians recruited as forced workers in the colonial period.
Nuevo indio	New Indian.
Ordinario	Alcalde (see above).
Oriente	The Orient or East. Refers to the lowlands, or Amazonian region, of Ecuador.
Parroquia	Parish, small administrative unit.
Prioste	Indian appointed by the priest or cacique to sponsor a fiesta.
Pueblo	Peoples.
Pueblo indio	Indigenous peoples.
Quishquero	Translator and mediator between Spanish speakers and monolingual Quichua speakers.
Recuperación	Recovery.
Riccharimui	To awaken.
Rocoto	Literally, "large pepper." Derogatory term applied to Indians.
Sub-suelo	Subsoil.
Teniente político	Political lieutenant. A type of sheriff who administers local disputes at the parish level. Serious criminal cases are handled by police authorities in the closest city.
Terrateniente	Large landowner.
Tinterillo	Mediator between Indians and mestizos; may act as translator, lawyer, or scribe.
Tu	Informal second person, you.
Usted	Formal second person, you.
Verdugo	Executioner; also a derogatory term for Indians.
Vos	Formal or plural second person, you.
Yachac	Wise man; medicine man.
Yaruqueño	Inhabitant of Yaruquíes.

REFERENCES

BOOKS, ARTICLES, DISSERTATIONS, AND MANUSCRIPTS

Adler Hellman, Judith. 1995. "The Riddle of New Social Movements: Who They are and What They Do." In *Capital, Power and Inequality in Latin America*, ed. Sandor Halebsky and Richard Harris. Boulder, Colo.: Westview Press.

Aguirre-Beltrán, Gonzalo. 1975. *Obra polémica*. Mexico: SEP-INAH.

Alberts, Tom. 1983. *Agrarian Reform and Rural Poverty: A Case Study of Peru*. Boulder, Colo.: Westview Press.

Albornoz, Osvaldo. 1971. *Las luchas indígenas en el Ecuador*. Guayaquil: Editorial Claridad.

Almeida, José. 1986. "Movilizaciones campesinas: 1925–1960." Paper presented at the Fourth Congress of the Faculty and School of Sociology, Quito.

Alvarez, Sonia. 1990. *Engendering Democracy in Brazil*. Princeton: Princeton University Press.

Andreski, S., ed. 1971. *Herbert Spencer: Structure, Function and Evolution*. London: Nelson.

Aronowitz, Stanley. 1981. *The Crisis in Historical Materialism*. New York: Praeger.

Arrieta, Modesto. 1984. *Cacha: Raíz de la nacionalidad ecuatoriana*. Quito: Ediciones del Banco Central del Ecuador–FODERUMA.

Ayala Mora, Enrique. 1978. *Lucha y origen de los partidos en Ecuador*. Quito: Publitécnica.

———. 1989. *Historia, compromiso y política*. Quito: Editorial Planeta.

Barsky, Osvaldo. 1984. *La reforma agraria ecuatoriana*. Quito: Corporación Editora Nacional.

Barta, Roger. 1975. *Estructura agraria y clases sociales en Mexico*. Mexico: Editorial Era.

Beck, Scott, and Kenneth Mijeski. 2000. "The Electoral Performance of Ecuador's Pachakutik Movement, 1996-1998." Unpublished manuscript.

Becker, Marc. 1997. "Class and Ethnicity in the Canton of Cayambe: the Roots of Ecuador's Modern Indian Movement." Ph.D. dissertation, University of Kansas.

Benítez, Lilyan, and Alicia Garcés. 1993. *Culturas ecuatoriana: Ayer y hoy*. 7th ed. Quito: Ediciones Abya-Yala.

Bentley, Carter. 1987. "Ethnicity and Practice." *Comparative Studies in Society and History* 29 (1): 24-55.

Bocco, Arnaldo. 1987. *Auge petrolero, modernización y desarrollo: El Ecuador de los años 70*. Quito: CEN.

Bonfil Batalla, Guillermo. 1992. *Identidad y pluralismo cultural en América Latina*. Buenos Aires: Fondo Editorial del CEHASS.

Bonifaz, Emilio. 1979. *Los indígenas de altura del Ecuador*. Quito: Publitécnica.

Bourdieu, Pierre. 1977. *Outline of a Theory of Practice*. Cambridge: Cambridge University Press.

———. 1984. *Distinction: A Social Critique of the Judgement of Taste*. Cambridge, Mass.: Harvard University Press.

Bourgois, Phillipe. 1989. *Ethnicity at Work*. Baltimore: Johns Hopkins University Press.

Brysk, Alison. 1994. "Acting Globally: Indian Rights and Information Politics in he Americas." In *Indigenous Peoples and Democracy in Latin America*, ed. Donna Lee Van Cott. London: St. Martin's Press.

———. 2000. *From Tribal Village to Global Village: Indian Rights and International Relations in Latin America*. Stanford: Stanford University Press.

Burgos, Dalton. 1985. *Historia de la luchas populares*. 4 vols. Quito: CEDIS.

Burgos, Elizabeth. 1984. *"I, Rigoberta Menchú": An Indian Woman in Guatemala*. Trans. Ann Wright. London: Verso.

Burgos Guevara, Hugo. 1977. *Relaciones interétnicas en Riobamba: Dominio y dependencia en una región indígena ecuatoriana*. Mexico: Instituto Indigenista Interamericano.

Calhoun, Craig. 1994. *Social Theory and the Politics of Identity*. Oxford: Blackwell.

Carrasco, Hernán. 1993. "Democratización de los poderes locales y levantamiento indígena." In *Sismo Etnico en el Ecuador*, ed. CEDIME. Quito: CEDIME.

Carrasco, Hernán, and Carola Lentz. 1985. *Migrantes: Campesinos de Licto y Flores*. Quito: Abya-Yala.

CEDIME. 1993. *Sismo etnico en el Ecuador: Varias perspectivas*. Quito: Abya-Yala.

Cervone, Emma. 1995. "El retorno del Inca." Ph.D. Dissertation, St. Andrew's University.

Cervone, Emma, and Freddy Rivera. 1999. *Ecuador racista: Imagenes e identidades*. Quito: FLACSO, sede Ecuador.

Cevallos, Pedro Fermín. 1887. *Resumen de la historia general del Ecuador desde su origen hasta 1845: Geografía política*. Vols. 14, 6.

Chantal Barre, Marie. 1982. "Políticas indigenistas y reivindicaciones indias en América Latina: 1940–1980." In *America Latina: Etnodesarrollo y etnocidio*, ed. Francisco Rojas, Guillermo Bonfil Batalla, and Guillermo Rojas Aravena. San José: Ediciones FLACSO.

Chiriboga, Manuel. 1987. "Movimento campesino e indígena y participación política en el Ecuador: La construcción de identidades en una sociedad heterogénea." *Ecuador Debate* (May): 87–121. Quito: CAAP.

———. 1988a. "La reforma agraria ecuatoriana y los cambios en la distribución de la propiedad agrícola, 1974-1985." In *Transformaciones agrarias en el Ecuador*, ed. CEDIG. Quito: CEDIG.

———. 1988b. "La reforma agraria en el Ecuador y en América Latina." *Nariz del Diablo* 11: 30-36.

Clark, Kim. 1998a. "Race, 'Culture' and Mestizaje: The Statistical Construction of the Ecuadorian Nation (1930-1950)." *Journal of Historical Sociology* 7 (1): 49-72.

———. 1998b. "Racial Ideologies and the Quest for National Development: Debating the Agrarian Problem in Ecuador (1930-1950)." *Journal of Latin American Studies* 30 (2): 373-93.

Cobb, John. 1989. "Double Consciousness: William James, W. E. Du Bois, and Current Discussion of Race and Gender." Ph.D. dissertation, Southern Illinois University, Carbondale.

Cohen, Jean. 1985. "Strategy or Identity: New Theoretical Paradigms and Contemporary Social Movements." *Social Research* 52 (4): 663-715.

Colburn, Forrest D., ed. 1989. *Everyday Forms of Peasant Resistance*. Armonk, N.Y.: M. E. Sharpe.

"Como indígenas tenemos nuestros planteamientos políticos." 1986. Interview with Alberto Andrango. *Ecuador Debate* 12: 247-60.

COMUNIDEC. 1992. *Actores de una década ganada: Tribus, comunidades y campesinos en la modernidad*. Quito: COMUNIDEC.

CONAIE. 1989. *Las nacionalidades indígenas en el Ecuador*. Quito: Abya-Yala.

Conejo, Mario. 1990. "Participación política de los indígenas." In *Análisis de los procesos electorales*, vol. 4. Quito: Tribunal Supremo Electoral.

Connor, Walker. 1994. *Ethnonationalism: The Quest for Understanding*. Princeton: Princeton University Press.

Cornejo Menacho, Diego, ed. 1993. *Los indios y el estado-país: Pluriculturalidad y multietnicidad en el Ecuador. Contribuciones al debate*. Quito: Abya-Yala.

CORPEA, ILDIS, and Taller Cultural Causana Cunchic. 1992. *Pueblos indios, estado y derecho*. Quito: Corporación Editora Nacional.

Cueva, Agustín. 1982. *The Process of Political Domination in Ecuador*. New Brunswick, N.J.: Transaction Books.

De Janvry, Alain. 1981. *The Agrarian Question and Reformism in Latin America*. Baltimore: Johns Hopkins University Press.

De la Torre, Carlos. 1996. *El racismo en el Ecuador: Experiencias de los indios de clase media*. Quito: Centro Andino de Acción Popular, Colección Estudios y Análisis.

Díaz-Polanco, Hector. 1997. *Indigenous Peoples in Latin America: The Quest for Self-Determination*. Boulder, Colo.: Westview Press.

Donovan, Patricio. 1989. "En torno a la resistencia indígena: Contextualizaciones y reformas teóricas." *IDIS* 23: 160-80.

Dorner, Peter. 1992. *Latin American Land Reforms in Theory and in Practice*. Madison: University of Wisconsin Press.

Du Bois, W. E. B. 1903. *The Souls of Black Folk: Essays and Sketches.* Chicago: A. C. McClurg.

Eisenstadt, Schmuel. 1998. "The Construction of Collective Identities in Latin America: Beyond the European Nation-State Model." In *Constructing Collective Identities and Shaping Public Spheres: Latin American Paths,* ed. Louis Roniger and Mario Sznajder. Brighton: Sussex Academic Press.

Enloe, Cynthia. 1972. *Ethnic Conflict and Political Development.* Boston: Little, Brown.

Escobar, Arturo, and Sonia Alvarez. 1992. *The Making of Social Movements in Latin America: Identity, Strategy, and Democracy.* Boulder, Colo.: Westview Press.

Esman, Milton J., and Itamar Rabinovich. 1988. *Ethnicity, Pluralism and the State in the Middle East.* Ithaca: Cornell University Press.

FEPP. 1993. *Versión corregida del diagnóstico de la regional Riobamba Parte Cacha.* Quito: FEPP.

Foweraker, Joe. 1995. *Theorizing Social Movements.* Boulder, Colo.: Pluto Press.

Friedman, Jonathan. 1992. "Myth, History and Political Identity." *Cultural Anthropology* 7 (2): 194–210.

Geertz, Clifford. 1971. *Myth, Symbol, and Culture.* New York: Norton.

———. 1973. *The Interpretation of Cultures: Selected Essays.* New York: Basic Books.

Gilroy, Paul. 1987. *There Ain't No Black in the Union Jack: The Cultural Politics of Race and Nation.* London: Hutchinson.

Gitlin, Todd. 1994. "From Universality to Difference: Notes on the Fragmentation of the Idea of the Left." In *Social Theory and the Politics of Identity,* ed. Craig Calhoun. Oxford: Blackwell.

Goffman, Erving. 1963. *Stigma: Notes on the Management of Spoiled Identity.* Englewood Cliffs, N.J.: Prentice Hall.

Goldberg, David Theo, ed. 1990. *Anatomy of Racism.* Minneapolis: University of Minnesota Press.

———. 1993. *Racist Culture: Philosophy and the Politics of Meaning.* Oxford: Blackwell.

Graham, Richard, ed. 1990. *The Idea of Race in Latin America.* Austin: University of Texas Press.

Guerrero, Andrés. 1983. *Haciendas, capital y lucha de clases andina: Disolución de la Hacienda Serrana y lucha política en los años 1960–1964.* Quito: Editorial El Conejo.

———. 1991. *La semántica de la dominación: El concertaje de indios.* Quito: Ediciones Libri-Mundi.

———. 1993. "La desintegración de la administración etnica en el Ecuador." In *Sismo Etnico en el Ecuador,* ed. CEDIME. Quito: CEDIME.

———. 1994. "Una imagen ventrílocua: El discurso liberal de la desgraciada raza indígena a fines del siglo XIX." In *Imagenes e imagineros: Representaciones de los indígenas ecuatorianos, siglos XIX y XX,* ed. Blanca Muratorio. Quito: FLACSO.

———. 2000. "El proceso de identificación: Sentido común ciudadano, ventriloquía y transescritura." In *Etnicidades.* Quito: FLACSO.

Gurr, Ted. 1970. *Why Men Rebel.* Princeton: Princeton University Press.

Haber, Paul. 1996. "Identity and Political Process: Recent Trends in the Study of Latin American Social Movements." *Latin American Research Review* 31 (1): 171–88.

Hale, Charles. 1992. "Between Che Guevara and the Pachamama: Mestizos, Indians and Identity Politics in the Anti-Quicentenary Campaign." Paper presented at the Seventeenth International Congress of the Latin American Studies Association, Los Angeles, September 24–27.

———. 1994. *Resistance and Contradiction: Meskitu Indians and the Nicaraguan State*. Stanford: Stanford University Press.

Hall, Stuart. 1986. "Gramsci's Relevance for the Study of Race and Ethnicity." *Journal of Communication Inquiry* 10 (2): 5–27.

Hanchard, Michael. 1991. "Racial Consciousness and Afro-Diasporic Experiences: Antonio Gramsci Reconsidered." *Socialism and Democracy* 7, no. 14 (Fall): 83–106.

———. 1994. *Orpheus and Power: The Movimento Negro and Rio de Janeiro and São Paolo, Brazil: 1945–1988*. Princeton: Princeton University Press.

Handelman, Howard. 1980. "Ecuadorian Agrarian Reform: The Politics of Limited Change." American Universities Field Staff Report, Hanover, N.H.

Harris, Marvin. 1974. *Patterns of Race in the Americas*. New York: Columbia University Press.

Hasenbalg, Carlos. 1985. "Race and Socioeconomic Inequalities in Brazil." In *Race, Class and Power in Brazil*, ed. Pierre Michel-Fontaine. Los Angeles: Center for African-American Studies, UCLA.

Hill, Jonathan. 1994. "Contested Pasts and the Practice of Anthropology." *American Anthropologist* 94 (4): 809–15.

Hobsbawm, Eric J. 1971. *Primitive Rebels: Studies in Archaic Forms of Social Movement in the 19th and 20th Centuries*. Manchester: Manchester University Press.

———. 1990. *Nations and Nationalism since 1870*. New York: Cambridge University Press.

Hobsbawm, Eric J., and Terence Ranger. 1983. *The Invention of Tradition*. Cambridge: Cambridge University Press.

Hopkins, Diane. 1985. "The Peruvian Agrarian Reform: Dissent from Below." *Human Organization* 44 (1): 18–32.

Horowitz, Donald. 1985. *Ethnic Groups in Conflict*. Berkeley: University of California Press.

Ibarra, Alicia. 1992. *Los indigenas y el estado en el Ecuador: La práctica neoindigenista*. Quito: Abya-Yala.

ILDIS. 1991. *Indios*. Quito: Abya-Yala.

Isaacs, Anita. 1993. *Military Rule and Transition in Ecuador, 1972–1992*. Pittsburgh, Pa.: University of Pittsburgh Press.

Iturralde, Diego. 1988. "Notas para una historia política del campesinado ecuatoriano." In *Nuevas investigaciones antropológicas*, ed. Lauris McKee and Sylvia Arguello. Quito: Abya-Yala.

IWGIA. 1971."Declaration of Barbados."

Jaquette, Jane S., ed. 1989. *The Women's Movement in Latin America*. Boston: Unwin and Hyman.
Jaramillo Alvarado, Pío. 1922. "El indio ecuatoriano." Selected text in *Pensamiento indigenista del Ecuador*, ed. Banco Central del Ecuador. Biblioteca Básica del Pensamiento Ecuatoriano 34. Quito: Corporación Editora Nacional.
Jimenez, Michael F. 1989. "Class, Gender and Peasant Resistance in Central America, 1900–1930." In *Everyday Forms of Peasant Resistance*, ed. Forrest D. Colburn. New York: M. E. Sharpe.
Knapp, Gregory. 1991. *Geografía quichua del Ecuador: Nucleos, dominios y esfera*. Quito: Abya-Yala.
Korokvin, Tania. 1992. *Los indígenas, los campesinos y el estado: El crecimiento del movimiento comunitario en la sierra ecuatoriana*. Monograph, Waterloo University, Canada.
Laclau, Ernest, and Chantal Mouffe. 1994. *The Making of Political Identities*. London: Verso.
Lehmann, David. 1990. *Democracy and Development in Latin America: Economics, Politics and Religion in Latin America in the Post-War Period*. Philadelphia: Temple University Press.
Lloyd, Rudolph, and Susanne Hoeber Rudolph. 1969. *The Modernity of Tradition: Political Development in India*. Chicago: University of Chicago Press.
Macas, Luis. 1991. *El levantimiento indígena visto por sus protagonistas*. Quito: ICCI.
Mallon, Florencia. "Indian Communities, Political Culture and the State in Latin America: 1780–1990." *Journal of Latin American Studies* (Suppl.) 24: 35–53.
Malo, Claudio, ed. 1988. *Pensamiento indigenista del Ecuador*. Biblioteca Básica del Pensamiento Ecuatoriano 34. Quito: Corporación Editora Nacional.
Mariátegui, José Carlos. 1928. *Siete ensayos de interpretación de la realidad peruana*. Lima: Biblioteca Amauta.
Martinez, Nicolás. 1926. "La condición actual de la raza indígena en Tungurahua." In *Indianistas, indianofilos, indigenistas: Entre el enigma y la fascinación. Una antología de textos sobre el "problema" indígena*, ed. Jorge L. Trujillo. Quito: Abya-Yala.
McAdam, Doug. 1982. *Political Process and the Development of Black Insurgency: 1930–1970*. Chicago: University of Chicago Press.
Melucci, Alberto. 1989. *Nomads of the Present: Social Movements and Individual Needs in Contemporary Society*. Ed. John Keane and Paul Mier. Philadelphia: Temple University Press.
Mijeski, Kenneth, and Scott Beck. 1998. "Mainstreaming the Indigenous Movement in Ecuador: The Electoral Strategy." Paper presented at the Twenty-fifth International Congress of the Latin American Studies Association, Chicago, September 24–26.
Ministerio de Bienestar Social. 1984. *Politica estatal y población indígena*. Quito: Abya-Yala.
Moncayo, Abelardo. [1895] 1986. "El concertaje de indios." In *Pensamiento agrario ecuatoriano*, ed. R. Marchan. Quito: BCE-CEN.

Monsalve Pozo, Luis. 1943. *El indio: Cuestiones de su vida y de su pasión*. Cuenca: Austral.
Moore, Barrington. 1969. *The Social Origins of Dictatorship and Democracy*. Harmondsworth: Penguin.
Moreno, Segundo, and José Figueroa. 1992. *El levantamiento indígena del Inti Raymi de 1990*. Quito: FESO, Abya-Yala.
Moreno, Segundo, and Udo Oberem. 1981. *Contribución a la etnohistoria ecuatoriana*. Otavalo: Instituto Otavaleño de Antropología.
Mörner, Magnus. 1967. *Race Mixture in the History of Latin America*. Boston: Little, Brown.
Muñoz, Jorge, and Isabel Lavadenz. 1997. "Reforming the Agrarian Reform in Bolivia." Development Discussion Paper no. 589. Harvard Institute for International Development.
Muratorio, Blanca. 1982. *Etnicidad, evangelización y protesta en el Ecuador: Una perspectiva antropológica*. Quito: CIESE.
———, ed. 1994. *Imagenes e imagineros: Representaciones de los indígenas ecuatorianos, siglos XIX y XX*. Quito: FLACSO.
Norval, Aletta J. 1996. "Thinking Identities: Against a Theory of Ethnicity." In *The Politics of Difference: Ethnic Premises in a World of Power*, ed. Edwin N. Wilmsen and Patrick McAllister. Chicago: University of Chicago Press.
Oboler, Suzanne. 1995. *Ethnic Labels, Latino Lives: Identity and the Politics of Representation in the United States*. Minneapolis: University of Minnesota Press.
Olano, J. 1983. "Programas de partidos vs. campesinos indígenas." *Ecuador Debate* (December): 73–82.
Omi, Michael, and Howard Winant. 1986. *Racial Formation in the United States from the 1960s to the 1990s*. New York: Routledge.
Pachano, Simon. 1986. *Pueblos de la sierra*. Quito: IEE-PISPAL.
———. 1993. "Imagen, identidad, desigualdad." In *Los indios y el estado-país: Pluriculturalidad y multietnicidad en el Ecuador. Contribuciones al debate*, ed. Diego Cornejo Menacho. Quito: Abya-Yala.
Padilla, Félix. 1985. *Latino Ethnic Consiousness: The Case of Mexican Americans and Puerto Ricans in Chicago*. Notre Dame, Ind.: University of Notre Dame Press.
Pareja Diezcanseco, Alfredo. 1979. *Ecuador: La república de 1830 a nuestros días*. Quito: Editorial Universitaria.
Pitt Rivers, Julian. 1971. "Race, Color and Class in Latin America and the Andes." In *Majority and Minority: The Dynamics of Racial and Ethnic Relations*, ed. Norman Yetman and C. Hay Steele. Boston: Allyn and Bacon.
Piven, Frances Fox, and Richard Cloward. 1979. *Poor Peoples' Movements: When They Succeed, How They Fail*. New York: Vintage Books.
Plummer, Ken. 1996. "Symbolic Interactionism in the Twentieth Century: The Rise of Empirical Social Theory." In *The Blackwell Companion to Social Theory*. Oxford: Blackwell.
Prieto, Mercedes. 1978. "Condicionamientos de la movilización campesina: El caso de las Haciendas Olmedo/Cayambe (1926–1948)." Thesis. Quito: PUCE.

Quijano, Anibal. 1979. *Problema agrario y movimientos campesinos en América Latina*. Lima: Mosca Azul Editors.

Radcliffe, Sarah. 1993. "People Have to Rise Up—Like the Great Women Fighters: The State and Peasant Women in Peru." In *Viva: Women and Popular Protest in Latin America*, ed. Sarah Radcliffe and Sallie Westwood. London: Routledge.

Ramón Valarezo, Galo. 1986. "La visión andina sobre el estado colonial." *Ecuador Debate* 12 (December): 79–100.

———. 1993. *El regreso de los runas: La potencialidad del proyecto indio en el Ecuador contemporáneo*. Quito: COMUNIDEC.

Reidinger, Jeff. 1993. "Agrarian Reform in the Phillipines." In *The Violence Within: Cultural and Political Opposition in Divided Nations*, ed. Kay Warren. Boulder, Colo.: Westview Press.

Rex, John. *Race and Ethnicity*. Milton Keyes, U.K.: Open University Press.

Rohn, Francisco. 1978. "Las movilizaciones campesinas en el Ecuador, 1968–1977: El caso de ECUARUNARI." Thesis, CLACSO-PUCE.

Rosero, Fernando. 1990. *Levantamiento indígena: Tierra y precios*. Quito: CEDIS.

Rothschild, Joseph. 1981. *Ethnopolitics: A Conceptual Framework*. New York: Columbia University Press.

Rudolph, Lloyd, and Suzanne Rudolph. 1967. *The Modernity of Tradition: Political Development in India*. Chicago: University of Chicago Press.

Salamea, Lucía. 1980. "La transformación de la hacienda y los cambios en la condición campesina." In *Ecuador: Cambios en el agro serrano*. Quito: FLACSO and Centro de Planificación y Estudios Sociales.

Sánchez-Parga, Jose. 1986. "Etnia y formación de clase." *Ecuador Debate* 12 (December): 25–77.

———. 1988. *Actores y discursos culturales: Ecuador, 1972-1988*. Quito: Centro Andino de Acción Popular.

———. 1990. *Etnia, poder y diferencia en los Andes Septentrionales*. Quito: Abya-Yala.

———. 1992a. "Comunidad indígena y estado nacional." In *Pueblos indios, estado, y derecho*, ed. CORPEA, ILDIS, and Taller Cultural Causana Cunchic. Quito: Corporación Editora Nacional.

———. 1992b. *Presente y futuro de los pueblos indígenas*. Quito: Siglo XXI.

San Juan, Epifanio. 1992. *Racial Formations/Critical Transformations: Articulations of Power in Ethnic and Racial Studies in the United States*. Atlantic Highlands, N.J.: Humanities Press.

Santana, Roberto. 1981. "El caso de ECURAUNARI." *Nariz del Diablo* 2 (7): 30–51.

———. 1984. "Actualidad de una confrontación: Cuestión indígena y cuestión campesina en el espacio interandino ecuatoriano." In *La cuestión indígena en el Ecuador*, ed. CIRE. Quito: CIRE.

———. 1986. "La cuestión etnica y la democracia en el Ecuador." *Ecuador Debate* 12 (December): 101–24.

———. 1993. "Actores y escenarios étnicos en Ecuador: El levantamiento de 1990." Unpublished manuscript.

Scott, James C. 1976. *The Moral Economy of the Peasant*. New Haven: Yale University Press.

———. 1985. *Weapons of the Weak: Everyday Forms of Peasant Resistance*. New Haven: Yale University Press.

Seligmann, Linda. 1995. *Reform or Revolution: Political Struggles in the Peruvian Andes, 1969–1991*. Stanford: Stanford University Press.

Selverston, Melina. 1994. "The 1990 Indigenous Uprising and the State in Ecuador." In *Indigenous Peoples and Democracy in Latin America*, ed. Donna Lee Van Cott. New York: St. Martin's Press in association with the Inter-American Dialogue.

Silva, Erika. 1992. *Mitos de la ecuatorianidad*. Quito: Abya-Yala.

Skidmore, Thomas. 1992. *Fact and Myth: Discovering a Racial Problem in Brazil*. Notre Dame, Ind.: Helen Kellog Institute for International Studies, University of Notre Dame.

Smith, Anthony. 1991. "The Nation: Invented, Imagined, Reconstructed?" *Millenium* 12 (2): 149–61.

Sollors, Werner, ed. 1989. *The Invention of Ethnicity*. New York: Oxford University Press.

Solomos, John. 1989. *Race and Racism in Contemporary Britain*. London: Macmillan.

Stavenhagen, Rodolfo. 1968. *Clases, colonialismo y aculturación*. Cuadernos del Seminario de Integración Guatemalteca. Guatemala: Ministerio de Educación.

———. 1992. "Challenging the Nation-State in Latin America." *Journal of International Affairs* 45 (Winter): 421–40.

Stepan, Alfred. 1978. *State and Society: Peru in Comparative Perspective*. Princeton: Princeton University Press.

Stepan, Nancy Leys. 1991. *The Hour of Eugenics in Latin America*. Ithaca: Cornell University Press.

Stern, Steve J., ed. 1987. *Resistance, Rebellion and Consciousness in the Andean Peasant World, Eighteenth to Twentieth Centuries*. Madison: University of Wisconsin Press.

Stokes, Susan. 1995. *Culture in Conflict: Social Movements and the State in Peru*. Berkeley: University of California Press.

Sylva, Paola. 1986. *Gamonalismo y lucha campesina: El caso de la provincia de Chimborazo*. Quito: Abya-Yala.

———. 1991. *La organización rural en el Ecuador*. Quito: CEPP-Abya-Yala.

Tarrow, Sidney. 1994. *Power in Movement: Social Movements, Collective Action and Politics*. Cambridge: Cambridge University Press.

Taylor, Charles. 1991. *The Malaise of Modernity*. Concord, Ont.: House of Anansi Press.

Todorov, Tzvetan. 1992. *The Conquest of America: The Question of the Other*. New York: Harper Perennial.

Trujillo, Jorge L. 1987. "Comentarios a la ponencia: Movimiento campesino e indígena y participación política." *Ecuador Debate* 13 (May): 123–28.

———, ed. 1993. *Indianistas, indianofilos, indigenistas: Entre el enigma y la fascinación. Una antología de textos sobre el problema indígena*. Quito: Abya-Yala.

UNESCO. 1977. *Race and Class in Post-Colonial Society: A Study of Ethnic Group Relations in the English-speaking Caribbean, Bolivia, Chile and Mexico.* Paris: UNESCO.

Valenzuela Arce, José Manuel. 1992. *Decadencia y auge de las identidades: Cultura nacional, identidad cultural y modernización.* Tijuana: Colegio de la Frontera Norte.

Van Cott, Donna Lee. 1994. "Indigenous Peoples and Democracy: Issues for Policymakers." In *Indigenous Peoples and Democracy in Latin America*, ed. Donna Lee Van Cott. New York: St. Martin's Press.

———. 2000. *The Friendly Liquidation of the Past: The Politics of Diversity in Latin America.* Pittsburgh, Pa.: University of Pittsburgh Press.

Van der Berge, Pierre. 1978. *Race and Racism: A Comparative Perspective.* New York: Wiley.

Varese, Stefano. 1996. "The Ethnopolitics of Indian Resistance in Latin America." *Latin American Perspectives* 23, no. 2 (Spring): 58–71.

Vasconcelos, José. 1948. *La raza cósmica: Misión de la raza iberoamericana, Argentina y Brazil.* Mexico: Espasa Colpe Mexicana.

Velasco, Fernando. 1979. *Reforma agraria y movimiento campesino indígena de la sierra.* Quito: El Conejo.

Wade, Peter. 1993. *Blackness and Race Mixture: The Dynamics of Racial Identity in Colombia.* Baltimore: Johns Hopkins University Press.

Wallerstein, Immanuel, and Etienne Balibar. 1991. *Race, Nation, Class: Ambigious Identities.* New York: Routledge, Chapman and Hall.

Warren, Kay. 1978. *The Symbolism of Subordination: Indian Identity in a Guatemalan Town.* Austin: University of Texas Press.

Weismantel, Mary. 1997. "White Cannibals: Fantasies of Racial Violence in the Andes." *Identities* 4 (1): 29–44.

West, Cornell. 1988. "Marxist Theory and the Specificity of Afro-American Oppression." In *Marxism and the Interpretation of Culture*, ed. Laurence Grossberg. Urbana: University of Illinois Press.

Whitten, Norman. 1981. *Cultural Transformations and Ethnicity in Ecuador.* Urbana: University of Illinois Press.

1997 "Return of the Yumbo: The Indigenous Caminata from Amazonia to Andean Quito." *American Ethnologist* 24 (2): 355–91.

Wiarda, Howard. 1981. *Corporatism and National Development in Latin America.* Boulder, Colo.: Westview Press.

Wright, Winthrop C. 1990. *Café con Leche: Race, Class and National Image in Venezuela.* Austin: University of Texas Press.

Yashar, Deborah. 1998. "Contesting Citizenship: Indigenous Movements and Democracy in Latin America." *Comparative Politics* 31, no. 1 (October): 23–42.

Young, Crawford. 1976. *The Politics of Cultural Pluralism.* Madison: University of Wisconsin Press.

Zamosc, Leon. 1995. *Estadística de las areas de predominio etnico de la sierra ecuatoriana.* Quito: Abya-Yala.

REFERENCES

ARCHIVES

Archivo de Arzobispado de Riobamba

Comisión Coordinadora del Seminario Nacional de Alfabetización Bilingue Quichua La Merced Nueva Vida. April 14–18, 1980. "Resoluciones generales."
"Curso de leyes para campesinos." September 1977. Hogar Santa Cruz.
"Curso sobre política para campesinos." May 1978.
"Encuentro Nacional de Comunidades Cristianas Campesinas." January 20–25, 1980.
Jatun Ayllu. N.d. "Evaluación del Jatun Ayllu y de los cabildos de cada comuna durante el año 1983 y programación para el año 1994."
"Otra vez sangre en el Páramo." 1974.
Segunda Jornada de Estudiantes Campesinos en Chimborazo. 1977.

Confederación de Nacionalidades Indígenas del Ecuador (CONAIE)

CONACNIE. "Las organizaciones indígenas del Ecuador denunciamos la división de las comunidades con el programa de alfabetización." N.d.
———. "Acuerdo puntual." N.d.
CONAIE. "A las organizaciones indígenas del país." May 19, 1983.
———. "A las organizaciones indígenas del país, dirigentes, promotores provinciales y nacionales de alfabetización." May 6, 1983.
———. "Comisión organizadora del Primer Congreso del CONAIE: Acuerdo puntual." N.d.
———. "Comisión política del Primer Congreso de las Nacionalidades Indígenas del Ecuador." 1986.

Archivos de la Jefatura Política de Cotacachi

Cotacachi Canton. "Jefe Político's Report to the Governor of Imbabura." 1960–80.

ECUARUNARI

"Causaimanta Allpamanta Quishpirinca caman tantanacushucnchi: Organizaciones indígenas del Ecuador." May 1984.
"Al Dr. Jaime Roldós Aguilera, presidente electo, y a los representantes a la Camara Nacional en un nuevo régimen político del Ecuador." June 18, 1979.
"Pueblo ecuatoriano únete a la gran marcha nacional campesina e indígena "Mártires de Aztra." 1979.
"Resoluciones generales del VI congreso nacional del Ecuarunari realizado en la ciudad de Riobamba en el mes de septiembre de 1981. Plataforma de Lucha." September 1981.
"VI Congreso Nacional Trabajo de la Comisión." No. 4. 1981.
"VII Congreso Nacional. Documento político." October 25–29, 1983.

Federación de Organizaciones Indígenas de Napo (FOIN)

FOIN. "La lucha de los Napo Runas." 1987.
Viteri, Alfredo. *Derechos del pueblo.* CEDHU, 1983.

Archivos de la Unión de Organizaciones Campesinas de Cotacachi (UNORCIC)

Andrango, Alberto. Speech. July 9, 1986.
Banco Central del Ecuador. *FODERUMA: Memoria 1978–1984.* N.d.
FODERUMA, Banco Central del Ecuador. "Informe semestral de labores." January-June 1985.
———. "Study of Thirty-Nine Communities." 1988.
Frente de Solidaridad con los Pueblos Indígenas. "Por que el Instituto Linguístico de Verano debe salir del país." Quito. June 30, 1981.
UNORCIC. Executive Committee's Report to the Fourth Congress, 1992.
———. Letter from the UNORCIC to the Provincial Director of Education in Imbabura, June 5, 1986.
———. Organizational meeting, n.d.
———. Report on Economic and Geographic Characteristics. UNORCIC archives, n.d.

GOVERNMENT DOCUMENTS

Oficina Nacional de Alfabetización. "La alfabetización bilingue bicultural." 1981.
———. "La alfabetización participatoria, como proceso socio-político." August 1981.
———. "Alfabetización: Hacia una auténtica participación popular." 1981.
———. "Alfabetización y pluralismo." 1981.
República del Ecuador. "Discurso presidencial a las FF.AA. segundo aniversario." February 1974.
———. "Ecuador: Filosofía y plan de acción del gobierno revolucionario." N.d.
———. *Filosofía y plan de acción del gobierno revolucionario y nacionalista del Ecuador.* N.d.
———. INEC. *III censo de población y vivienda: Imbabura, 1974.*
———. INEC. *IV censo de poblacion 1980.*
———. INEC. *V censo de población y IV de vivienda, 1992.*
———. Tribunal Supremo Electoral. *Electoral Statistics.* 1979–92.
Rodriguez Lara, Guillermo. Gobierno Nacionalista Revolucionario. 1974.

INTERVIEWS

All interviews were conducted by the author unless otherwise specified.

Abagalla, Manuel, November 9, 1993, Riobamba.
Andrango, Alberto, July 8, 1993, Topo Chico, Cotacachi.
Andrango, Segundo, July 7, 1993, Topo Chico, Cotacachi.

Aro, Carmen, August 1993, Cotacachi.
Asqui, Agustina, and José Janeta, November 7, 1993, Cacha-Obraje.
Chancoso, Blanca, October 8, 1993, Quito.
Cocha, Silverio, August 24, 1993, Guamote. Interview by Marta Roldós.
de la Cruz, Pedro, July 5 and August 6, 1993, Cotacachi.
Gladys, August 16, 1993, Riobamba.
Guamachi, Rafael, August 10, 1993, Tixán.
Guacho, Ana María, August 20, 1993, Riobamba.
Guamán, José, July 14, 1992, Quito.
Housse, Rogelio, October 1993, Quito.
Janeta, Manuel, November 3, 1993, Cacha.
Lima, Alberto, August 5, 1993, Cotacachi.
Lovato, Hector, n.d., Riobamba.
Llucu, Miguel, July 1, 1993, Quito.
Macas, Luis, May 11 and August 6, 1993, Quito.
Maldonado, Pedro Vicente, November 10, 1993, Cacha.
Morán, Enrique, August 1993, Cotacachi.
Morán, Lucas, August 1993, Cotacachi.
Morocho, José, November 1, 1993, Cacha-Machángara.
Morocho, Pedro, November, 1993, Cacha-Machángara.
Paca, Manuel, August 13, 1994, Tixán.
Pacari, Nina, September 1, 1993, Riobamba.
Perez, Juan, August 10, 1993, Riobamba.
Rodriguez, Genoveva, August 16, 1993, Riobamba.
Tapuy, Cristobal, September 20, 1993, Quito.
Tatamues, Mesías, June 28, 1993, Quito.
Tenesaca, Delfín, August 10, 1993, Santa Cruz, Riobamba.
Tiopul, Tomás, November 7, 1993, Cacha-Machángara.
Tituaña, Auqui, October 8, 1993, Quito.
Vallejo, Manuel, November 12, 1993, Yaruquíes.
Verduga, Cesar, August 1993, Quito. Interview by Marta Roldós.

PERIODICALS AND NEWSPAPERS

"Una administración a lo interno." 1990. *Hoy*, August 31.
"Alfabetización o proselitismo?" 1980. *Nueva* 72 (December).
"Borja entregó Sistema Electrico." 1990. *Hoy*, September 10.
"El campesinado indígena y la alfabetización." 1980. *Acción 5: Boletín Informativo Agrario* (May–June). Quito: CIESE.
"Campesinos de Llín-Llín: La justicia tarda pero llega." *Nueva* 62 (February 1980): 20–25.
"Campesinos de Quinchuquí: Morir luchando antes que morir en casa." 1978. *Nueva* 53 (November).

"Una condena al racismo." 1990. Transcript of a Chimborazo Indian's speech. *Punto de Vista* 421 (June 11).
"Ecuador defiende estado multi-étnico." 1989. *Hoy*, June 11, 1989.
"Derecho tradicional." 1990. *Hoy*, August 31.
"El despertar indígena se da en la lucha por la tierra." 1983. *Nueva* (June).
"Ecuador: Indigenous Peoples Create Political Movements." 1995. *ALAI*, August 21.
Flores, Antonio B. A. 1961. "Los indios y los montuvios han despertado." *Mañana* 2, no. 98 (December 21).
"Gobierno crea dirección de pueblos indígenas." 1985. *Amanecer Indio*, December 30.
"El grito en el cielo." 1983. *Nueva* 94 (January–February): 30.
"La iglesia y la inquisición militar." 1976. *Nueva* 33 (September).
"Indians of Ecuador Coalescing in Quest for Political Power." 1996. *Washington Post*, July 23.
"Investigarán las culturas vernáculas." 1984. *El Comercio*, June 1.
KIPU: El mundo indígena el la prensa ecuatoriana, nos. 1–24. Quito: Abya-Yala.
"Lázaro Condo no murió en vano." 1978. *Nueva* 52 (October 8).
Moscoso, Gladys. 1986. "El pueblo ya se pronunció." *Nueva* 127 (June).
Proaño, Octavio. 1985. "La alfabetización se extranjeriza." *Nueva* 118 (September).
"Quinchuquí: El alto precio de la lucha." 1979. *Nueva* 59 (November): 51.
"Quinchuquí: Ya basta!" 1980. *Nueva* 67 (July).
"Quinchuquí: Hasta cuando patrón IERAC?" 1981. *Nueva* 76 (April).
Ramirez, Fausto. 1978. "Denuncian: Penetración de la CIA en el movimiento indígena." *Nueva* 45, 46, 47, 48.
Ramón, Galo. 1980. "La comunidad indígena ecuatoriana: Planteos políticos." *Nariz del Diablo* 1, no. 3 (July-August).
"Recursos son de todos." 1990. *Hoy*, August 31.
"Reflexiones sobre el movimiento popular ecuatoriano." 1985. *Punto de Vista* 5 (September 2).
"Seminario sobre política estatal y población indígena." 1984. *El Mercurio*, February 21.
"VI Congreso de Ecuarunari: Contra política anticampesina." 1981. *Punto de Vista*, October 8.
"Soplan vientos de una guerra racial." 1990. *La Otra*, August 16.
"El Tribunal Indígena de Cotopaxi." 1990. *Punto de Vista* 424 (July 2).
Vera, Hugo. 1977. "Sangre sobre el azúcar." *Vistazo* (November).
"Vías no están militarizadas." 1990. *Hoy*, August 29.

Index

Achuar, 6
Agrarian Development Promotion Law of 1979, 56–58
Agrarian reform, 3–16, 20, 26–29, 37–56, 60–61, 74, 88, 146, 148, 154, 166, 189, 228; 1964 reform, 15–16, 38–39, 77, 45, 123; 1973 reform, 15–16, 123
Alcaldes, 115–19, 124–26, 240n.7
Alliance, 13, 36, 96, 142, 147, 223; indigenous-mestizo, 87, 93, 143; interracial, 26, 73, 98, peasant-worker, 13; popular, 168, 181. *See also* Coalitions; Coalition politics
Amulag, 113, 133–34
Andrango, Alberto, 72–73, 83, 86, 91–96, 101–102, 105, 108
Annexes, 42, definition of, 232n.8
Anticapitalism, 33, 157–59
Anti-imperialism, 24, 34, 176
Antiracism, 5, 24, 84, 143, 154–60, 163, 181, 201, 219
Arranche, 66, 122
Arrieta, Father Modesto, 125–33, 240n.15
Autonomy, 19–20, 23–24, 34, 72, 110, 127, 129, 136, 142–43, 154–57, 173, 182, 195, 198, 199, 220–21, 226; political, 5, 19, 42, 156–60, 162–63, 168, 171–72, 201, 211–12, 215
Azuay, province of, 6, 163, 230, 242n.3

Barbados, declaration of, 188–89, 195, 207. *See also* Indigenismo
Barsky, Osvaldo, 232n.4, 236n.6
Bolivar, province of, 6, 17

Bolivia, 10, 33, 42; land reform in 37, 39, 51–52
Borja, Rodrigo, 20, 216; administration of, 16, 184, 203, 208, 248n.35
Bourdieu, Pierre, 111–12, 118, 123, 139. *See also* Doxa

Cacha, Chimborazo, 110–44, 155, 193, 246n.7; ethnic identity, 110, 132–41; parish, 127–31, 142; population, 112, 240nn.6,8,15
Caciques, 12, 115–23, 125, 246n.7
Campesinismo, 4, 29, 33–34, 84, 87, 149, 160–62, 165, 173–76, 179, 183, 186, 201, 218–19; definition of, 14–15. *See also* Campesinista
Campesinista, 147, 150, 159–61, 164–66, 169, 173–75, 179–83, 208, 222; discourse, 141; organizations, 14, 22, 143; politics, 14, 28, 108, 201. *See also* Campesinismo
Cañar, province of, 6, 155; Cañaris, 8, 160–63
Capitalism, 13, 45, 158–59. *See also* Development
Carchi, province of, 6, 66, 242n.3
Cayambe, canton of, 12, 14, 230nn.6,9
Central Intelligence Agency (CIA), 164, 167
Central de Organizaciones Clasistas (CEDOC), 167–69, 242n.4
Centro de Investigación para la Educación Indígena (CIEI), 191, 205
Chamber of Agriculture, 20, 48, 212
Chancoso, Blanca, 155, 162, 165, 177

Chicha, 58; stores (*chicherías*), 155; vendors of (*chicheros*), 61, 118, 120, 240n.4
Chimborazo, province of, 6, 17, 62–63, 110, 125, 138, 150–51, 155, 163, 240n.8, 241n.21, 243n.15
Chulqueros, 61, 118, 120, 129, 240n.15
Church, 12, 22, 62, 128, 131, 150, 152; Catholic, 18, 125–26, 148
Citizenship, 11, 14, 16, 33, 40, 67, 70, 72, 80–81, 95, 126, 140, 143, 148, 157, 159, 189, 197, 201, 216, 226
Civil registry, 114, 122, 131, 134, 200
Civil rights, 163, 169, 184–85
Class, 5, 8, 26, 30, 34–35, 60, 68, 73, 84–85, 92–95, 141, 146, 164, 222–23; consciousness, 14, 85, 107, 144, 163; difference, 8, 85; discourse, 15, 87; identity, 144, 179, 207; politics, 23, 109, 144, 146, 226–27
Class-centered approach, 25–27, 29
Coalitions, 73, 89, 98, 142–43, 147, 165, 181, 218, 221, 237n.28; Indian-Left, 87, 26; highland-lowland, 173–78
Coalition politics, 15, 21, 37
Colombia, 185, 188
Colonization of lowlands, 55–56, 59, 189, 202
Communist, 26, 48; Party, 13, 15, 21, 233n.13. *See also* Left
Communities, 7, 12, 18, 27–28, 36, 42, 61, 124–27, 233n.10; definition of, 232n.8, 243n.13; free, 11, 14, 39, 116, 121, 123, 139–40, 231nn.1(chap. 3),3(chap. 3)
Conciertos (concertaje), 10, 12. *See also* Debt peonage
Confederación de Nacionalidades Indígenas del Ecuador (CONAIE), 3, 17–19, 21, 73, 92, 98, 100–104, 107–109, 148, 184, 196, 203–12, 219–24, 228, 234n.28, 236n.6, 246n.11; history,174–78
Confederación Ecuatoriana de Organizaciones Clasistas (CEDOC), 15, 149
Confederación Nacional de Indígenas Amazónicos (CONFENIAE), 17, 174, 210
Congress, 20, 192, 205, 208, 248n.34
Consciousness, 5, 23, 25–27, 29–33, 69, 85, 134, 162, 182, 198, 200; double, 24, 32–34, 146, 161, 174, 178, 181–83, 199, 218, 222; ethnic, 145, 165; false, 32, 35, 119, 132, 179, 201; racial, 31, 85–86, 107, 218–19, 225. *See also* Dubois, W. E.
Constitution, 20, 246n.8

Cooperatives, 13, 15, 41–42, 47, 52–53, 58. *See also* Agrarian reform
Coordinadora de Indígenas de la Costa Ecuatoriana (COICE), 17
Coordinadora Nacional de Organizaciones Indígenas del Ecuador (CONACNIE), 92, 148, 173, 178, 205, 207
Cotacachi: canton of, 19, 65, 67, 72–109, 142–44, 154–55, 161, 179, 182, 219–20, 234n.22, 235n.2, 236nn.6,7, 237n.28; and electoral politics, 90–98. *See also* Unión de Organizaciones Campesinas de Cotacachi
Cotopaxi, province of, 6, 17–18, 151, 230n.5
Council: city, 90–91, 96, 99–100; community 38, 42, 126, 232n.8, 243n.13
Cultural: difference, 43, 59, 115; policy, 186–88, 193–95, 199, 204–206, 210, 214–15, 245n.4; recovery, 5, 21, 86, 132, 143, 163, 194, 219; rights, 3, 17, 190, 206, 210
Culture, 15, 27 , 46, 76, 86–87, 99, 163, 170, 207, 230n.8

Daquilema, Fernando, 132–34, 241n.28
De la Cruz, Pedro, 67, 95–96, 99, 102, 105–109
Democracia Popular (DP), 88, 91, 104
Debt peonage, 14, 60. *See also Conciertos*
Development, 36, 150, 184; national, 44–45, 49, 54, 189, 197; rural, 14, 16, 29, 34, 40–41, 44–47, 52, 54, 68–71, 89, 149, 186, 191, 199, 207, 210, 233n.21, 245n.4, 246n.5
Domination, 111, 116, 118
Doxa, 111–12, 116, 119, 134, 139. *See also* Bourdieu, Pierre
Dubois, W. E., 32–33. *See also* Consciousness, double
Duchicela dynasty, 132–33, 241n.30

Ecuador, 3–6, 12, 16, 19, 53, 59, 219
Ecuarunapac Riccharimui (ECUARUNARI), 21–22, 41, 68, 87, 145–81, 204–207, 210, 232n.7, 233n.21, 242n.8, 243n.15; history, 5, 16–17, 149–50; relationship with church, 150–53; relationship with other organizations, 147, 152–53
ECUARUNARI–Pichincha, 153, 162
Education, 46, 62, 79, 86, 125, 127, 132, 134, 148, 163, 172, 175, 187, 191–92, 196–200, 203, 206–207; bilingual and

INDEX

bicultural, 3, 16, 86, 186, 189–90, 197, 204–205, 208, 210, 228, 235n.40, 247n.26; discrimination in, 64–65. *See also* Literacy
Elections: in Cotacachi, 87, 90–91, 94–96, 104–106, 143; in Ecuador, 143, 187
Ethnicity, 10, 26, 30, 34–35, 70, 173, 179, 207, 222–23, 244n.28
Ethnicity-centered approach, 25, 27–28
Ethnic groups, 7, 59, 132, 170, 198, 213
Exclusion, 18, 27, 62, 68–69, 83

Febres Cordero, León, administration, 191–92, 203, 208, 230n.10, 248n.34
Federación de Cabildos Indígenas de la Parroquia de Cacha (FECAIPAC), 23, 127–31, 135, 138–43
Federación de Organizaciones Indígenas de Napo (FOIN), 169–70, 245n.39
Federación Ecuatoriana de Indios (FEI), 13, 15, 22, 39, 41, 149–51, 164, 166, 175, 232n.7, 242n.9
Federación Indígena y Campesina de Imbabura (FICI), 76, 87
Federación Nacional de Organizaciones Campesinas (FENOC), 14–15, 22, 41, 73, 87, 88–89, 92, 100–103, 106–109, 141–42, 149–50, 154, 164, 166–68, 175, 178, 232n.7, 239n.46, 242nn.4,5
Fiestas, 115–20, 123, 125–29, 131; definition of, 239n.1
Fondo para el Desarrollo Rural Marginal (FODERUMA), 137, 148, 191, 196, 231n.2(chap. 3), 234n.22, 237n.22, 246nn.4,5
Frente Amplio de Izquierda (FADI), 73, 87–88, 90–91, 166, 174, 238nn.30,35. *See also* Left
Frente Unido de Trabajadores (FUT), 166–68, 177–78

Gamonalismo, 12–13, 49, 51
Government, 16, 40–41, 49, 78, 124–25, 130, 138
Guatemala, 33, 70
Guerrero, Andrés, 11, 232n.4

Hacienda, 7, 10–13, 16–17, 29, 39–42, 52, 56–57, 60, 66–69, 74, 77, 139, 142, 230n.8, 232n.3. *See also* Hacendado
Hacendado, 49, 61. *See also* Hacienda
Hale, Charles, 31, 111

Highlands, 6, 8, 12–14, 18, 48, 53, 86, 93, 115, 123, 144, 145, 149, 155–56, 187, 193, 201, 203, 205, 246n.5; Indians, 8, 10, 11, 25, 36, 171, 181; organizations, 13–14, 38, 148, 151, 160, 169, 176
Huaoranis, 6, 170, 244n.39
Huasipungo, 12, 14, 16, 27, 35, 38, 78, 231n.1(chap. 3). *See also* Debt peonage; Huasipungueros
Huasipungueros, 10–11, 14–15, 39–40, 43, 47, 51–53, 57, 60–61, 66, 69, 74, 230n.8, 231nn.1(chap. 3),3(chap. 3), 232n.5. *See also* Huasipungo
Human rights, 172, 176; movements, 21, 157, organizations, 148, 177
Hurtado, Osvaldo, 205; administration, 16, 184, 191–94, 203

Ideology, 5, 72; political, 30, 32, 86
Identity, 5, 7, 16, 24, 34, 67, 88, 185, 227; collective, 36, 135, 149, 217; ethnic, 10, 23, 43, 140–41, 144, 179; Indian, 4–5, 16, 21, 28, 34, 70, 86, 150, 187, 218, 220, 227; indianista, 25, 145; national, 32, 147, 177; political, 10, 22, 24–25, 30–31, 34–36, 43, 140, 149, 170, 182, 196; racial, 32, 138, 202. *See also* Indigenous, identity
Illiteracy, 8, 16, 187, 240n.4; in Cotacachi, 78–79, 81, 84
Imbabura, province of, 6, 17, 19, 73, 86, 91, 93, 155, 162, 206, 230n.5, 236n.5, 242n.2
Import Substitution Industrialization, 45, 51
Indianismo, 5, 16, 34, 149,154, 165, 170, 172, 178–83, 186, 218–20, 223; definition of, 21–25, 29. *See also* Indianista
Indianista, 36, 70, 98, 147, 148, 150, 163, 179–83, 207, 208, 218, 222, 232n.7; organizations, 22, 141, 143; politics, 108, 165, 180. *See also* Indianismo
Indian movement, 4, 20, 28, 36–37, 141, 164, 192, 214–15, 222. *See also* Indigenous, mobilizations; Indigenous movement
Indianness, 54, 85, 147, 158, 170, 179, 220
Indians, 11–12,18–19, 21, 40, 48, 51, 58–70, 77–81, 91–92, 118, 139, 146, 161, 167, 173, 207, 220, 223–24; definition of, 229n.1; repression of 55–59, urban, 6, 79. *See also* Indigenous
Indigenismo, 45, 164, 186–88, 233n.14, 244n.30; neo-,148, 177, 184, 186–88, 196, 200, 201, 217

Indigenous, definition of, 229n.1. *See also* Identity, Indian; Indians
Indigenous activism and activists, 4, 16, 17, 19, 21, 25, 28, 29, 32, 33–34, 41, 47, 60, 94, 124, 147–50, 152, 155, 160, 163, 167–68, 173–75, 179–83, 186, 188–89, 193–94, 196, 198–201, 203, 207, 209, 211, 220, 225, 246n.8
Indigenous candidates, 94–95
Indigenous communities, 19, 32, 38–39, 41, 45, 53, 61, 73, 91, 94, 96–97, 105, 123, 124, 126, 133, 138, 154, 196, 198, 201–203, 205, 207, 216, 246n.7; leaders, 41. *See also* Communities
Indigenous identity, 32, 85, 143. *See also* Identity, Indian
Indigenous issues, 95–96, 161–62
Indigenous mobilizations, 12, 14, 23, 27, 215, 231nn.1(chap. 2),2(chap. 2)
Indigenous movement, 3, 30, 34, 53, 184, 203, 218, 220, 225–27, 242n.2; local and national, 3, 29, 72. *See also* Indian movement; Mobilization; Resistance
Indigenous organization, 3, 12, 23, 27, 43–46, 67, 85, 93, 146, 148, 156, 165, 184, 192–94, 196, 199–200, 203, 215, 220, 223, 230n.7, 233n.21; definition of, 229; intercommunal, 22, 29, 41, 88, 139, 154; local, 16–17, 158; national, 16, 138; regional, 17, 22. *See also* Highlands, organizations; Lowland Indians, organizations
Indigenous people, 16, 28, 86, 91, 114, 130, 135, 168, 170, 216
Indigenous politics, 72, 218, 220
Indigenous population, 6, 8, 188, 191
Indigenous resistance, 66
Indigenous struggle, 26, 34
Instituto Ecuatoriano de Reforma Agraria (IERAC), 38–39, 41, 58, 196. *See also* Agrarian reform
Intag, 89, 93
Integration, 44, 70, 206
Izquierda Democrática (ID), 21, 88, 91, 203

Jefe Político, 80, 81, 236n.13

Labor, 5, 11, 43, 53; forced, 66–67, 120–21, 236n.17; wage, 10, 78. *See also* Mita
Labor market, 10, 70
Land, 5, 8, 11, 14, 160, 182, 199, 207; communal, 10; conflict, 16, 18, 20, 210;
expropriation, 38, 50–51; reform (*see* Agrarian reform); rights, 13, 50, 147, 177, 206, 211
Landowners, 15–16, 19, 38–40, 45–48, 50, 53–58, 82, 124–26, 230n.8, 233n.9
Language, 59, 161, 170, 200, 207. *See also* Quichua; Spanish
Latin America, 33, 51, 54, 59–60, 187, 195, 218, 222–25, 246n.8
Left, 5, 15, 22, 26–27, 31, 33, 72–73, 90–92, 144, 148–49, 165, 172, 212, 220, 222, 238n.30; leftists, 13–14, 219. *See also* Frente Amplio de Izquierda; Movimento Popular Democrático; Partido Socialista Ecuatoriano
Liberation theology, 16, 125, 150–51. *See also* Church, Catholic
Literacy, 22, 124, 127, 149, 166, 186–87, 190, 196–203, 206, 247n.23. *See also* Education
Loja, province of, 6, 151, 162, 206
Lowland Indians, 36, 56, 145, 149, 165, 171, 176, 189; 1992 march, 17, 20, 28, 213, 215; organizations, 147–48, 165, 168–73, 244n.39. *See also* Federación de Organizaciones Indígenas del Napo; Organización de Pueblos Indígenas de Pastaza; Shuar Indians, Shuar Federation
Lowlands, 56, 201

Macas, Luis, 21, 104, 107, 174, 246n.11
Mahuad, Jamil, 225
Maldonado Lince, Jorge, 49–50
Maltrato (mistreatment), 59–69, 76–77, 91, 155, 234n.34
Meskitu Indians, 31–32, 111
Mestizo, 6, 7, 11, 22, 32, 34, 38, 53, 58–60, 62–67, 74, 78, 81–86, 90–92, 105, 114, 118–21, 124, 134–38, 143, 153, 202, 223, 225; authorities, 29, 43, candidates, 89, 91–94, 97; communities, 89, 96, definition of, 229n.4; intermediaries, 43, 61, 65, 129, 154, 202; towns, 6, 38, 78; townspeoples, 61, 116, 122, 151
Mexico, 28, 37
Migrant workers, 12, 21, 47, 76, 78, 122, 127, 151
Migration, 7, 43, 53, 85, 124, 233n.11
Military, 4, 18, 20, 44, 57, 211–12, 223; government, 14, 40, 45, 55; regime, 44, 189, 247n.12; triumvirate, 56, 59, 162, 187

INDEX

Minga, 66, definition of, 232n.8
Minifundios, 8, 49
Mita, 11, 121, 225. *See also* Labor, forced
Mobilization, 5, 14, 17, 21, 25, 34, 39, 70, 99, 138, 155, 185–86, 197, 218, 220–21, 230n.7. *See also* Indian movement; Indigenous, activism; Indigenous, mobilizations; Resistance
Modernity, 43, 48, 54, 59, 147, 157, 227
Modernization, 4, 6, 8, 16, 233n.9; economic and political, 36, 43; rural, 29, 36, 38, 49, 54, 60, 123, 145–46
Morocho, Pedro, 130, 137
Movimiento Indígena de Tunguragua (MIT), 155–56
Movimiento Popular Democrático (MPD), 73. *See also* Left
Multiculturalism, 130, 160, 172, 224, 226. *See also* Pluriculturalism

Napo, province of, 17, 176, 193, 245n.39
Nation, 46, 70, 184, 214, 223; nation-state, 25, 32, 62, 187–88, 213–14, 221
Nationalism, 24, 32–33, 160, 214–16
Nationalities, 24, 173, 179, 213, 217, 228
Negotiation, 34, 111, 148, 168, 185, 200–201, 212, 218; of 1990 uprising, 18–19
NGOs, 22, 41, 53, 84, 89, 124, 137, 176–77, 219, 242n.2
Nicaragua, 31, 33, 111
Nueva Vida Seminar, 199–200, 247n.22. *See also* Literacy

Oil, 45, 176; exploration, 16, 20, 212
Organización de Pueblos Indígenas de Pastaza (OPIP), 19–20, 169–70, 211–12, 215–16, 245n.39
Otavalo, 8, 160, 205

Pachakutik-Nuevo País, 3, 21–22, 104–106, 221, 224; 1996 elections, 21
Parishes, 8, 23, 114, 157
Partido Roldosista Ecuatoriano (PRE), 88, 104, 192
Partido Socialista Ecuatoriano (PSE), 12, 15, 21, 73, 87–88, 93, 100, 104, 106, 168, 238n.35, 247n.18, 248n.34. *See also* Left
Pastaza, province of, 3, 20, 193, 211
Peasant, 16, 26, 39, 47, 49–50, 53, 58, 61, 71, 78, 88, 103, 146, 149, 159, 167, 173, 192, 206–207, 222, 232n.7; indigenous, 8, 37–38, 41–42, 49, 51–54, 57, 67; mestizo, 8, 92
Peru, 10, 42, 44, 215; land reform in, 38, 47, 51–53
Perugachi, Rafael, 81–84, 237n.20. *See also* Police, brutality
Pichincha, province of, 6, 12, 17, 47, 163, 230n.5
Pluriculturalism, 19–20, 34, 184, 186, 189–209, 213–17, 246n.5, 248n.34. *See also* Multiculturalism
Plurinationalism, 184–85, 213–14, 217, 221, 228
Police, 11, 78, 136; brutality, 57–58, 65, 68, 81–84, 237n.20
Policy, 17, 43, 46, 53
Political ideology, 23, 28, 30, 34, 72, 77, 206, 218
Political movement, 20, 29, 143
Political parties, 27, 76, 146, 166, 202, 221, 226
Politics, 34, 148, 164, 179; of disruption, 186, 218, 223–25; electoral, 33, 90–99
Poor, 69, 85, 91, 94
Poverty, 8, 51, 55, 84–85, 95, 150
Power, 33, 192; political, 17, 100, 216; relations, 18–19, 31, 42, 69, 110–11, 128, 162
Prioste, 116–17
Proaño, Leonidas, Monsignor, 125–26; literacy campaign, 203
Producers, 48–50, 54–57, 69
Production, 45, 56, 70; agrarian, 48–54, 80
Productivity, 44–45, 48–52, 59, 191
Property, social function of, 48–50
Public offices, 63, 67–68, 78, 80, 120
Public officials, 11, 18–19, 25, 40–41, 76, 90, 114, 120, 124, 155, 189, 192

Querag, 113, 133–34
Quichua: ethnic identity, 229n.3; Indians, 6–8, 29, 170–71, 193, 244n.39; language, 64, 67–68, 79, 120, 187, 193, 199–202, 248n.27
Quishqueros, 123, 135, 240nn.9,15
Quito, 3, 13, 17, 20, 63–64, 125

Race, 10, 30, 34, 60, 69, 84–85, 92, 107, 134, 141, 179, 222–23
Racial consciousness. *See* Consciousness, racial
Racial difference, 37, 43, 69–70, 151, 162–63, 214

INDEX

Racial discrimination, 18–19, 60, 62, 64, 68, 70, 76–80, 83–85, 107, 142–43, 150, 152, 154, 156, 181
Racial exceptionalism, 60, 226
Racialization, 6, 11, 53
Racial politics, 36, 68, 85, 87
Racial relations, 23, 36, 43, 68, 119, 127, 221, 225
Racial segregation, 62–64, 68, 142
Racial subordination, 27, 37, 67, 69, 109–10, 151, 169. *See also* Consciousness, racial
Racism, 18, 23, 54, 60, 68, 85, 94–95, 152, 154, 163, 168
Redistribution, 45, 47, 49, 51, 58, 70. *See also* Agrarian reform
Resistance, 5, 23–24, 30, 36, 40, 72, 110–12, 139, 200, 214, 217, 222; social construction of, 110, 112, 135, 138, 140. *See also* Indigenous mobilizations; Indigenous movement; Indigenous organization; Indigenous resistance; Mobilization
Respeto, 76, 91, 161
Revolution, 13, 33, 44, 110, 233n.21
Right, 33, 225
Riobamba, city of, 18, 114, 121–22, 124, 126, 128–30, 135, 148, 153
Rodriguez Lara, Guillermo, 44, 49–50, administration, 45–51, 56, 59, 233nn.13,21. *See also* Military, regime
Rohn, Francisco, 144, 179
Roldós, Jaime, 58, 130, 184, 193, 246n.11; administration, 16, 187, 189, 194–97, 203

Salasacas, 8, 160, 244n.25
Santana, Roberto, 144, 198
Saraguro: city of, 19, 154; Indians, 8, 160, 244n.25
Schools, 40–41, 65, 67, 78, 86. *See also* Education
Self-determination, 16–17, 20–21, 34, 179, 211–12. *See also* Autonomy
Shuar Indians, 6, 170–71, 244n.39; Shuar Federation, 16, 160, 169, 244n.39
Sionas and Secoyas, 6, 244n.39
Social Movements, 3–4, 15, 21–25, 34, 140, 143, 168, 184–85, 219–20, 224, 226. *See also* Indian movement; Indigenous, resistance; Indigenous movement; Resistance
Spanish: colonialism, 10, 59, 115, 121; language, 200
State, 13, 20, 22, 26, 28, 31, 40–41, 47, 53, 70, 110, 130, 135, 146, 184, 187, 190, 194, 196, 206, 211–15, 230n.8; discourse, 70, 201
Summer Institute of Linguisitics (SIL), 176, 200, 228, 244n.36

Teachers, 64–65, 69, 85, 235n.40. *See also* Education; Schools
Tenientes Político, 19, 61, 69, 156–57, 234n.34, 241n.25, 243n.17; in Cacha 114–15, 118, 121–25, 129–30, 134–37
Territory, 19, 24, 171, 173, 207
Tituaña, Auqui, 104, 239n.49
Tungurahua, province of, 6, 17, 151, 160, 162–63, 198, 230n.5

Unión Campesina del Azuay (UNASAY), 73
Unión de Organizaciones Campesinas de Cotacachi, (UNORCIC or UNORCAC), 23, 72–109,141–43, 156, 161, 183, 234n.22, 236nn.7,11, 237nn.22,26, 238nn.28,35,40, 239n.42; and CONAIE, 73, 92, 98, 100–104, 107–109 and FENOC, 73, 88–92, 100–103, 106–109, 141–42
Unions, 13–14, 27, 89, 156, 165
Uprisings, 209, 222, 230n.12; in 1990, 17, 19, 28–29, 73, 141, 185–86, 210–12, 215; in 1994, 3, 17, 20, 28, 215, 248n.41

Velasco, Fernando, 25–26
Verduga, Cesar, 208–209
Violence, 81–82, 116

Water, 40, 169; conflicts, 16; rights, 13, 20, 228
White-mestizos, 21, 43, 97, 114–15, 120, 122, 125, 139, 146, 171, 209, 225; definition of, 229n.4; towns, 12, 16, 94
Whites, 32, 53, 59, 67, 74, 134; definition of, 229n.4
Women, 5, 13, 58
Workers, 45, 147, 166

Yaruquíes, Chimborazo: inhabitants of, 120, 127–31; town of 113–18, 121–36, 139

Zamosc, Leon, 6